religious belief and ethical values of rigveda

A Book on Rigveda

Vedas Are Eternal

Vedas Are Spreaded All Over the Universe

dr. surbhi parashar

notionpress.com

INDIA • SINGAPORE • MALAYSIA

Notion Press

Old No. 38, New No. 6
McNichols Road, Chetpet
Chennai - 600 031

First Published by Notion Press 2018

ISBN 978-93-86295-93-4

Contents

Foreword

The research work elaborately deals with religious belief and ethical values of Rigveda, it throws light on Vedic Gods; fire (agni), the Sun (surya), the Dawn (ushas), the Earth (prithvi), the Raincloud (parjanya), the Storm (maruts), the Winds (vayu, vata) the Sky (dyaus), the bright sky and day (mitra), the dark sky and night (varuna) the morning sun (savitra). Vedic Gods are spirit presiding over the diverse powers of nature. Religious belief and ethical values of rigveda enlighten the path of people specially young people and by its scientific reasoning bringing out some fundamental principles on which they should mold their outlook and approach towards better life.

I acknowledge my profound indebtedness to Dr. S.P. Panday prof. arts and commerce college Devi ahilya university Indore, and Dr. S.P. Vyas a renouned ex professor of Banaras Hindu University Varanasi.

I offer my profound thanks to my family member, specially my husband Mr. Sharad Parashar and very special to my son Mr. Varun Parashar, without whom I could not have come so far.

I am confident that this book will prove of immense value not only to students but also to the social reformers and spiritual people. It would be of considerable help to those who are interested to have the knowledge of Vedas.

– Dr. Surbhi Parashar

Preface

Many people are closed off to their own potential because they do not know the infinite power and intelligence of this miraculous universe and that of themselves. The power of the universe and human being are same in quality but different in quantity. As long as I started the practices to obtain, I experienced that an unseen power first created my interest in Vedas. First I have gone through philosophy of swami Vivekananda, Jadunath sinha, Tagore, Aurobindo, Sayanachrya and many others like Deepak Chopada and Radheshyam kaushal, the study shown me the path to go to the original source of knowledge that is 'Rigveda.' The same unseen power has inspired me to bring out the thought that, the truth about action must be shown; the truth of prohibited action also be known. For mysterious are the ways of action. And I started to find out the Religious belief and Ethical values of Rigveda.

A modest attempt is made in this book perhaps the first time to know religious belief and ethical values of RigVeda in so simple manner that people can understand and follow these practices in their life to bring happiness, peace and prosperity.

Appendix

List of Abbreviation

RV – RIGVEDA

YV – YAJURVEDA

SV – SAMAVEDA

AV – ATHARVAVEDA

CHU – CHHANDOGYOPNISHAD

CB – CHHANDOGYOBRAHMANA

SB – SATPATHA BRAHMANA

AB – ASHVALOYUNA BRAHMANA

KB – KAUSHITAKI BRAHMANA

KA – KATHA ARANYAKA

SHA – SHANKHYAYANA ARANYAKA RTA – RITA (LAW OF NATURE)

BCE – BEFORE CHRISTE

Definitions

VEDA – The word 'Veda' means knowledge derived from the Sanskrit word 'Vid' which means to know, to see, to intuite.

RIGVEDA – The Rigveda (Sanskrit. ऋग्वेद) Rig-Veda, a compound of re "praise, verse"[6] and Veda knowledge.

SAMVEDA – The samveda, the 'Veda of melodies' which are used for invoking prosperity from deities.

VEDA TRAYI – the combination of three vedas; RIGVEDA, SAMVEDA, AND YAJURVEDA are called VEDA-TRAYI.

HYMN – a religious song or poem of praise to God or a god., A religious song or antheme. A Vedic hymn, in short, may be said to consist of praises of, and complaints to the gods.

MANDALA – The hymns are arranged in eight Astakas or ten mandalas. Mandalas 2 to 8 contain groups of hymns, each group ascribed to one author or member of a particular Rishi family.

RIC AND PADA – The Suktas in term consist of individual stanzas called rc (praise Pl. reas), which are further analyzed into units of verse called pada (foot).

METRE – jagati (a pada consists of 12 syllables) trishtubh (11) virat (10) Gayatri and anushtubh (8) (in each pada).

SUKTA – Each mandla consists of hymns called sukta (su-ukta, literary "well recited" ecology.

MANTRA DRISHTA – Swami Vivekananda described 'Rishi' as Mantra Drishtas or 'The seers of thought.' He told, "The truth came to the Rishis of India – the mantra drishtas, the seers of thoughts."

RISHI – In the Vedas the term Rishi (Sanskrit ऋषि) denotes an inspired poet of Rig Vedic hymns, who alone or with other invokes the deities with poetry. Post Vedic tradition regards the Rishis as sages or saints.

SAMHITA – The term samhita in Sanskrit means 'putting together,' and refers to a collection or compilation The Samhita of a Veda is a composition of hymns.

BRAHMANA – Brahmana: The Brahmanas (/bramana/Sanskrit/ब्राह्मणम्) are collection of ancient Indian text with commentaries on the four Vedas The Brahmanas is commentaries in prose.

ARANYAKA – The Aranyakas are forest treatises.

UPNISHADS – The upnishads are mostly parts of Aranyakas.

Ekam evadvitiyam – One without a second.

Religious belief – Religious belief refers to attitudes towards mythological supernatural, or spiritual aspects of metaphysical facts, that is a religion, religious belief is distinct from common religious practice or religious behaviors with some believers not practicing religion and some practioners not believing religion. Religions belief, being derived from ideas that are exclusive to religion often relate to the existence characteristics and worship of a deity or deities, divine intervention in the universe and human life and gain logical explanations for the values and practices centered on the teaching of a spiritual leader or group.

Ethics – The word 'Ethics' means system of moral principles.

Rita-Rta is the moral law. It is truth and righteousness.

Chapter - I

Introduction of Rig-Veda

An Overview

The most ancient and most precious hindu scriptures for indian religion is the collection of 1,028 hymns known as Rig Veda Samhita, which has been handed down to generation to generation by oral traidition. The growth of the religious thought is shown by the occurance of philosophical and cosmogonic hymns, preserved in its early stages by oral tradition and long regarded as to secred to be reduced for writing, the text afford abundant internal proof of the accuracy with it, was preserved as one of the most stupendous manifestation of the spirit and handed down to us under the generic name of RIGVEDA.

These are universal in their approach and message. The Vedas are not only imagination of Vedic rishis but their intuition of impersonal truth too, the knowledge at their highest level of consciousness and soul. These are monument of universal religion and deep human experience that is still virtuous and capable of enriching and challenging the modern man. The Vedas disclose their authentic authority. The Vedic revelation is neither the voice of an anthropomorphic revealer nor the unveiling of the veil that covers reality. In point of fact, we can see the reality the truth if we become able to see 'maya,' to understand 'maya,' and recognize it in its true sense. The shruti is shruti when that which is heard in it's true sense. The shruti is shruti when that which is actually heard is not merely the sound but all that there is to be heard, perceived, understood, realized human beings discover, our process of discovery is part of the revelation itself. Only in the spirit are the Vedas. And now we can understand why for centuries they were neither written down nor expanded to outsiders.

The word 'Veda' means knowledge derived from the Sanskrit word 'Vid' which means to know, to see, to intuite. These are large body of texts originating in ancient India, composed in Vedic Sanskrit. Ancient Hindu Rishis (seers) considered the Vedas to be 'Apaurusheya' (अपौरूषेय) which means "not of a man, superman and" impersonal, but the exploration of the secret power of the whole universe. Vedas are authorless. These are called 'Shruti' (What is heard). The seers of Vedic period obtained knowledge of the secret of miraculous universe; its beginning, maintenance, controlling, ruling, knowledge of celestial, atmospherically and terrestrial bodies, nature and spirit by hearing the words during meditation and contemplation through their intuition. So Vedas are called shruti. The knowledge had been handed down to the next generation in the form of hymns (songs). The Vedic rishis obtained knowledge and they had seen 'mantras' (mantra Dristas) they constructed hymns and by oral practice they taught the knowledge in the form of hymns to their next generation. Thus Vedas are called 'smritis.' The Veda, for orthodox Indian theologian are considered revelations, some or other the work of the deity. These are eternal utterances of God.

Vedas are four in number; Rig-Veda, Sam Aveda, Yajurveda, and Atharvaveda. The first three constitute the triad (trayi), which are the original Vedas, and which enjoy higher authority. The atharva Veda is a later addition. Each Veda has three divisions viz. the samhitas, the Brahmanas, and the Aranyakas. The smhitas are mostly verses. The Brahmans are commentaries in prose. The Aranyakas are forest treaties. The Upanishads are mostly parts of the Aranyakasas. The samveda contains the hymns of Rig-Veda, which are to be chanted to be in sacrifices. The Yajurveda contains large portions of Rig-Veda. The Atharvaveda also contains many mantras of the Rig-Veda, which is the earliest. The various Indian philosophies and denominations have taken different positions on the Vedas. Schools of Indian philosophies, which cite the Vedas as their scriptural authority, are classified as 'orthodox' (astika). Other sramana traditions such as lokayata chariaka Ajivika, Buddhism and Jainism, which did not regard Vedas as authorities are referred to as 'heterodox' or non-orthodox (nastika) schools.

The Rig-Veda belonged to the hotr priests contains chants and melodies (saman), chanted the priest of that name. The Yajurveda consists of vid of sacrificial hymns of the Adhvaryu priest, and many of these also are taken from Rig-Veda. It has came down to us in several recensions the Krishna or black yajurveda whose samhita are taittriya, the matrayani, and kathaka, and while or sukla yajurveda whose samhita is the vajasamei. The Atharvaveda is some what removed from the other three by virtue of the popular character of many of the prayers against ills, incantations, and spells which is contained in it.

Meaning of Veda

The Sanskrit word Veda 'knowledge, wisdom' is derived from the Sanskrit word 'vid' which means 'to know,' 'to see,' 'to intuite.' This is reconstructed as being derived from the proto-indo European root 'ueid' – meaning, "see," know. The Sanskrit term Veda as a common noun means 'knowledge, but can also be used to refer to field of study unrelated to liturgy or ritual e.g. in agada-veda medical science Sasya-veda. Science of agriculture or sarpa Veda "Science of Snakes," durveda means with evil, evil knowledge, ignorant.[1]

It should be distinctly understood that every Veda is in two fold, – one side citing the 'mantra' intended for incantation at the time of the prayer and praise or chant the glory of the powerful deity'[2] and on the other side is laid down 'Brahmana' setting out the procedural matters and directives at length for achieving the exacting performance on the eve of ceremony where the mantras have to be recited, in loud voice[3]. The very term 'vedvakaya'[4] must be constructed as an unchallengeable truth, irrefutable fact and in controvertible assertion of divine sermon for the entire Aryan. Vedas are sound vibrations, which specify the path for the living being to achieve their goal. Vedas insistently on respect and praying of supreme Reality and nature.[5] Vedas encompasses all that is essential for ensuring correct way of life, peace and prosperity and spiritual progress. They contain mantras, which on recitation generate positive vibrations in and around the surroundings.

Meaning of Rigveda

The Rigveda (Sanskrit. ऋग्वेद) Rig-Veda, a compound of re "praise, verse"[6] and Veda knowledge. The most celebrated and well-known part of the Vedas is undoubtedly the Rigveda. Rc – means actually a *sacred verse* recited in praise of deity – Thus we can understand the direct meaning of Rigveda to be "The knowledge of sacred recitation," "Veda of praise. Rigveda, which is most likely the most ancient literature of the world, consists of 1028 hymns. The hymns are arranged in eight Astakas or ten mandalas. Mandalas 2 to 8 contain groups of hymns, each group ascribed to one author or member of a particular Rishi family.[7] The ninth mandla contain the hymns sung at the soma ceremonies. The first and the tenth mandals are somewhat different in their language and thought to be composed by a larger variety of individual authors.

"Rigveda Samhita" is a collection of hymns and songs originated by the ancient Rishis and handed down by generation to generation to the Hindus who lived in the banks of the River Indus where they had been used in adoration of Agni, Indra, Surya, Usha, Varuna-Mitra etc. in prayers for health, wealth, longevity, victory in battles and war between Indra (the rain-Gods) and the malevolent power of darkness and demons of draught who withheld the rain of heaven. Rigveda has earliest evidence of the religious, philosophical, and social thoughts of human beings that are preserved in the form of hymns. The pyramids of Eygpt can tell us only about the art of ancient man. But the thought aspects of life of primitive man can be seen only in the Rigveda. According to the Maxmuller "there is nothing more ancient than the hymns of the Rigveda." In reality the Mantra and the Brahman portions are termed as the Vedas "mantra Brahmanyorvedanamadheyam"

In Rigveda, religion was considered to be sustainer of the world. Religion is born when the virat or the unlimited is worshipped by the wise. The Rigveda mentions thirty-three gods[8] but in fact it puts its faith in one supreme Lord alone. They call him Indra, Mitra-Varuna, Agni and the heavenly noble-winged Garutman: sages call the one Reality by many names.

The Hymns of the Rigveda are arranged in collections each dealing with particular deity: Agni comes first; Indra comes second and so on. Within each collection, hymns are arranged in the descending order in the number of stanzas per hymns. It two hymns in the same collection have equal number of stanzas than they are arranged so that the number of syllabus in the meter are in descending order.[9]

Each mandla consists of hymns called sukta (su-ukta, literary "well recited' ecology)" intended for various sacrificial rituals. The Suktas in term consist of individual stanzas called rc ("praise Pl. reas), which are further analyzed into units of verse called pada (foot). Meters most used in the years are the jagati (a pada consists of 12 syllables) trishtubh (11) virat (10) Gayatri and anushtubh (8) (in each pada).

For pedagogical convenience, each mandla is synthetically divided into roughly equal section of several suktas, called anuvakya "recitation."

Recensions[10] several shakhas (branches i.e. recensions) of Rigveda are known to have existed in the past of these shakhas is the only, One to have survived in its entirety. Another shakha that may have surived is the Baskala.[11]

The sakala recension has 1,017 regular hymns and an appendix of 11-valakhilya hymns.[12] The Baskala recension has its own appendix of 98 hymns, the khilani.[13]

In the 1877 edition of Aufrecht the 1028 hymns of Rigveda contain a total of 10,552 RCS or 39,831 padas. The satpadha Brahmana gives the number of syllables to be 432,000[14], while the metrical text of van Nooten and Holland (1994) has a total of 395,563.

Rishis

In the Vedas the term Rishi (Sanskrit ऋषि) denotes an inspired poet of Rig Vedic hymns, who alone or with other invokes the deities with poetry. Post Vedic tradition regards the Rishis as sages or saints.[15]

When Etymologically described, the word may be derived from two different meanings of root 'rsh.' Sanskrit grammarians' derive this word from the second meaning 'to go to move.' Another form of this root means 'to flow,' to move near by flowing.[16] Like River' which flows to achieve its goal to be mingled in the sea as the mind and spirit of Rishi flow to achieve the goal of liberation. That's why Rishis sit to meditate at the bank of river to get the motivation from the Rivers to go forward… Monier Williams also quotes Tarana-ha who compiled the great (Sanskrit to Sanskrit) dictionary named "rati jnanena samsara-param) (i.e. one who reaches beyond this mundane would by means of spiritual knowledge).

More than a century ago, Monier-Williams tentatively suggested a derivation from drs 'to see.' Manier-Williams also quotes the Hibernian (Irish form) arsan (a sage, a man old in wisdom, as related to rshi. He also conjectures that the root drish (to see) might have given rise to an obsolete root rish meaning to see post-Vedic tradition regards the Rishis as sages' or staints, constituting a peculiar class of divine human beings in the early mythical system, as distinct from Asuras, Devas and mortanmen Swami Vivekananda described 'Rishi' as Mantra Drishtas or 'the seers of thought.' He told the truth came to the Rishis of India – the mantra drishtas, the seers of thoughts.

The man rishis recorded in the Brahmanas and the Rigveda Brahmanas and later works as typical representatives of the prehistorik, or mythical period.

In Rigveda most suktas are attributed to single composer. The family books (2–7) are so called because they have hymns by members of the same clan in each book but others clans are also represented in the Rigveda. In all, 10 families of rishis account for more than 95% of the rcs, for each of them the Rigveda includes a lincage specific aprihymn (a special sukta of rigidity formulaic structure used for animal sacrifice in the soma rithaul).[17]

Families	Apri	Rcas
Angiras	1.142	3619 (Mandala 6)
Kanva	1.13	1315 (Mandala 8)
Vashishta	111.2	1276 (Mandala 7)
Atri	III4	983 (Mandala 3)
Bhrgu	V.5	885 (Mandala 5)
Kashyapa	IX.0	415 Part of Mandala 9
Grtsamada	11.3	401 M. 02
Agastya Bharata	1.188 X70	316 170

Time of Rig Vedic Period

The Vedic period refers to that time period when Vedic Sanskrit text were the commonly proposed period of earlier Vedic age is dated back to 2nd millennium BCE. There always been a great disputation about the period of Rigveda. During the early part of Vedic period, the Indo-Aryans settled into northern India, brining with them their specific religious tradition.

The associated culture (Vedic-civilization) was initially a tribal. They occupied the north western part of the Indian subcontinent. It spread after 1200 BCE to the Ganges plain. The society that emerged during that time is known as Vedic period or the Vedic Age, civilization. The Vedic civilization flourished between 1500 BC and 500 BC. On the Indo-Gangetic plains, plains of Indian subcontinent.

The Indo-Aryan migration started approximately 1800 BCE, after the invention of the war chariot and also brought Indo-Aryan language into inner Asia. The oldest scriptures Vedas, were compiled during CA 1750–500 BCE.

The knowledge about the Aryans comes mostly from the Rigveda Samhita,[18] which was composed between ca 1500–1200 BCE. According to Anthony, the old Indic religion probably emerged among Indo-European immigrants in the contact zone between the Zeravshan River (zeraveshan river is a in Tajikistan central asia) (present day crbdicictem) and present day Iran.[19] It was a synergetic mixture of old central Asian and new Indo-European element. Bal Gangadhar Tilak assigns the Vedic hymns to 4500 BC; the Brahmanas to 2500 BC, and early upnishads to 1600 BC. Maxmuller dates the Vedas 1200 BC. Hang puts them at 2400 BC, and Jacobi assigns them to 4500 BC.

Intervene military conflicts between the various tribes of Vedic Aryans are also described in the Rigveda. Most notable of such conflicts was the battle of Ten kings which took place on the banks of the river parushni (modern day Ravi).

After the 12th Century BCE, as the Rigveda had taken its final form, the Vedic society transitioned from semi-nomad life to silted agriculture, philosophical estimates tend to tend to date the bulk of the text to the second half of the second millennium. Being compassed in an early Indo-Aryan language the hymn must post date the Indo-Iranian separation, dated to roughly 2000 BC. A reasonable date close to that of the composition of the core the Rigveda is that of the Indo-Aryan Mitanni documents of 1400 BC.

The Rigveda is far more ancient than any other Indo-Aryan text. For this reason, it was in the center of attention of western scholarship from the times of Max-Muller and Rudolf Roth onwards. The Rigveda Records an early stage of Vedic religion.

In writing appears in India around the 3rd century BC in the form of the Brahmi script but text of the length of the Rigveda were likely not written down until much later, while written manuscript were used for teaching in medieval times, which decompose fairly quickly in the topical climate, until the advent of the printing press from the 16th century.

Vedas are the Sources of Indian Philosophy

Indian philosophy is based on logical reason subordinate to the authority of the Vedas, which are believed to embody in the intuitions of seers of truth. The authorities of the Vedas are that of intuition. Logical reason is subordinate to intuition. So Indian philosophy is based on rational speculation in harmony with the Vedas, and consciously aims at achieving the highest perfection (moksha) attainable in human life.

Hinduism and Indian philosophy is directly nurtured by the Vedas and are a continuation of Vedic spirit. It is well-known fact that long recognized and now confirmed by the recent studies that, Indian philosophical system, not only the orthodox schools (Astikas) but also the most heterodox one (nasticas) have drawn very minute reflections from the Vedas. A contradictory study and explanation needs more attention and minute observation to the pre existing literature (i.e. Vedas).

For about 4000 years India's civilization has developed in a continuous tradition. The same general attitudes which inspired the India of the middle ages and that of the modern times is already, in its salient lines evident in the ancient Vedic period of the second millennium BC. The main traits of Vedic texts are still very much alive and still binding for the orthodox Indian of today.

The monism adumbrated in Rigveda is developed into idealistic monism in the Upanishads, which regard Brahman, the infinite, eternal, omnipresent, omniscient, and pure spirit as the ultimate reality. The temporal, spatial, and causality-bound the world is the manifestation of this infinite and eternal spirit. Brahma permeates it. It shines by its light. It is sometimes regarded as a mere appearance, a name, and form.

Vedas are the foundation of Upanishad and the whole Indian philosophy based on upnishad. Indian philosophy is essentially spiritual. Philosophy and religion are ultimately connected with each-other in India. Religion is not a system of Dogmas, but a living experience. It is the spiritual truth, which is practically realized. It is an insight into the nature of the reality, which leads to liberation. The Ramayana, the Mahabharata, and the Puranas contain religious and philosophical concepts without any attempt at systematization. They are popular treaties, which profoundly influence the minds of Hindus. They draw their inspiration from the upnishads, which teach spiritual monism and mysticism.

Monotheism leads to monism. "The vedic poets conceived one Reality which is manifested in diverse ways" There is one Reality; sages call it by various names; they call it Agni, yama, matarisvan, "that one" (tad ekam) is not personal. The Nasadiya sakta clearly brings out the monism of Rigveda. That one (tad ekam) was later identified with the Atma in the Upanishad.

The Vedic Rishis are called mantra Drishta (seers of mantras and philosophy means "Darshana,' which means vision. Philosophy is the vision of reality as a whole, which was first seen by Vedic Rishis.

The upnishad speaks of Para Brahma and Apra Brahma. The former is higher Brahma. The later is lower. Brahma, the former is indeterminate, unconditioned, and devoid of attributes. The latter is determinate, conditioned and endowed with attributes. The former is transcendental and non phenomenal (nisprapanch). The latter is immanent in the phenomenal world (saprapench). The former is transcendental. Being (sat), consciousness (chit), Ananda (Bliss) that constitute its essence. To connect human mind with such transcendental '*Sat chit Ananda*' stage, there is a need to mediate and contemplate on the infinite, eternal, omnipresent, omniscient and omnipotent creator, preserver, and destroyer of the world, the universe, the lord of the law of Karma, which is "*Apara Brahma.*" That is why the seers of Vedic period worshipped personification and deification of phenomenonal (saprapanch) Gods, which is formed by the transcendental Brahma (Para Brahma). The Para Brahma transcends them as their knower, governor, and guide and called both immanent and transcendent in relation to the world and individual soul. Para Brahma is without beginning and end. The hymn of Rigveda X 90 Purusha Sukta describes the formation of the world from the body of the primordial man who is so vast that he covers and even overlaps, the earth, not only in space but also in time. For, he covers the three ages of the past, present and future. Onlyone quarter of the cosmic person is visible and emerges into the sphere of manifested. Temporal life is only a quarter of the whole man. The four-quarter of the reality remains same which is formless, beginning less a endless, space less, which has had a long history in the cosmological conception of man up to the present day.

Rigvedas religious relief monotheism leads to monism. One reality is conceived, which is manifested in diverse ways. There is one reality. Sages call it by various names; they call it Agni yanja matarishvan[20]

Ekam Sat Vipra Vahuda Vadani agninm Yamam, matarishvan[21]

"Three fourth of man ascended high,

One fourth took birth again down here.

From this he spread in all direction

Into animate and inanimate things"[22]

Para Brahma is the Atma, the witness (sakshin), the seer (Drastra), and the knower (vijnatra). It is not an object (Idiom). It is not comprehended by manas, which is enlightened by it. It is not grasp by life, which is urged by it to perform its functions.[23] "How can the knower be known."[24] It is experienced through spiritual realization.

The philosophy of Mahabharata and the purana is a synthesis of the absolutism of the Upanishad and samkhya dualism of Prakriti and Purusha. The blend of absolutism and dualism is funnel in svetashvatara upnishad. It is a later upnishad, which advocates theism. It regards 'Shiva' as 'Brahma.' The samkhya dualism of Prakriti and Purusha can be traced to the upnishads. If the concept of God is excluded from the philosophy of svetasvatra upnishad, it becomes the samkhya a philosophy.

The yoga philosophy also can be traced to the svetasvatara Upanishad. God is the lord of Prakriti and Purusha. He devoid of Satva, rajas and tamas, taintless and free from merits and demerits. The Nyava ontology also can be traced to the upnishads. The world is composed of earth, water, fire, air, ether, time, space, life and organisms. The Nyava doctrine of A satkaryavada is found in upnishad.[25] "There was non-being first (3/4 power of the universe), the being was produced out of non-being (1/4 power of the universe)."

The Charvaka doctrine of the self as a identical with the body, non-existence of future, and pleasure as the highest good is mentioned in the Upanishads, and it is criticized by them.[26] The Buddhist doctrine of empowerance is the arithihesis of the upnishadic doctrine of eternity of Brahma or Atman. It is a variant of the upnishadic doctrine of non-eternity of all that is not Atma.

The Veda and the Upanishads form the background of the Vedanta. They are called shruti. The Hindus implicitly believe in the authority.

The orthodox systems of philosophy, the Nayava, Vaisheshika, the Minansa, the Samkhya, the Yoga, and the vedant employ reason in the subordination to the authority of the Vedas. But the heterodox systems, the Charvaka the Buddhist, and the Jaina repudiate their authority. They are believed to be revelation of truths to the seers (rshi). They embody their intuition. This is the truth that an individual self resides in the supreme self. The upnishads advocates Transcendental Eudemonism, realization of Atman as the Highest Good/God. The individual self is seer, toucher, hearer, determiner, and doer. It resides in the transcendental Aksara Atman, supremeself[27] Atma, supreme self, shines as the universal life in all embodied individual selves. One who knows this truth plays with the Atma, delights in the Atma, performs all acts for the Atma. This person is the upnishadic doctrine of Transcendental Eudemonism. It is not the Hegelian and neo-Hegelian doctrine of self-realization. Here the word 'Atma' means universal, supreme self as distinguished from the individual self. Self-realization means realization of the same transcended self which resides. Within every individual self. If the intellect of individual self pays whole attention with pure consciousness, he realized the supreme soul the Atma what our Vedic seer did.

The Jaina philosophy is dualism of the soul (jiva) and the non-soul (Ajiva). There are innumerable souls. The earth-soul, human souls, and god souls. The soul is an eternal spiritual substance. The soul and matter are entirely heterogeneous. The eternal spiritual substance is transcendental soul, which is Third quarter part of the universe as said in Rigveda Purusha Sukta. And matter is ¼ of the part of the universe. This is dualism. All the objects of the world are multiform (anekanta) and endued with infinite qualities and relations (anantadharmata). The reality can be considered from the different point of views. Jainism is the complete view of the reality. It embodies the absolute truth. All judgments are relative and probable. This is "Syadvada." Jainism agrees with Samkhyas in denying the existence of God, and advocating dualism of matter and spirit.[28]

Lord Buddha says, All existences are essence less and impermanent. This is the universal law. The empirical individual is an aggregate of the body, perception, feelings, dispositions, and self-consciousness, which are in permanent. Heracliftus said, "All things are in a flux." Bergson holds that all is flow and flux. The upnishad stress eternal being of Brahma.

Buddhism stresses impermanent becoming. It gives a dynamic view of reality. Buddha reconciles being and non-being in becoming. He says everything is – this is one extreme. Everything not is another extreme.

Whatever exists arises from causes and condition and is in every respect impermanent. Buddha says, "He who knows dependent origination, knows dharma. He, who knows dharma, knows dependent origination. But some scholars opine that Buddha believed in the eternal self. Dr. Radhakrishnan says "Buddha clearly tells us what the self is no, though he does not give any clear account of what it is." It is however wrong to think that there is no self at all according to Buddha. The discussion of the burden and his bearer moksha out that the skandhas which are the burdens and the pudgala which is the bearer are distinct entities." The Buddha implies the reality of a universal spirit which is not to be confused with changing empirical aggraates.[29] This interpretation involves the here of extremism (shashvata vada).

'Mahayanasradhotpadasastra' is ascribed by tradition to Asvaghosha, the famous author of Buddha Charita. Asvaghosha was a Brahman converted into Buddhism. The doctrine of Tathata or such ness elaborated Absolute monism of the upnishads and Advaita Vedanta. It is believed that Ashvaghosha smuggled upnishadic Absolutism into the Mahayana Buddhism. The ultimate reality is called suchness (Tathata). It is the supreme transcendental realtiy. It is the Absolute. Samkara emphasizes the monistic tendency in the upnishads and develops it into a systematic Advaitavada. He emphasizes the reality of the unconditioned and unqualified (nirguna) Brahma, and regards God (Ishvara), the individual souls (Jiva) and he world (Jagat) as appearances due to an indefinable principle called 'Maya' (cosmic nescience) which is neither real nor unreal, nor both, nor neither. God is Brahma associated with Maya in its excellent aspect.

The samkhya maintains that prakriti, the triad of sattva, rajas, and tamas, is stimulated to activity by the transcendental influence of the purushas or individual souls and evolves into the world to effect their experience (bhoga) and liberation (apavarga). Shamkara also argues that the Atma, the one, eternal, pure consciousness (vijnanasvarupamatra) cannot be the cause of activity. Shamkara argues that the inactive Lord (Ishvara), who is ubiquitous, immanent in the entire universe, omniscient, omnipresent, and omnipotent, can act and create the world, even as an inactive magnet can move a piece of iron, or inactive objects can move the sense organs. Shamkara opines that the diverse names and forms (namarupa) presented by Maya, Avidhya, or cosmic nescience are acted upon (pravartya) by the Lord who is the active agent (Pravartaka). "God is the efficient cause of the world. Maya the power of God is its material cause."[30] Thus God is both the efficient cause and the material cause of the world.

The Bhagvata maintain that God is the efficient cause and the material cause of the world. Shankara also holds that God is the efficient cause and the material cause of the world. This doctrine is taught by the upnishads. So Shamkara criticize the Bhagvata doctrine of fourfold manifestation (caturvyuha) of God, which revolts against their monism.

Atma according to Samkara is the universal self. It is Brahmana, the absolute, the supreme reality. The Atamn is the transcendental, nonempirical, metaphysical self. The Jiva is the empirical, phenomenal, psychological self. The Atam is the reality in the Jiva. It is the foundational consciousness which sustains the Jiva. Its existence cannot be denied. One who denies its existence is the Atman.[31] The Atma is one eternal, homogeneous consciousness in its essential nature (nityaikarasavijamaptimatrasattaka). It is of the nature of consciousness (nityabodhasvarupa). But the Atma is the eternal principle of consciousness, which reveals and apprehends them. The Nyaya-Vaishesika holds the knowledge (Jnana) is a quality of the Atman. Brahma is the only ontological reality.[32] The concept of one reality (tad ekam), the Brahma the supreme soul is discussed and believed right from Vedic literature to different philosophical schools and to contemporary age also so it must be concluded that Vedas are the source of Indian philosophy.

The philosophy of the Epics is theistic. The belief, in Prakriti and Purusha or souls, which are real forms of Brahman. They conceive of Brahman as a lord of Prakriti and Purusha. Manusmhita is held in great respect among the Dharmashastras. Maxmuller opines that Manusmriti is based on an ancient Dharma Sutra. Sir William Jones dates the code of many, 1250 BC. Manu is mentioned in 'Ramayana' and the Mahabharata. The Manusmriti appears to be prior to the Mahabharata. Common ethical concept occurs in the Manusmriti and Bhagwad Gita, both of which are mainly ethical. The ethics of Bhagwat Gita is more comprehensive, personal and reflective then Manu's ethics. Dharma is the prescribed by the Vedas. It is a means to the highest good.[33] Rik, Yajus, Sama and Athrava, Smriti, Good conduct (sila) of persons well-versed in them, conduct (achara) of virtuous persons, and satisfaction of the self (atmanah trusti) are the sources of Dharma. The Brahmanas of good conduct, well-versed in the Vedas, Brahma revealed the three Vedas, Rig, Sama, and Yahus.[34] The Mahabharata refers to the upnishads, Manu, Kpila, Asuri, Punchshikha, Samkhya, Yoga, Pancharatra, vaisheshika, and Vedanta. It advocates theistic Samkhya. Philosophy like Puranas. It preaches the cult of Narayana, Vasudeva or

Vishnu or Shiva. But it does not regard them as polytheism (different deities).

The Bhagwadgita is a part of Mahabharata. It is attributed to Vyasa. It is regarded as most sacred books of the Hindus. It has exerted profound influence on their minds. Samkara, Anandgiri, Madhusudana, Saraswati, Ramayana. Madhav, Sridhara and others wrote commentary on it. Bal Gangadhar Tilak's "Gitarahasya," Mahatama Gandhi's "Anasaktiyoga," Shri Aurobinda's "Essays on the Gita" are contemporary works on the Gita.

Dr. S.N. Dasgupta opines that he Bhagvadgita is the earliest work on the Bhagvata school written long before the composition of the Mahabharata. It was written before the sutras of the different system of the philosophy were composed and after the earlier Upanishads were composed (500 BC)[35] Ramayana Refers to the Vedas, the Vedangas, Manu, the Puranas, and Vedanlas.[36]

Ramayana mentions the deities of Vedas and puranas. It mentions Indra, Varuna, Aditya, Brahma, Vishnu, Rudra, Agni, Vivasvat, Maruts, Soma, Savita, Prajapati, Yama, Uma, Lakshmi, Saraswati, Gayatri and Skandha. It appears to believe in henotheism. Ramayana believes in pantheism and monotheism, which is prescribed in Vedas.

The contemporary philosopher Rajaram Mohan Roy described Vedas in an easy way. He studied Shamkaras Advaitvedant and Upanishad very well and form concept that there is only one reality, the supreme soul. 'Shri Ramkrishnakathamrit' is an excellent book. He believed that there is different way of expression of God, but the goal is one. Swami Vivekananda gave concept of practical Vedanta.

Swami Vivekananda says, "Philosophy must be practical."[37] Bhagwad Gita is the best commentary on Vedanta Philosophy. As scene is laid on battlefield, where Krishna teaches Arjuna, 'Do your duty' (Dharma) and pay your whole attention to the goal of life (Moksha). Vedanta preaches the ideal. But there are two tendencies in human nature. One to harmonize the ideal with the life, and the other is to elevate the life to the ideal. In the Chhandoyga Upanishad we read that a sage called Narada came to another called Sanat Kumara, and asked him various questions, of which one was, if religion was the cause of things as they are. And Sanat Kumar leads him, as it were, step by step, telling him that there is something higher than this earth, and something higher than that, and so on, till comes Aakasha, ether, Eather is higher than light, then the question arises "is there higher than that (Sun)," and Sanat Kumar replies yes "Prana" Prnaa (breath) is higher than all as Vedanta describes. Prana (breath) means 'Atma' is Vedas, and this is the principle of life.

Pythagoras came to India and studied "Samkhya" philosophy and that was the beginning of Greek Philosophy.[38] Later, it formed the Alexandrian school, and still later, the Gnostic. It become divided into two: one part went to Europe and Alexandria, and the other remained in India, and out of this, the system of Vyasa was developed.[39] The Samkhya philosophy of Kapila was the first rational system that the world ever saw. The authority of the knowledge is word (Shabda). Shabda is Brahma by which knowledge can be obtained. And seers of Vedic period had seen the Shabdas, Mantras so that they called Mantra Drishtas. Vedic words are authentic doubtless. By recognizing all the above facts it becomes clear that "Vedas are the source of all Philosophies."

* * * * *

References

1. Monier Williams, 1899.
2. Sanskrit; समिधा य आहुति यो वेदेन ददाष मर्तो अग्नये। योनमसा स्वध्वरः ।।5।। Rigveda Sukta, 8–19.
3. Wikipedia Free Encyclopedia.[en.wikipedia.org/wiki/Vedas)
4. Words of Vedic Hymn.
5. Mantramanjari p.19.

6. Derived from the root rc "to precise: (f. Dhatupatha 28.19 monier Williams).
7. J.N. Sinha, Indian philosophy.
8. RV 10.92.4.
9. Mantra Manjari by Pannikar, p.30.
10. Wikipedia Free Encyclopedia.
11. Wikipedia (The Free Encyclopedia)
12. Mantra of Khila hymns were called schalika and not y.cas (Khila means distinct part of Rigveda separate from regular hymns: All regular hymns are Akhila (The whole).
13. These Khilani hymns have also been found in a manuscript of Skala revision of the Kashmir Rigveda.
14. J.S. Sinha, I. Ph. VI.I.
15. Dictionary Monier-Williams.
16. Wikipedia Free Encyclopedia.
17. Pletcher Kennth (2010) The History of India, panniker mantramanjari.
18. Flood 1996, p.31. Anthony 2007 p.454–455.
19. Jadunath Sinha, Indian Philosophy, Vol. II, p.418.
20. Jadunath sinha Indian Philosophy vol ii pg 418–420
21. Ekam Sat Vipra Vahuda Vadani agninm Yamam, mata rishvan RV I, 64, 46.
22. Pannikar, Mantramanjari, p.74., Purusha Sukta RV X 90
23. Parnikar mantramanjari, p.75.
24. Kena up, 1, 2, 3, 5–8.
25. Vijnataram are kena vijaniyat adhi up.11 4.14.
26. Anyadeva tad viditad athaviditad adhikena up. i,4.
27. Jadunath Sinha, Indian Philosophy, Vol. I, p.31.
28. Jadunath sinha indian philosophy, p.41.
29. Katha up, I, 2.6.22
30. Jadunath Sinha, I. Ph. I, p.181.
31. J.S. Sinha, I. Ph. p.298.
32. J.S. Sinha, II.

33. Atmandh pratyadkhyaatum asakyatad ya eva nirakata tasyavia at matut SBS i, 1.4.
34. Ekameva hi parmarthatyam brahma S.B. Tait up 4.6.
35. Veda Pramankah Sreyasadhianam dharmah-II.
36. Hrdayena bhyanujnatah ii I.
37. J.S. II, I.Ph. p.612.
38. J N. Sinha Pg.146.
39. The complete work of By Swami Viveka nanda

Chapter - II

Introduction of Vedic Literature

The term "Vedic literature" simply means literature based on or derived from the Vedas. The text which constitutes the Vedic literature are: I The four Vedas; RIGVEDA, YAJURVEDA, SAMVEDA, ATHRVAVEDA with their divisions; 1. The Samhitas, 2. The Brahmams, 3. Aranykas, 4. The Upanishads. The samhitas are verses in text. The Brahmanas are commentaries in prose. The Aranyakas are forest treatises. The upnishads are mostly parts of Aranyakas.

The Rigveda, Samveda and Yajurveda are collectively known as Vedatrayi. AtharrvaVeda is considered later addition. Bharatbhumis Natyasastra is considered to be the panchama Veda (fifth Veda). Rigveda is the oldest and original one, which had been compiled over several centuries. Some of the earliest hymns are said to have been composed around 1500 BC. These were passed on from teacher to disciple, orally. All these texts are foundation for Vedic literature.[1]

When we seek to understand the essential truths in Vedic literature, then we must obtain an expansion of knowledge hidden in Samhita, Brahmana, Aranyaka and Upanishad. This knowledge possess the secret of the universe and reveals the secrets of Tad ekam, the only one ultimate reality of Brahma, Atma (Soul, breath, prana) and origin and derivation of this empirical world and revelation of secrets hidden in human mind which is part and parcel of this ultimate power, same in quality but different in quantity.[2]

The Samhita of a Veda is a composition of hymns (mantras) or prayers, which are used for invoking prosperity on themselves and their folks, in their adoration of the dawn, in celebrating of the struggle between the god who wields lighting and the power of darkness and rendering thanks to the heavenly beings for preservation in battle.[3] A Vedic hymn, in short, may be said to consist of praises of, and complaints to the gods. A hymn in ritual act, is always utilized for the accomplishment of some material aim and therefore, is addressed to a god (devata). There are other hymns too, which have no religious functions and are completely secular. Such hymns were mostly written in praise of aristocrats who have bestowed riches upon the poets.[4] ex. Hymns to surya Starts with-

Udshay devh savita savay shashvattam tadpa varhirsthat|

Nunm devebhyo vi hi dhati ratnamthamjad vitihotram savasto||

Uprisen is savitar, this God, to quiken, priests who neglects not this most constant duties.

Udy taym jatvedasm devm vahanti ketayah|

Darshe vishvay suryam||

His bright rays bear him up aloft, the God who knoweth all that lives, surya, that all may look on him).[5] RV. I, 50.

Hymn to Pusan:

The man who pusan designates
With words like these, 'Pushanyi, cause to thrive,'
By him the god is not described.
With pusan joined to unison
The best of warriors, truest Lord,
Indra, the evil demon slays.

The brahmanas, on the other hand, are not so much concentrated with the goals, as they are concentrated with the sacrifices. Their sole concern is ritualistic and they are related only to those part of samhitas which are dedicated to the sacrifice. They are, in a word, Exclamatory notes on the samhitas. They are written in prose and are filled with wearsome prolixity of exposition, characterized by dogmatic assertions and flimsy symbolism rather than by serious reasoning. The word Brahmana has many meanings: prayer, devotion, incantation, magic, knowledge etc.

The Rigveda samhita has come down to us in the sakala school recenssion. The first hymn is usually addressed to Agni:

ऋषिः मधुच्छन्दाः वैष्वामित्रः छन्दगायत्री देवताअग्नि (अग्नी)

ॐ अग्नीमीले पुरोहितं यज्ञस्य देवमृत्विजम होतारं रत्नधातमम्।।1।।

अग्निनो पूर्वोभिऋर्षिभिरीयो नूतंनैरूत। स देवाँ एह वंक्षति।।2।।

अग्निोतो रयिमेश्रवत्पोर्षमेव दिवेदिवे। यषसं वीरवंत्तमम्।।3।।

अग्नेयं यज्ञमेध्वरं विष्वतेः परिभूरसि। स इद्देवेषु गच्छति।।4।।

I adore Agni, the chosen priest, God, Minister of sacrifice, the hoter, laviast of wealth.[6]

The next comes Indra, and then come the hymns addressed to be visva-devatas and special deities. The composition of the Rigveda Samhita does not seem to have been liturgical. Although many of the hymns of the Rigveda do not the ritualistic stamp. Yet a good number of the hymns have definitely a magical and liturgical in character.

The Rigveda is a mystical text contains knowledge in its abstract imagery of what the seers had realized.

The samveda, the 'Veda of melodies' contain 1549 verses meant to be used as songs in various ceremonies, primarily for the udgata priest. Most of them are taken from Rigveda and arranged according to their use as utilized in particular rituals.

The yajurveda is "the veda of Rituals, and contain 1975 verse-mantras in 40 chapters, many of which are similar to those in Rigveda and used in rituals, usually by the adhvarya priest." These contain different level of knowledge and wisdom. Yajurveda has two samhitas, or collection of verses, known as the white yajurveda or (vajasmeyi-samhita) with hymns and rituals, and the black yajurveda (or Taittiriya-Samhita) with their interpretations. The Atharva Veda is Veda of Chants and once had 50 branches of which we have only shaunak branch today. It has a book of 5977 verses in 20 chapters containing prayers, spells, and incontentations which is some respects resemble magical instructions found in Tantras and even various magical incantations found in Europe.[7] The Atharva-Veda contains a small section of verses of instructions, wisdom, descriptions of the soul and God, but the majority of it consists of it rules for worshipping the planets rules for oblation and sacrifice, prayers for averting evil and disease, incantation for the destruction of foes, for fulfilling personal desires etc. mostly for the material needs of people.

In Brief

Name of Samhita	Name of the Brahmans	Name of Upanishad
Rigveda;	Aiteraya Brahmana Aiteraya-aranyaka	Kaushitaki Brahmana, Kaushitaki Upanishad
Samveda;	Praudha Brahmana, Chandogyapnishad, Sadvamsa Brahmana, Samavidhi Brahmana, Arsheya Brahmana, Detadhyaya Brahmana, Vamsa Brahmana, Samhitopnishad Brahmana,	Kena Upanishad Taittiriya BrahmanaTaittiriya- aranyak Upanishad Narayaniya
Yajurveda black	Satapatha Brahmana	Upnishad. Svetsvettar Upnishad Katha Brihadaraya Upnishad
Yajurveda white	Gopatha Brahmana	Mundaka Upnishad, Naupnishad Prasana Upnishad anduckya Upnishad[7]

The four primary Vedas represent the accomplishment of a highly developed religious system and encourage satisfaction of material desires through worship of the demigods. They contain many directions for increasing ones power and position or for reaching the heavens in one's future by properly performing particular sacrifices in worship to the devas (demigods and so on).

The very common question arises in the mind of some of the Hindus that "why these seems to be so many gods within Hinduism or Vedic cultures." If we just peer into the Vedic religion and literature, we come to analyze the situation, and through study we understood that there is but one supreme reality, supreme being who has many agents or demigods who assist in managing the creation and natural forces within. All the deified and personified deities of Veda has individual divine importance without the working of which the universe can't be exist, but that alone can't maintain the phenomenal and cosmic process of the universe. They are all correlated and connected with each-other keenly. They are bounded with each other by the "law of (rta) Rita,"[8] which is cosmic, moral social and physical law of the universe. Think, without Agni, how can the process of the universe go on. Which is cosmic, atmospheric and domestic god (deity), which is the messenger, the mediator between the man and the God which is the preserver, destroyer and maintainer of the universe. Just think, without 'sun' (surya) can life exists? Which is the source of light, heat and life of all types of plants. Which is the source of rain. The sun rays convert the water into steam, which become light in weight and goes upwards and form clouds. The Usha, which spread mild light and flourish the earth. The Mitra and varuna which causes and control seasons. Varuna controls the law of physical and moral order. So the each and every deity of the universe as well as each and every material thing of the world has it's own importance. When each deity properly approached with prayer or worship, they may help facilitated the person by granting certain wishes that may be within the jurisdiction of that demigods. The four principles 'Vedas' include the concept of spiritual perfection or liberation.

The term samhita in Sanskrit means 'putting together,' and refers to a collection or compilation. The first sections of the Vedas, which have hymns or verses, are known as samhitas. The samhitas and Brahmanas are called Karmakanda, the portion pertaining to rituals. The Aramyakas are called Upasanakand, the portion relating to meditation. The upnishads are called Jnanakand, the portion dealing with supreme knowledge.

Etymologically samhita is a Sanskrit word from the roots sam (स) and hita (हित) which means 'correct,' 'proper,' and wholesome, arranged. In order to study the Vedas in detail, six shastras are helpful. These shastras are known as the Vedang. The six Vedangs are: Shiksha, Kalp, Vyakrana, Nirukta, Jyotish and chhanda. The samhita forms the first part of each Vedas. A samhita is a collection of Mantras, so the samhita are sometimes also referred to as the 'mantras.'

Swami Dayananda Saraswati made extraordinary effort to bring out the significance of the mantra of the Vedas. Shri Aurobindo also challenged the western philosopher and opined that the mantras are found to express esoteric truths which west ness cannot grasp. He strove hard to elevate the cryptic meaning of the Vedic words and the hymns. The Rigveda samhitas hymns known as *'richas.'* These hymns are metered verses. Thc same samhita contains mantras in the form of songs meant for liturgy or public worship. The yajur samhita contains verities of mantras composed in the poetical and prose forms. The Atharva Samhita contains mantras meant for routine rites and rituals.

As it is discussed previously that Rig-Samhita contains 10 mandalas. Each mandala is divided in various Adhyayas (chapters). The rchas (hymns), which are for praising and invocation of different deities are written in the padas as:

In first mandal, the very first chapter ।।अथ प्रथमोष्टकः (प्रथमोध्यायः।। वर्गा. 1–37) (म.1. अनु.1)

ऋषिः मधुच्छन्दाः वैष्वामित्रः छन्दगायत्री देवताअग्नि

ऊँ "अग्नीमीले पुरोहितं यज्ञस्य देवमृत्विजम होतारं रत्नधातमम्।" ।1।।

अग्निनो पूर्वोभिऋर्षिभिरीयो नूतंनैरूत। स देवाँ एह वंक्षति।।2।।

अग्निोतो रयिमेश्रवत्पोर्षमेव दिवेदिवे। यषसं वीरवंत्तमम्।।3।।

अग्नेयं यज्ञमेध्वरं विष्वतेः परिभूरसि। स इद्देवेषु गच्छति।।4।।

The very mark (-,.,) small horizontal line(-), the vertical line(|) above the word and dot(.) have their importance while pronouncing every pada, sukta and mantra. The small vertical line put above the letter is called "स्वरिता" Swarita (high pitch), the two vertical lines called "दीर्घ स्वरिता" big higher pitch, the letter which has no line is called "उदात्त" (medium pitch) and the letter with line put below it is called "अनुदात्त" (lower pitch). Pure word, pure pronunciation of mantras are very important in Rig-veda Samhita – As it is obviously well known that the Rig Veda-Samhita's hymns are spoken by seers, which has been pronounced with proper stress and intonation which has deep meaning of themselves. The true meaning of hymns are hidden in right pronunciation which awaken the different chakras[9] of human body. And if shastrar chakra awakens it connects with universal power and the prayer sounds reaches to the God (deities).

The meaning of above mantra is:

1. Laud (adore, invoke) Agni, the chosen priest, God, minister of Sacrifice, the hotar, lavishest of wealth.
2. Worthy is Agni to be praised by living as by ancient seers. He shall bring hitherward the Gods.
3. Through Agni man obtains wealth, yea, plenty, waxing day by day.
4. The most rich in heroes, glorious.
5. Agni, the perfect sacrifice which than encompasses about verity goeth to the Gods.[10]

ऋषिः मेधातिथिकाण्वः छन्दगायत्री देवता इन्द्रः 1, 5, मरुतः 2, त्वष्टा 3, अग्नि 4.1

मित्रावरूणो 6, द्रविणोदाः 7–10, अष्विनो।।

एषायुक्त परावतः सूर्यस्योद्यनादाधि

शतं रथेभिः सुभगोषा इयं पि यात्यापि भायुमान।।

In this way every letter of Sanskrit has written with sound as the hymns of Rigveda were taught orally before 3rd century BCE.

Brahmana: The Brahmanas (/bramana/Sanskrit/ब्राह्मणम्) are collection of ancient Indian text with commentaries on the four Vedas. They are primarily a digest incorporating facts, legends, the explanation of Vedic rituals and in some cases philosophy.[11] They are attached to each veda, and form a part of Hindu 'sruti' literature.

The Brahmanas are particularly noted for their instructions on the proper performance of rituals, as well as explain the symbolic importance of sacred words and rituals actions in the main text. The oldest Brahmanas dated to about 900 BC while youngest Brahmanas (such as the satapatha Brahmana) were completed by about 700 BC. According to Jan Gonda the final codification of the fore Vedas, Brahmanas, Aranyakas and early Upanishads took place in pre-Buddhist times (ca 600 BCE).

The Brahmanas are primarily a digest incorporating facts, legends, the exposition of rituals in the Vedas and in some cases philosophy.

Brahmanas are a storehouse of the most ancient sacrifices of the Aryans. Sacrifices, magic and asceticism are a theory greater in power than the heavenly gods. Priest and ritualism are more important than beauty, human affection, and religion. The whole religious spirit is expressed and explained in ritualistic terms. It is the priest and the aristocrat who are to be revered and the rest of the people are to be treated as 'food of nobility.'[12] One who offers cows to the Brahmanas gets whatever he wants.[13] It is believed that by shaving the head one can consume foes on all sides like the Sun.[14] Holiness can be won only by those who offer seasonal sacrifices. The one who offers such sacrifices winds the year, and the year is a complete whole, and a complete whole is indestructive; hence his holiness is indestructible, and the theory becomes a part of a year and goes to the gods; but as there is no destruction in the gods, his holiness is therefore indestructible.[15]

The fee for the sacrifices is also fixed. It must consist of one thousand cows. But one could give more if one desired so. The priest performs the sacrifices, not because it is his religious duty, but for the fee alone, and it must be paid in the form of cows, gold, valuable garments, and so on. The most coveted thing is the gold, for it is immortality the seed of Agni.[16]

In the first chapter of Chandoyoga Brahmana, who is one of the oldest Brahmana, includes eight Suktas (hymns) for the ceremony of marriage and rituals at the birth of a child.[17]

The first hymns is recitation that accompanies offering a Yajna oblation to deity Agni (fire) on the occasion of marriage, and the hymn prays for prosperity of the couple getting married. The second hymn wishes for their long life, kind relatives, and a numerous progeny. The third hymn is a mutual marriage pledge, between the bride and groom, by which the two bind themselves to each other-as mentioned.

यदेतद्धदयं तव् तदस्तु हृदयं मम।

यदिदं हृदयं मम तदस्तु हृदयं तव।।

That heart of thine shall be mine,

and this heart of mine shall be thine – Chandogya Bramana, Ch.1 [18]

Brahmanas mentions instruction for the performing rituals as well as explain the symbolic importance of sacred words and rituals actions. These instructions insist on exact pronunciation (accent), Chhandas (छन्दः meters), precise pitch, with coordinated movement of hand and fingers any mistake makes it powerless.

The language of the Brahmanas is Sanskrit. Dating of the Brahmanas is controversial, with oldest being dated about 900 BCE, while the youngest Brahmanas (shatapatha Br.) were completed by about 700 BCE.[19]

Rigveda Brahmana: i. Shakala Shakha Aitareya Brahmana, rarely knowns as Ashvalayana Brahmana (AB).[20] It consist of 40 Adhyayas

(Chapters) dealing with soma-sacrifice and in particular the fire sacrifice rituals.[21]

ii. Bhaskala Shukha-Kaushitaki Brahmana (khayana Brahmana) consist of 30 chapters.

The Aranyakas: Aranyakas are sacred writings that are supposed to frame the essence of the upnishads and are considered to be secret and dangerous to the uninitiated. The Aranyakas revealed more of the esotery aspects of the rituals and their purposes than the Brahmanas. They are meant only for the brahmana priest and kshatrya worriers who have renounced all materialistic activities and retired to the solitude of the forests, which is the meaning of 'aranyaka.'

Etymologically, Aranyakas (Sanskrit aranyaka आरण्यक) literary means "Produced, born, relating to a forest" derived from the root Aranya (अरण्य) which means 'forest, wilderness.'[22] Two theories have been proposed to the origin of the word 'Aranyakas.' One theory holds that these were meant to be studied in a forest, while other holds that the name came from these being the manuals of allegorical interpretation of sacrifice, for those in vanaprastha (forest dwelling) stage of their life.

Aranyakas describes and discuss rituals and sacrifices from various perspectives. As Kotha Aranyakas describes rituals such as the mahavrata and pravargyana.[23] Aitareya Aranyaka includes explanation of the Mahavrata ritual. They are identified as karmakand. In Aitraeya Aranyaka there are five chapters each of which is even considered as a full Arenyaka. It is in Aranyaka that one finds specific statements about how one who follows the Vedic injustices and performs the scarifies goes to become the God of Fire, or the Sun or Air and how one who transgresses the Vedic prescription is born into lower levels of being, namely, as birds and reptiles. In second chapter of Aiteriya Aranyaka "Pramna-Vidhya-meins" prana, the vital Air that constitutes the life-breath of a living body is mentioned, which are also called breath of mantras, all Vedas and Vedic declarations. The third is known as "Samhitapanishad."

The fourth as Madhyandina Taittiriya Aranyaka: There are Ten Chapters, one to six from Aranyaka proper. Chapter I is very late Vedic chapter, which even has some puranic names; it is usually called the Arana prajna for the particular style of fire bricks. It is also known as surya-Namaskar chapter. Chapter 2 discussed the five Maha-Yajnas that every Brahman has to do daily. Most importantly the daily recitatation of the Veda (SV adhyya). Further the sacred thread, the yajnopvita, sandhya worship, that of the ancestors (pitra), the Brahman yajna, and cleansing homa-sacrifice are treated in detail.

Katha Aranyaka: It is fairly parallel to the text of the Taittiriyas.

Shankhyayana Aranyaka

There are 15 chapters, which deals with Mahavirta, 3–6 constitute Kaushiki upnishad, 7–8 are known as samhitopanishad. 9, describes "Prana," 10 of Agnihotra ritual. 11 for dream 12 for fruits of prayer, 13 about discarding bodily attachment and on 'shavana' and practice of discipline of penance, faith, self-control etc. Ch.14 gives two mantras "I am Brahm; अहम् ब्रह्मास्मि," it is the Apex of Vedic mantra, signifies about the meaning of hymns of Vedas.

Brihadaranyaka: The Aranyaka of the while yajur veda is part of its Brahmana: Satpatha Br. 14.1.3 is the madhyaandina version.[24]

Upnishads: Upnishad (Sanskrit उपनिषद, plural उपनिषद) are collection of Vedic text, contain the earliest emergence of some of central concept of Hinduism, some of which Buddhism and Jainism.[25] Upanishads are constituted by the last part of the Vedas. They are mystical and theosophical in nature. They form the end of the Vedic literature and are a, therefore, referred to as the Vedanta (the end of the Vedas).

The word 'Upanishad' is rendered by most of the scholars as that which speaks of mystery. According to shankara, the word is formed by adding u-at pa-foot nishat – sitting down, the suffix 'kvip' and the prefixes 'upa' and 'ni' to the root 'sad,' which means that which destroys ignorance.[26] Modern scholars on the other had/hand are of the opinion that the word means the art of sitting near a teacher, of submissively listening to him. Etymologically described 'upnishad' (u-at, pa-foot, nishat-sitting down) sitting at the foot of teacher.[27]

The upnishads do not give us a systematic philosophy in the modern sense of the word. We find in the magic coupled with philosophy. The early speculation is materialistic; the ground of the universe is identified with food (anna), breath, (prana) and water (apa). In them we find a variety of doctrine. Another contradicts the doctrines of one sage. We find advocates both of a personal god and of an impersonal absolute. In the final analysis of the word, the Upanishad do not give us one particular system of thought, but a medley of doctrines. It would be of benefit to us if we keep the warning of Prof. Dasgupta in view when he writes that 'we must turn a deaf ear to the absolute claims of these exponents, and look upon the upnishat not as systematic treatises but repositories of diverse currents of thought – the melting-pot on which all later philosophic ideas were still in a state of fusion.[28]

Generally speaking the main thesis of the Upanishads is this that, behind the objective world there is an absolute and impersonal principle, known as Brahma; that the self (atman) is identical with the Brahma; that we are in this cycle of sansara due to our non-recognition, i.e. because we do not realize that we are identified the ground of being. This non reorganization of identity is referred to as ignorance (avidhya). Man is striving, therefore, should be directed towards this realization. The self and Brahma are one. The world and all its objects animate and inanimate are to be considered unreal, because Brahma alone is real. The absolute is without a second (ekam eve advaitiyam). This theory of identify is described is "mahavakya." They are: "Thou art that." This individual soul is absolute.[29] I am Brahma and consciousness is Brahma.

Sarvapalli Radhakrishnan states that the Upanishads have dominated Indian Philosophy, religion and life ever since their appearance. The Upanishads describes ethical values also as in chhandogyauponshad, there is a declaration of (Ahinsa) non-violence as an ethical percept.

Description of other premises such as Damah (temperance, self-restrain), satya (truthfulness) Dana (charity), Ayaver (non hypocrisy) Daya (compassion) and others are found in the oldest Upanishads. The Upanishads prefer knowledge of the 'self,' more important than performing rituals and worshipping gods. The Kaushitake upnishad asserts that external rituals such as ritual Agnihotram offered in the morning and in the evening must be replaced with inner 'Agnihotram,' the ritual of introspection. And that not rituals, but knowledge should be one's pursuit. The Mundaka upnishad declares how man has been called upon, promised benefits for, scare dun to and misled into performing sacrifices, oblation and pious works.

"The performance of all sacrifices, described in the Maitrayana-Brahmana, is to lead up in the end to a knowledge of Brahman, to prepare a man for meditation. Therefore, let such man, after he has laid those fires meditate on the self, to become complete and perfect.

– Maitri upnishad[30]

The opposition to rituals is not explicit in the oldest Upanishads. The Brihadaranyaka interprets the practice of horse. Sacrifice or ashvamedha allegorically. It states that the over-lordship of the earth may be acquired by sacrifice a horse. Similarly Vedic gods such as the Agni, Indra, Vishu, Rudra, Brahma and others equated in the upnishads to the supreme, immortal and incorporeal Brahman Atman of the upnishads. God become synonyms with self concept of Brahma and Atman: Two words that are of paramount importance in grasping the Upanishads are 'Brahma' and 'Atman.' The Brahman is the ultimate reality and the Atman is individual self. Differing opinions exist amongst scholars regarding the etymology of these words. Brahmah probably comes from the root brhm, which means 'The Biggest' the greatest – The All "Brahma" is the infinite spirit source and fabric and core and destiny of all existence, both manifested and destiny of all existence, both manifested and un-manifested and the formless infinite subtraction and from whom the universe has grown. Brahma is the ultimate, both transcendent and immanent, the sum total of all that ever is, was or shall be. The word 'Atma' means the immortal perfect spirit of any living creature, all beings, including animals and trees. Atman is the idea in all upnishads, and "know your Atman" their thematic frus.[31] some states that Brahma (Highest Reality, universal principle. Being consciousness bliss) is identical with atman, while other states that 'Atman' is part of Brahman but not identical. This ancient debate flowered into various dual, non-dual theories in Hinduism. The Brahmsutra by Badaryama (-100 BC) synthesized and unified these somewhat conflicting theories, stating that Atman and Brahman are different in some respects, particularly during the state of ignorance, but at the deepest level and in the state of self realization, Atma and Brahman are identical, no different.[32]

Aum: The upnishads also contain the first and most definite explications of the divine syllable Aum, the cosmic vibration that underlies all existence. The mantra Aum Shanti, shanty, Shanti, translated as 'the soundless sound, peace-peace, is often found in the upnishads.[33]

The upnishad form one of three main sources for all schools of Vedanta, together with the Bhagwadgita and the Brahmsutra.[34] The schools of Vedanta" seek to answer questions about relation between 'Atman' and 'Brahman' and the relation between 'Brahma' and the world.[35]

- According to Advaita verdant there is no difference between Atman and Brahma, both are identical.
- According to vishisthadvaida, the jvatma is a part of Brahma, and hence is similar, but not identical.
- According to Dvaita, all individual souls ('jivatmas') and matter as eternal and mutually separate entities.[36]

Advait Vedanta: Advait literary means non-duality, and it is a monistic system of thought. It deals with the non-dual nature of Brahma and Atman Gandapada was the first person to expound the basic principles of the Advaita philosophy in a commentary on the conflicting statements of the upnishads.[37] Gandpada's Advaita ideas were further developed by Shankara.[38] Radhakrishnan on the other hand, suggests that Shankara's views of Advaita were straight forward developments of the upnishads and Brahmasutra.[39]

Shankra (788–820 AD) was the greatest philosopher among the Indian thinkers. He wrote commentaries on Kena, Katha, Isha, Prasna, Mundaka, Mondukya, Chandogya, Brahadaranyaka, Svetasvetara, Aiteriya, and Taiteriya upnishads. He emphasizes monistic tendency in upnishads and develops it into a systematic Advaitavada according to him Atman is one, eternal homogeneous consciousness in essential nature (nityakarasavijnapatma trasattka). It is of the nature of the eternal consciousness (nityabodha swaroopa).[40] Brahma is eternally fulfilled (nityatrpta)[41]

In upnishads the concept of Bondage and liberation (vidhya and Avidhya) described well. Ignoraned (Avidhya) is non-discrimination of the eternal and the non eternal. Knowledge (vidhya) is discrimination between them. Avidhya is knowledge of distinction, plurality, and individuality. It is intellectual knowledge invoking distinction of subject and object. It is knowledge of things limited by time, space, and determined by causality. Vidhya (libration) is intuition of identity. It is above intellectual knowledge. Avidhya is the sphere of actions, which spring from the knowledge of identity. Avidyha is the cause of bondage and transmigration. Vidhya is the cause of liberation.[42]

Action (karma) concentration of mind (yoga) devotion (bhakti), and knowledge (jnana) are the means to the attainment of libration (moksha). The mind is cause of bondage and liberation. An impure mind is cause of bondage. A pure mind is cause of liberation. A mind free from taint for desire for pleasure is pure. A mind attached to objects of enjoyment produces bondage. A mind detached from them produced liberation. Discipline of body and mind and practice of Yoga purify the mind, and make it fit for acquiring knowledge of the Atman. Penance (Tapas), mind control (dama), withdrawal of the senses from their objects (uparati), endurance of physical hardship (titiksha) and trance due to meditation

(Samadhi) are pre-requisites for the intuitive realization of the Atman within individual self.[43]

The philosophy of Mahabharta and Purana's is a synthesis of the absolutism of the upnishads and the Samkhya a dualism of Prakriti and Purusha or individual soul.[44]

The knower of the Brahma becomes Brahma. The soul knowing the God washes off merits and demerits, and achieves supreme reality with the Brahma.

* * * * *

References

1. Jadunath Sinha Indian philosophy voi ii
2. Panniker Mantramanjari
3. A glimpse of vedic literature – Kumar Sanjay Jha (ignca.nic.in)
4. Stephen Knapp – "A Complete Review of Vedic literature."
5. Ruth Zur: Literature and Geschichte desweda, p.8.
6. Colebrooke, Miscellaneous Essays, p.308.
7. Rigveda the oldest Divine book, RTH Griffith, p.79.
8. Vedic Hinduism, Motilal Pandit, p.12.
9. Rigveda the oldest Divine Book, Griffith, p.36–37/Vedic Hinduism, M.L. Pandit, p.18.
10. The human body possess 7 chakras namely; Muladhar, Swadhisthan, Manipur, Arahat, Ahnan, and Shsastrar.
11. Rigveda Oldest Divine Book, T.H. Griffith, p.37.
12. Brahmana Encyclopedia Britanica, 2013.
13. ibid
14. Klaus Klostermaier (1994) A Survey of Hinduism, p.67.
15. Sathapatha Brahmana, No. 1.2.25.
16. Ibid, 1.93.6, Yam Kama, Kamyata 50 asmit Kamah Samridhyate, 53 Ibid III 6.3.14–17.
17. Rigveda, viii, 51.2.

18. Max Muller, Chandogya Upnishads, Part I, p. LXXXVII.
19. Brahmana Encyclopedia Britannica.
20. Theodor Aufrecht Bonn (1879).
21. PMuriz Wintermits (2010).
22. Paul Deussen "The Philosophy of the Upnishads," p.4–6.
23. aranya – Sanskrit Eng. Dictionary, Koeln Uni. Germany.
24. M. WItzel, Katha Aranyaka, s, 2001, xxviii.
25. Em.m.wikipedia.org. Which has taken from film "Aranyaka," 1994.
26. These include, rebirth, karma, moksha, ascetic techniques and renunciation,/65 Samkara Bhashya on katha upnishad...and monier Sanskrit dictionary.
27. Maxmuller, "Ancient Sanskrit Literature," p.319.
28. Monier-William – Sanskrit Dictionary.
29. S.N. Dasgupta, History of Indian Philosophy, Vol. II, p.45.
30. Chandgoya upnishad, iv.
31. Mandukya upnishad 2.
32. Brahdaroryak upnishad, iii, 2.
33. Aiteriya upnishad, 5.3.
34. S. Radhakrishnan, The Principle upnishads, p. 17–19.
35. "Laid those fires" is a phrases in Vedic Literature that implies 'Yajna' and ancient religious rituals: EB Cowell.
36. Maxmuller, 'the upnishads, Part 2,' Maitrayana-Brahmana upnishads.
37. Mahadevam, 1956, p.59.
38. PT Raju (1985) Structural depth of Indian thought, p.35–36.
39. Soul is synonymous with self in Hindu Philosophy (translation).
40. Radhkrishnan, 1956, p.272.
41. Raju, 1992, p.176–177.
42. King, 1999, p.129.
43. King, 1999, p.221.
44. Radhakrishnan, 1956, p.284.

Chapter - III

Philosophical Concept of Rigveda

The philosophical concept of Rigveda is *cosmological, spiritual* metaphysical and *phenomenal* in nature. The Vedic seers saw that, life is strongly associated with nature and they were trying to understand the world they lived, in terms of their association with matter, energy, air, water, animals, the good and the bad. The Rigvedic concept of philosophy and of ultimate reality is unique. It has monistic as well as dualistic components. The whole process of creation and evolution of the concept of reality[1].

The Rigvedic philosophy provides the answer to all unanswered questions; how did this universe begin? When did this universe originated? What is the nature of the ultimate reality? What is the nature of God, Soul (Atman), Brahma. The Rigvedic poets began to wonder about creations, which was said to have originated in a "Golden Embryo" (Hiranyagarbha). The Hymn of creation, which is the oldest surviving record of the philosophical speculation on the origin of the universe, describes mysterious chaos before creation.

"*Hyranyagarbha,*" hymn of Rigveda X 121 elaborates the beginning of the universe. It is said that Hiranyagarbha arouse in the beginning. According to the "Sayan's interpretation" Hiranyayi means golden. The word hiranmyayi is irregularly formed by dropping 'ma' of mayat by Ritvyariastuya (Pan 6.4.175).[2]

Hiranyagarbha, arouse in the beginning. He alone was the Lord of all that exists. He established the earth and the heaven. He gives breath and strength; his commands are followed by other gods. His shadow is death and immortality. He is the sole king of the whole universe. He rules the mountains the sea, and the rivers. He governs men and beasts. He alone is God above all gods. He began the earth, the heaven, and the mighty waters. He is no other than prajapati, the Lord of the creature. Hiranyagarbha and prajapati may claim the rank of the supreme gods.

The hymn "Hiranyagarbha" of Rigveda chants the majesty of the cosmos and the glory of its master whom it is incumbent upon man to adore. One feels, however, that the rsi is tormented as well as enchanted by the splendor of the world so near and tangible, yet so in explicable and elusive. In the hymn "Hiranyagarbha." Three closely related concepts connected with each other are; (a) the origin of reality (In the beginning arose the golden germ); (b) the Lordship of God ("He was, as soon as born, the Lord of Beings"); (c) the human adventure of returning to the primeval stage ("What God shall we adore with our oblation").

हिरण्यगर्भः समवर्तताग्रे भूतस्य जातः पतिरेक आसीत्।

स दाधार पृथिवीं द्यामुतेमां कस्मै देवाय हविषा विधेम[3] ।।

In the beginning arose the Golden Germ; he was, as soon as born, become the Lord of Being sustainer of the earth and of his heaven. What God shall we adore with our oblation. a) Verses 1, 7 and 8 explain the divine origin in terms of the cosmic egg, well known to both the Indian and other cosmogonies. Something happened in the womb of the supreme, it stirred, evolved, it came to be, it manifested itself.[4] Theological thinking will later say that the movement, if any, is seen only from our human point of view but the Rigveda is not concerned with systematic development and the language is both poetical and mystical, using symbols that disclose themselves only to a meditative gaze, the most powerful symbol for the hyranyagarbha, the Golden germ, we cannot call this first step a creation. God is not created, nor can we call it evolution in the usual sense of the word, nor a becoming, as if God first were not and later come to be vedic thought here struggles with the primordial problem of the piercing into a very nature of the God head and the aluminiferous discovery of its dynamism and life. God as God is only coextensive with beings; God is a relative term, related to the creature; God is not God himself; being appears when the beings are also there. And yet, 'previous,' to all this there seems to be an internal "divine" life, a disclosure, an explosion, a birth inside the ultimate mystery itself.[5]

HYMN CXXI. Ka. HIRNYAGARBHA

1. IN the beginning rose Hiranyagarbha, born Only Lord of all created beings.

   He fixed and holdeth up this earth and heaven. What God shall we adore with our oblation?

2. Giver of vital breath, of power and vigour, he whose commandments all the Gods acknowledge–.

   The Lord of death, whose shade is life immortal. What God shall we adore with our oblation?

3. Who by his grandeur hath become Sole Ruler of all the moving world that breathes and slumbers;

   He who is Lord of men and Lord of cattle. What God shall we adore with our oblation?

4. His, through his might, are these snow-covered mountains, and men call sea and Rasā his possession:

   His arms are these, his are these heavenly regions. What God shall we adore with our oblation?

5. By him the heavens are strong and earth is stedfast, by him light's realm and sky-vault are supported:

   By him the regions in mid-air were measured. What God shall we adore with our oblation?

6. To him, supported by his help, two armies embattled look while trembling in their spirit,

When over them the risen Sun is shining. What God shall we adore with our oblation?

7. What time the mighty waters came, containing the universal germ, producing Agni,

   Thence sprang the Gods' one spirit into being. What God shall we adore with our oblation?

8. He in his might surveyed the floods containing productive force and generating Worship.

   He is the God of gods, and none beside him. What God shall we adore with our oblation?

9. Neer may he harm us who is earth's Begetter, nor he whose laws are sure, the heavens' Creator,

   He who brought forth the great and lucid waters. What God shall we adore with our oblation?

10. Prajāpati! thou only comprehendest all these created things, and none beside thee.

    Grant us our hearts' desire when we invoke thee: may we have store of riches in possession.

The Hiranyagarbha Sukta RV 10:121: EXPLANATION

In the beginning was the Divinity in his splendour,

manifested as the sole Lord of land, skies, water, space and that beneath

and he upheld the earth and the heavens.

Who is the Deity we shall worship with our offerings?

It is he who bestows soul-force and vigour, whose guidance all men invoke,

the Devas invoke whose shadow is immortal life-and death.

Who is the Deity we shall worship with our offerings?

It is he who by his greatness became the one King of the breathing and the seeing,

who is the Lord of man and bird and beast.

Who is the Deity we shall worship with our offerings?

It is he through whose glory the snow-clad mountains rose,

and the ocean spread with the river, they say.

His arms are the quarters of the sky.

Who is the Deity we shall worship with our offerings?

It is he through whom the heaven is strong and the earth firm,

who has steadied the light and the sky's vault,

and measured out the sphere of clouds in the mid-region.

Who is the Deity we shall worship with our offering?

It is he to whom heaven and earth, placed in the lightby his grace, look up,

radiant with the mind while over them the sun, rising, brightly shines.

Who is the deity we shall worship with our offerings?

When the mighty waters came, carrying the universal germ, producing the flame of life,

then dwelt there in harmony the One Spirit of the Devas.

Who is the Deity we shall worship with our offerings?

It is he who in his might surveyed the waters, conferring skill and creating worship-he,

the God of Gods, the One and only One.

Who is the Deity we shall worship with our offerings?

Father of the world – may he not destroy us who with Truth as his Law made the heavens and produced waters, vast and beautiful.

Who is the Deity we shall worship with our offerings?

Lord of creation! no one other than thee pervades all these that have come into being.

May that be ours, for which our prayers rise, may we be masters of many treasures![6]

Scientifically, it is also proved that the universe is about 13.7 billion years old. The origin of the universe came into being by the process of explosion. 'Big bang' that would not only go on to produce all the matter in the universe but also marked the beginning of time.at the start the universe was a hot and dense ball of radiation energy. In one thousand of a second, tiny radiation particles produced tiny particles of matter. These combined to form the first ever chemical elements hydrogen and helium. Nuclear reaction inside the stars produced many other chemical elements including carbon and oxygen.[7] The term "Big-band" was coined in 1950 by Fred Hoyle. In 1959 a survey was conducted of scientists across American concerning their understanding of the physical sciences one particular question asked "what is our concept of age of the universe?" More than two thirds of the scientists polled responded that, "There was no origin of the universe. They believed that the universe is eternal. And I also believe that the universe is eternal as it is said in our Purusha Sukta that

> Three fourth of man ascended high,
> one fourth took birth again down here
> from this he spread in all directions
> into animate and inanimate things."[8]

The three fourth of param-purusha (cosmic person) whose body is the whole universe. He has a thousand heads, a thousand eyes, a thousand feet. He pervades the whole terrestrial space and transcends it.

> "A thousand-headed is the man
> with a thousand eyes, a thousand feet;
> encompassing the Earth all sides,
> he exceeded it by ten fingers' breadth."

Then five years later, in 1964, radio astronomer Arno Arno Penzias and Robert Wilson discovered a microwave signal buried in their data. They attempted to filter out the signal, assuming that it was merely unwanted noise. However they soon realized what the signal actually was; they had inadvertently discovered the Cosmic Microwave Background (CMB). The CMB had been predicated by a theory that few believed at the time called 'Big-Bang.' This discovery was the first evidence that the universe had a beginning.[9]

The basic question arises in the mind of every philosopher and scientists that "How did the universe came into existence?" And what existed before it? The seers of Vedic periods found out the answer in their intuition during deep meditation and contemplation. It is well known fact that chit (cit) or consciousness is fundamental or primary and that everything else is secondary to it or dependent upon it. The great ocean of consciousness exists timelessly and spinelessly as the being without becoming. The word 'consciousness' means 'awareness of something within oneself, and the state or fault of being aware of an external object, state or fact.' The consciousness means 'the state of being characterized by sensation, by emotion, volition and thought.' The pure conscious state of minds of vedic seers intuited that the whole universe is formed out of one fourth of the supreme, ultimate power of ultimate Brahma (supreme soul).

Most scientists now believe that the universe sprang into existence from a singularity. Scientists question "what existed before the Big-Bang." To answer this question scientist baffled "Nothing Existed prior to the beginning." This 'Nothing' of scientists can't be seen or observed by open eyes, can't be discovered by observation and researches, but it can only be seen by intuition; by pure consciousness, which has to be obtained by taps' deep meditation and contemplation.

"There was neither-existence nor nonexistence in the beginning; there was no sky, nor heaven beyond. Then there was neither day nor light. Neither death nor immortality. There was sole one (tad ekam),[10] [what scientists call 'singularity'] that breath by itself without breath; there was nothing other than one. Then there was darkness without light. All was engulfed in the primal cause. That one was born by the power of austerity (tapas). There first arose desire or will in the cosmic mind and from the first one sprang the seed of creation. The wise songs realized in their heart the bond of what is in what is not. He from whom this creation arose, the highest seer in the highest heaven knowns.This is pure spiritualistic monism. That one (Tad Ekam) was later identified with Brahma, Atman.[11]

The Advaita Vedanta holds that Brahma is existence (sat) consciousness (Chit) and Bliss (ananda)[12] Carl Friedrich Von Welzsacker, the famous German Physicist and philosopher, on the concept of sacidananda, writes that "In the Indian Vedanta doctrine, the one is sat-chit-ananda, which we can translate as being-awareness-bliss.

Brahma is existence (satya).[13] This statement has special meaning. It does not mean Brahma exists. The etymodogical meaning of the Sanskrit word Satya (as + kyap, derived from the Sanskrit verb root 'sat' is that which exists." When we say 'Brahma is existence, we do not specify and quality what exists. A proposition may be formed in Sanskrit language as "Yadasti tatsatyam (whatever exists is existent). This is a tautology, or in other words, an analytical statement like 'A' is 'A.' All analytical statements, without any exception, are true, we give a name to that which exists. The name we give is 'Brahma,' which is a verbal symbol of the ontological being. The Sanskrit word Brahma (bramh+manin) has been framed by adding the kvt affix minim to the verb root bramh; Grammatically, it means that which is great or big, the lexical meaning being 'the supreme Being.' The word Brahmin has been classical and hence it is retained. But we could give any other name to the ontological being without any alternation of the connotation. How we frame another proposition in Sanskrit viz., Yatsatyam tadbrahma (what ever exists is Brahma). This is also a true statement. Although it is not analytical like 'A triangle has three angles' is not a synthetic statement. The question of truth or felicity is not relevant to such a statement. Thus the significance of the statement "The Brahma is existence" is established. Both the Advaita Vedanta and the non-dualistic philosopher of Kashmiri savism say that 'Brahma' (Paramshiva) is pure consciousness when the human mind reduces at the state of pure consciousness become one with 'Brahma' and also become able to know 'Brahma,' the ultimate reality of the universe. So vedic seers known the Brahma in their consciousness and obtain the knowledge of Purusha-Sukta of Rigveda.

The theory of Higgs-Bason. In November 2012, in a conference in Kyota researchers said, "The findings of the researches meant that, scientists were very sure they had found an unknown particle of mass ~ 125 Gev/c^2 and had not been misled by experimental error or a chance result. The search for, and ultimate discovery of, the Higgs boson is a triumph of modern physics-a global, half-century effort whose outcomes would make or break the vaunted standard model of particle physics. The hunt for the Higgs was the subject of wide media attention due to the cost of the project, the complexity of the experiment, and the importance of the result. And when it was announced with great fanfare in 2012 that physicist has succeeded in creating and identifying this all-important new particle, the theory (research) help us to understand the rules for the universe which our seers visioned during Rigvedic period. They were very scientific in nature and believed that the whole universe immanantes from very true, 'Being,' the Brahma, which identified the quantum field theory."

The systematic attempt to discern the basic building blocks of matter and the fundamental forces than art born from the forest and herbs;

Thou art born bright, O Lord of men, to men.[14] Agni is intent upon right (rta) and true. In him all commands all wishes dwell. He protects us from sin that defiles us. He reigns over immortality.[15] The hymn for the god of Sky "The Sun, as awakener of all from slumber, throws off the dark cloak with his rudicut beams. He bestows upon people life and cheerfulness, creating the morning beauty of dawn."

Another God of sky is savitra, who has the same traits as the sun and is usually conceived in material form. Most of the hymns, which are composed in his honor, were intended to be recited at morning and evening savifield. The god savitra is said to be, like Varuna, the forgiver of sins. In the following hymn the spiritual aspect of the god is developed.

> Today, with guiding word, let men directed him here
> He, who distributes gifts unto the sons of men,
> Shall thou, O savitra, dost first upon the gods
> Who sacrifice deserve, lay immortality,
> The highest gift, and then to mortals dost[15]

In another hymn we find savitra designated as priest of priests, arranger of sacrifice, and one with Pusan, and for this deed he became very famous. Another sky god Pusan, is praised and extolled because he bestow riches on all, brings secret treasures to light, softness those whose hearts are hard, makes miser generous, and shower joy and happiness up his adores. He sits in the middle of heaven, guards all animate and inanimate objects, and is careful of his cattle. He clears all roads from danger and obstruction and protects men on their journey. Being the god of fertility, he is invoked in the marriage rite.[16]

Vishnu is prepared for his bravery, because he measured all the earth in three strides. His foot prints are very sweet and a secure of a great joy. He lives in the highest realm, a place where the departed spirits go. Here is a hymn in which Vishnu is prevised.[17]

> None born god Vishnu, and none born hereafter
> Ever reaches the limit of thy greatness;
> It was thou who established your high value of heaven.[18]

The Maruts are the storm gods. They are endowed with terrible vigor and strength. They cause men and mountains to tremble. They drench the earth with rain. They wash away all sins of men. They are bristle, active indefatigable, powerful, and impetuous. They throw down what is firm. They are all all-knowing, true, flowness searches and purges of sins.

They raise the rain from the sea, and rain it down on earth. They are great, bounty, immortal, righteous, and merciful to the worshippers. Their greatness is infinite.[19]

Indra holds the earth, the sky, and the heaven. He unites the immeasurable earth and the sky. He is the father of the Maruts, the Sun, the dawn, and the fire god. He is the terrific destroyer of enemies in the battle-field. He is the killer of the demon vritra. He is the Lord of the world. He is resplendent, every young, and infinitely great. He is a voracious drunker of soma juice. He is the giver of food, wealth, prosperity, victory and long life. He entered into the earth and the sky, and created the world. He is the creator of the waters. He is bountiful, generous, self-controlled, and immortal. He is great grave, and fierce. He pervades the world. He is the protector of the worshippers.[20]

Varuna is the chief Aditya. It is he who made heaven and earth stand firm. He is the curer of all diseases. His realm of habitation is so high that not even birds can venture to ascend there. It is due to him that the stars and the moon are regulated. He is the personification of heaven.[21]

> "His actions bear witness to his might and wisdom,
> Who fashioned firm supports fro earth, and heaven,
> And set on high the firmament uplifted,
> And fixed the starts and spread out earth's exances."[22]

The Sun's sure courses Varuna appointed. He sent the streaming waters flowing on ward. The mighty path of days he first created. And rules them as the riders guide their horses.[23]

Then we have the goddess dawn who is the daughter of heaven. She has a beautiful face and lives among men. Her sister is night, whose color is different from hers; but they are equal in mind. She is the opener of the gates of heaven for every creature. Her golden colored chariot is driven by beautiful steeds. She brings, with her luminous light, everything to life and creates in them motion.[24]

The Asvins, the Horsemen, are twin sons of Dayus. Brothers of the Dawn perhaps.[25] In the last book of Rigveda they are spoken of as the sons of saranyy and vivasvant and are also referred to as the youngest of gods.[26]

The Asvins are the physicians of heaven and to men give herbs and save them in times of danger. Their chariot is drawn by birds, which are as swift and agile as thoughts. They help lovers in procreating. They visit sacrifices three times a day; morning, noon and evening.

Soma, which was originally a plant, is now raised to the position of God. The juice of this plant was offered thrice daily, in a sacrifice, and it was believed that the soma-plant grew on the Mujavat mountain. Parianya, the rain god, is said to be his father, and waters are his sisters.[27] Indra when intoxicated by soma, does great and extraordinary deeds. We also find that soma too is given all the attributes which were given to Indra. So we find soma destroying towns, begetting gods, upholding the sky, prolonging the life of the mortals, and so on. Initially he was associated with Indra, Agni, Rudra, and Pushan. Later he was identified with beauty, fierceness, intelligence, wisdom, Omniscience, mercifulness, benevolence, justice, and righteousness. They are not confined to a particular place. They are pervasive entities. They are supernatural and superhuman spirits governing the phenomena of nature, friendly and benevolent to the worshipped, and terrific and deadly to their haters. They are mighty fierce, invincible, wise, merciful, omniscient, pervasive, righteous, truthful and benevolent. They are easily propitiated by hymns, adoration, prayer, oblation offerings and sacrifices. They are giver of wealth, strength, happiness, sons and grandsons, victory in battles and a life of a hundred years. They are also givers of wisdom and moral qualities. They are born of father and mother and yet immortal. Mortals are elevated to the rank of immortals. There is a kinship between mortals and immortals.

The fire god, Agni is the domestic god. He is the Lord of the house. He is the youngest, resplendent, and beautiful god. He is mighty, great, invincible, and destructive. He is wise, righteous, omniscient and benevolent. He is the mediator between men and gods. He is the messenger of gods.

He carries the oblation to the gods. He brings them to the sacrifices. He is the steward of both worlds. He shines on heaven and earth. He has a twofold birth, celestial and terrestrial.

> "Thou O Agni, the flaming one (here thou means "you")
> Art born of the heaven thou art
> born from the waters and the flint."

Existence of God

The gods of fire (Agni), the Sun (Surya), the dawn (Usas), the earth Prithvi, the rain cloud (Parjanya) the storms (Maruts), the winds (Vayu, Vata), the bright sky and day (Mitra) the dark sky and evening (Varena), the morning Sun savitra and the like.

According to the Yaskas, there are the three kinds of gods according to the 'three regions' over which they are distributed. They dwell in the region of the sky, of the atmosphere and of the earth. Agni dwells on the earth; Indra in the atmosphere and, surya in the sky. But Yaskas' distribution does not seem feasible on the ground that the gods do not strictly keep to their natural homes; they intrude, time and again, into one another region.

Gods of Sky

Surya, the shining one, in habits the highest region of the sky. He has the power of en livening and bestowing all good things on the matters on earth. He is spoken of as the shining one, surya, and the enliveners, savitra. He rises on the slope of the sky as the swift going steed carries him… Seven sisters steeds carry him. In some places the Sun's independence, as a giver of life, is destroyed by making him simply on 'eye of Mitra-Varuna'[28] who rouse the sun.

The vedic gods endowed with great physical power.

> नमं स्नानं स क्रनवो में अद्य मित्रो अर्थमा वरूणो जुषन्ता।
>
> आदित्यासः शुचयो धारयता अवृजिना अनवद्या अरिष्टाः।।

What becomes clear is that there is conceived as first existing one thing, which is described as breathing without wind, an effort to express a primitive nature different in severe from anything known to the priest, conceived perhaps metaphorically only as a dark ocean or chaos. Through Tapus which is cosmic than refer to the activity of seers or other human power by inward fervor, springs up the being enveloped in a shell, which is later conception is the golden world egg. The next step in the development of the universe is the appearance of desire, unless that is to be taken as born of mind, when, when it is described as the first seed of mind. If so the mind must be deemed to be an attribute of the one, which develops in a shell, whence springs desire. In Taittriiya Aranyaka we find that mind is given as prior to desire. The Kama was conceived as unconscious will: it is rather the natural expression for conscious desire, which would rise from the existence of mind as a substratum.

Tapas is the cosmic order; ascetic fire, arduous penance, concentration, which here amounts to an antic condensation, which is said in the hymn of the Rigveda to be the energy giving birth to cosmic order and to truth.

There was neither death nor immortality nor night not day. There was nothing else in the world save the one, which breathed, but without wind, of its own power. There was however darkness, and a moving ocean without light: through the might of ferver. Tapas, was born a living force enveloped in a shell. Then there developed desire, kama, the first seed of mind: the sages found the root of not-being in being, searching for it in the heart. The fifth verse is a puzzle: it may be referred to the sages who drove a division through the universe and distinguished the upper and the lower the world of nature above, the principle of nature below: The next two verses end with a deep expression of doubt: the gods are later than the creation and cannot know its origin. Whether, the creating was made by itself or not, the overseer of it is the highest space of heaven be knows of it, or perhaps, he knows not.

सुक्त – 129

(ऋषि–प्रजापति परमेष्ठी। देवता–भाववृत्त। छन्द त्रिष्टुप्1)

1. नासदासीन्नो सदसीत्तदानी नासीद्रजोनो प्योमा परो यत्।
2. किमावरीवः कुह कस्य शर्मन्नभ्भः किमासी द्रहनं गभीरम्।।3।।
3. कास्तदग्रे समवर्तताही मनसो रेतः प्रथमं यदासीता।
4. सतो बन्धुमसति निरविन्दन्हादि प्रतीन्य कवयो मनीषा।।4।।[29]

The idea behind hiranyagarbha is that, there is a production, a processes within the "wombs" of the ultimate. Because there is life, there is birth in and of God.

Verse 7 and 8 of Hiranyagarbha describes

"When came the mighty waters, bringing with them

the universal Germ, whence sprang the fire,

thence leapt the? Gods one spirit into being

What God shall we adore with out oblation?[30]

"This one who in his might surveyed the water

Pregnant with vital forces, producing sacrifice,

he is the God of Gods and none without him

What God shall we adore with our oblation."[31]

a. Once-born, the golden German become the Lord, the Lord of Being and of beings, in the general and also in the portative sense. Lord of Being and of non-being. He is the only king, and the poet raises his voice in praise and celebration of the lordship both cosmic and human, of this unknown and nameless God, who, being a father of all creation, transcends it. It is the Lordship that gives unity and harmony to the whole world.

b. Who, what, shall be the object of our worship?
To whom shall be direct it?[32] This question encompasses the whole of human destiny. Man's struggle to overcome all existential hazards in order to reach his final goal, which, in a way, is a recovery of his primordial divine stage. The main philosophical concept

> contained in the hymn is that, first "what is God, Second our relation with him" The following fact is mentioned in the Rigveda that "Indra, the last born of prajapati," was appointed by his father Lord of the Gods, but they would not accept him. Indra then asked his father to give him the splendor that is in the Sun, so as to be able to be Lord over the Gods. Prajapati answered: "If I give it to you, then who shall I be?" You shall be what you say: Who (Ka), and from them on this was his name. God is an interrogation in the dative, to whom? Toward whom all our actions, thoughts, desire, are directed. God is the problematic and interrogative end of all our dynamism. If the proper form of the Greek none for the God is the vocative, the Vedic name is a adaptive it is not only the term of invocation. It is also the receiver of sacrifice. The contemplative slant will prevail, however, and the same will be the pure nominative and ultimately 'Aham.'

"To whom," brings our to be more contemplative on. It is not only a theoretical question. It is the object of our adoration, the term of our worship, the aim of sacrifice, 'God' cannot be 'known,' if by knowledge we understand a merely mental consciousness; he can be reached only by sacrifice, by holy action, by orthoparxis, the ultimate concern of all religion. Sacrifice, moreover, needs to know only the interrogative of God. The living God with whom the sacrifice is concerned is not a concept, not a definite and graspable reality, but rather the term of the actual sacrifice which, though constantly running the risk of missing the target finds in the dynamic to whom its justification and its reward. Sacrifice is not a manipulation of the divine but the existential leap by which man plunges, as it were, into the not yet-existent with the cosmic confidence that the very plunge effects the emergence of that reality into which he plunges. The only oblation that the Lord of the Gods, of Men and of the universe, can fittingly accept is the oblation that enables him to go on creating the world by reenactment of the sacrifice of himself, that sacrifice by which the world is called upon to be. By this act Man shares in the cosmic process by which God creates the world.

The hymn of the origin, "The Nasadiya Sukta" provides vision of a profound insight in the mystery of reality. It is the product of a mystical experience that for transcends the limits of logical thinking; it is a religious chant-a The hymn commences with an assertion in the beginning there was neither-being not non-being: there was no atmosphere nor sky. As Baggott explains "the elements were judged to be eternal and indestructible, joined together in rather romantic combinations through the attractive force of Love and split apart through the repulsive force of strife, to make up everything in the world."[33]

Just like the physicists of today, the Ancient Greeks used their powers of observation, intuition and reasoning to try and out the true nature of reality. The Rigvedic philosophy had tried to intuit the nature of cosmic as well as material substance from their speculative thinking.

Rigvedic sages (seers) had the vision of the hymn "Nassadiya sukta" which comes out of profound insight into the mystery of reality. It is the product of a mystical experience that far transcends the limits of logical thinking; it is a religious chant.

> 'In the beginning Love arose,
> Which was the primal germ cell of the mind,'

The seers, searching in their hearts with wisdom, discovered the connection of Being non-being. The starting point of the hymn is not a piece of caused thinking seeking the cause of this world or of Gods or God, but rather an intuitive vision of a whole.

Philosophy of Life, According to Rigveda

The Vedic poets conceived one Reality; sages call it by various names; they call it Agni, Yama, Matarishvan 'That One' (tad ekam). The Rigveda points toward the mysterious "One," eka, which underlies and makes possible all multiplicity. There is one transcendental reality before creation of the world. There was one Atman in the beginning. It is the cause of all created things. It is their substratum in which they subsist. It is their ultimate ground and essence. It is one devoid of plurality. It is one beyond many then it. It is one without a second. The supreme principal is called Brahma because it is the up questions cosmic principle.

Tad ekam RV I. 164, 6.46

1.6. Not understanding, and yet desirous to do so, I ask the wise who know, myself not knowing; who may he be, the one in the form of the unborn who props in their place the six universal regions? [34]

4.6. They call him Indra, Mitra, Varuna,
Agni no the heavenly sumbird Garutmat.
The seers call in many ways that which is one;
they speak of Agni, Yama, Matarisvan.[35]

RV III. 54, 8–9.

That One (ted ekam) is not personal; it is neither male or female; it is neuter. It is an impersonal principle which breathed by itself without breath.

ii.8. All beings they unite and separate
They support the mighty God, but do not tremble.
The one is Lord over all things fixed or moving,
Walking or flying – this whole multi formation.[36]

9. From afar I perceive the Ancient one, the
father of mighty power, the generator, our connection,
singing the praise of whom the Gods, stationed
on their own board pathway, go about their business.

RV III. 56 20ab 4

iii. The one, without moving, supports six burdens.
The cows have gone to him, the highest instance.

RV VIII. 58.2[37]

iv. Only one is the Fire, enkindled in numerous ways;
Only one is the sun, pervading this whole universe;

Only one is the Dawn, illuminating all things.
In very truth, the one has become the whole world.

RV X. 114, 5ab

v. By their words the inspired sages impart
manifold forms to that Bird which is one.[38]

vi. Assemble all, with prayer to the Lord of heaven,
He is the one, the all-pervading, the guest of men.
He, the ancient of days, abides in the present.
Him, the one, the many follow on their path.

Av XIII. 4 12.21 6

Ekam Evadvitiyam

One without a second. It is the saying in chhandyoga upnishad as our first utterance, for it is in its light that we find the true perspective for viewing all the others. Likewise, in the Decalogue of the Bible, the opening sentence "I am Yahweh your God" through not incorporated into any of Ten Commandments constitutes the background that makes them meaningful. Similarly, in the Indian context, the ten command ments or tenfold law of Manu. Firmness, forgiveness, self-control, not stealing, inner and outer purity, sense mastery, insight, wisdom, truthfulness, and meekness[39], I must all be understood as being both the manifestation of dhamma and its fulfillment. Thus the four mahavakyas of the upnishads make sense only if viewed against the background of this first utterance, which affirms the uncompromising primary of the one. Nothing short of the one can be ultimate truth. Chhandogya upnishad significantly enough, also contain the mahavakya which is considered the zenith of the upnishadic teaching. Further more, both these teachings are imparted to sveltely by his own father uddaaka Aruni, teacher of famous yajnavalkya.

The setting is delightful. The young Svetketu, following the best Brahmanical tradition that Brahmanhood is not just a privilege of birth, goes away for twelve long years to study the Vedas. Coming back puffed up with pride, after spreading half of his total sum of years in academia, he is cross-examined by his father who asks him whether he knows how that which has not been heard becomes heard, that which has not been understood becomes understood. The learned young man knows noting of any such teaching. The vedic sage's fundamental question of the search of the infinite. In a period when information has reached its saturation point, when it is practically impossible to know and understand all the details of the constantly proliferating sciences and discoveries, when people begin to question the efficacy and even the possibility of a way out, of a comprehensive world view then the upnishadic "way in" of sitting quietly and trying to reach the roots of all things appears again in all its effectiveness. If there is any answer to such a quest in can come only from an attitude like that of the upnishads. Our minds must go in right direction in order to find right answer. Only in this way we can grasp the ungraspable, because we seize it before it is grasped, see in the uncared block all its potentialities, seized all music at its root before it is played. In other words, the unnishadic seer leads us to consider the identity of things and not their diversity.

When you come to central point regarding that one only without a second! There are two opinions. One says in the beginning the world was 'Being' one. Only without a second, and the other affirms, on the contrary, that at the beginning there was just non-being, one only without a second. By closer examination, however, we discover there is no contradiction in say that Being on the one hand and non-being on the other are one without a second, because the subject of both sentences is not being or nonbeing but idum, this, the nominative singular neuter of the demonstrative pronoun.

This, the idam, whether you consider it to be at the beginning Being or Nonbeing, is one. If somebody were to object that the idom is not one, the upnishadic. Seers would reply that the "Purvapaksha," the opponent, says to precisely because he has identified the idam with his particular conception of it, it is no longer an idam that can be applied to everything and every person who is capable of uttering idam sensibly. Idam is anything that that can full within the range of any possible experience.

The word advitiya or nondual has sometimes been considered to stem from a monistic world view. Even grammatically the word is painstakingly chosen to denote, not ekatva, kaivalya, ekaitama, and like but a a-dvita, that is, negation of all duality.

The One Only: Ekam eva: One of the questions of the great yajnavalkya, the 'clever' vidagha, does not know the danger of asking questions with out realizing their implications. And yet we owe to his searching spirit one of the most striking. 'reductions" of the multiplicity of Gods (1) He will not stop at anything before one, the only to which all powers all Gods, can be ultimately reduced which is both known as (Prana), the breath of life and unclench (as tyad, that)

But, as if he had to demonstrate by his life that these questions are far from being rhetorical, his ignorance of the true upnishadic 'Purusha' costs him his head. The warming that yajnavalkya had given to Gurgi for her unrestrained questioning has here come true. Vidogdha dies probably because he did not understand that the atman is not another but the only, one and one only.

Ekam eva [41]

BU III 9, 1–9

1. Then Vidagha Salaya asked him, "How many Gods are there Yajnavalkya?"
   He replied according to the Nivid, quoting the number mentioned in the Nivid of All Gods; "Three hundred and three and three thousand and three, Yes," he said, "but how many Gods are there really, Yajnavalkya?"
   Thirty three.[42]
   'Yes' he said 'but how many gods are there really, Yajnavalkya?
   Six,
   Yes, he said, "but how many Gods are there really Yajnavalkya?"
   Three
   Yes, "but how many Gods are there rally, Yajnavalkya?"

"Two."

"Yes," he said, but how many Gods are there really, Yajnavalkya?

'One and a half.'

'Yes,' he said, but had many Gods are there really, Yajnavalkya?

'One,'

'Yes,' he said, "but which are those three hundred and three and tree thousand and three?"[43]

2. Yajnavalkya replied: 'There are but their powers; there are only thirty-three Gods?'

   'The eight Vasus, eleven Rudras, and twelve Atityas make thirty-one; thus with Indra and Prajapati there are thirty-three all told.'[44]

3. "Which are the Vasus?"

   "Fire, the earth, space, the Sun, the sky, the moon, and the starts – these are the Vasus. In them is stored all treasure; hence they are called Vasus."[45]

4. "Which are the Rudras?"

   "The Ten breath that are in man, and the "atman" is the eleventh. When they leave the mortal body, cause men, to weep. Because they cause men to weep they are Rudras."[46]

5. "Which are the Atityas?"

   'The twelve months of the year, these are the Adityas they move onward, carrying along all that is; hence they are called Adityas.'[47]

6. "Who is Indra," Who is Prajapati?

   "The Thunder is Indra, The sacrifice is Prajapati."

   What is thunder?

   Lightening.

   What is sacrifice?

   "The Victim."

7. Which are the six?

   "Fire, the earth, the wind, space, the sun and the sky – these are the six, for these six are all."

8. Which are the three Gods?

   "The three Gods are three world's, in them all those Gods exists."

   Which are the two Gods?

"Food and life breath."
Which are the one and a half?
"The One who blows."

9. About this God they say: as the one who bellows (the air) is one only, why speak of one and a half? Because in him all this has developed, hence it is called one and a half.
Which is the one God?
Life Breath; he is Brahma, which the call that (tyad)
For me there is no earth, no water, and not fire.
For me there is neither wind nor ether.
The one who has discovered the supreme "atman"
dwelling in heart, without parts, without a second,
the universal witness, neither being nor non being
attains the pure form of the supreme atman.

The Vedic poets were simple children of nature. The wondered at the great and sublime, beautiful and useful aspects of nature, and thrilled into ecstasy. They clothed the powers of nature with the glory of supernatural and super human spirits akin to mankind. They broke forth into songs in honor of the gods;

Agni-

O shining one, cause now the sun,
that unaging star, to climb the sky,
imparting light to men.
You, O Lord, are mankind's bright sign,
Best, most beloved of the people, Awake!
Give strength to the singer!

RV X. 156, 4–5

Vishvedevah

1 with all the pleasing skill we may;
the birth of Gods we now proclaim
in chanted hymns, that men to come
may know of what be fell.

RV X. 72

Ushas

1 Now the Dawns have made their bright appearance,
Unfurling their splendor in the eastern firemaranment.
Like strong men preparing their weapons, these mothers,
the reddish morning clouds, arise.

RV I. 92

Pushon 1

Shorten our path, O God, remove
all stumbling blocks Deliver,
Be at hand to guide.

RV I. 42

Soma – 1

O Cleansing sacred Drink,
conqueror of high renown,
make us perfect.

RV IX. 4

Isavasyam

That is fullness, this is fullness,
From Fullness, comes fullness,
When fullness is taken from fullness.
Fullness remains.
Om peace, peace, peace.

ISU – 1–3

1. This whole universe is, all that lives
and moves on earth, is enveloped by the Lord.
Therefore find a joy in abandoning, the transient.
Do not hanker for another man's lot.
May the wind blow sweetness,
the river flow sweetness,

the herbs grow sweetness,
For the Man of truth'[48]
Sweet be the night,
Sweet the dawn
Sweet be earth15 fragrance,
Sweet father Heaven.
May the tree afford us sweetness,
the sun shine sweetness,
our cows yield sweetness.
milk in plenty!

RV I. 90, 6–8

The Gitā, as usual, adds its own touch of practicality. There distress of the human predicament can be overcome and sorrow can be eliminated. The process is, precisely, the true yoga. It consists not only in adjusting to the inevitable or in acquiring a sense of proportion, as is tempted to say; it is more than an ascetic detachment. It is the positive and disciplined act of cutting the knot that connects our existence with all that is perishable. *Sukha* and *duhkha* are not primordially ethical and much less eudemonistic categories, as if everything were on the level of pleasure and pain. It is rather a question of being or not being, or salvation, or realization.

A refreshing feature of the Vedic way of life, as we have already seen, is its healthy combination of the sacred and the secular. The intuitions underlying the concept of sacrifice demonstrate this to the full. Sacrifice is sacred, for it effects a breakthrough from the human plane to the divine and leads us to a new dimension of human existence; but it is also secular, for it requires human collaboration and engages the whole world in its performance. The three hymns in this subsection emphasize this idea and, though coming from differing backgrounds, all refer to sacrifice. The first one, RV X, 101, is a hymn addressed to the priests who offer the Soma-juice. It does not devote itself, as one might expect, to praise of the sacred office of the priest and to a detailed account of the various rites he must piously perform, but to a vivid and realistic description of the sacrifice in full swing with its atmosphere of busy activity, the various ritual acts being coordinated with careful precision.

At daybreak the sacred fire is lit and then, to use the accustomed phrase, the sacrifice is "set out," "stretched," just as threads may be set out on a loom. Sacrifice is next compared to a boat that transports the sacrificer to the opposite, that is, the heavenly, shore. Verses 3 and 4 compare sacrifice to ploughing. It is the priests who, being knowledgeable in the art of winning divine favor, yoke the ploughs. Verse 5 alludes in some detail to Soma, the "fount unfailing." Verse 7 goes on to compare sacrifice to a chariot and its ritual performance to a racecourse, while further mention is also made of the pressing stones which, under this new symbolism, become the chariot wheels. Verse 9 is a prayer that the divinity may be pleased to lend his ear, show himself favorable to the one who offers sacrifice, and shower abundant blessing upon him, "like milk from a bountiful cow."

The second hymn, which we have entitled "The Diverse Callings of Men," is dedicated to Soma and seems to be in a humorous vein. The third refers to the controversial *purusamedha* or human sacrifice, whether performed actually or symbolically. All three give a vivid picture of the highly organized Vedic society and the performance within it of a wide range of human activities.

There is no question here of presenting any human age of the past as a model for the present, nor of extolling the past to the detriment of the present. The importance lies in our observing how past ages have managed to deal with the human condition in the most variegated situations and to what extent a certain degree of specialization ha enhanced or harmed human harmony and wholeness.

Work is not regarded in the Vedas as unworthy of Man or as the occupation of slaves alone; nor, on the other hand, is it the highest human activity. Of this these hymns are a proof. In the first everythingh is concentrated upon a higher action; in the second the poet is sufficiently far removed from the scene to view it with a humorous eye. In the third text the seer seems to be so convinced that the highest values lie on another level as to suggest that Man's proper course consists in the sacrifice of his activities, at least as a sincere token of total surrender.

In the third hymn, which is concerned with human sacrifice, we have inserted some explanations in square brackets, so as to make more specific the range of human activities uunder consideration. The rite of human sacrifice consists in binding representatives of all classes, professions, and types of men and women to the sacrificial stake and offering them symbolically to Prajapati (v.22). Collective fice. This rite was considered to be even more efficacious than the famous *asvamedha,* horse sacrifice, Man being the most noble of all victims.[1] The irony, the relation among the different human trades, and the value each represents are obvious and require no commentary. It goes without saying that we are taking this hymn out of its context. We simply give it as an example of the many human activities of Vedic Man.

Cosmic Splendor in Man

Yasas

Modern Man tends to define himself as a bundle of needs and he asserts his right to the fulfillmetn of such needs. He needs food clothing, shelter, "education," and work, and modern society is theoretically organized so as to provide for his needs. The Vedic view seems to be concerned less with organizing society and more with personal fulfillment. Instead of justice, glory seems to be the central value: a glorious Man and a glorious community.

Human glory sems here to be less an imitation of the divine glory than a participation in the universal and indeed divine splendor of creation. Man's glory is not a reflection of God's glory but a sharing in the very splendor of God by a full realization of the but a sharing in the very splendor of God by a full realization fo the human function in the universal adventure of reality. In other words, the underlying pattern is not a dualistic one, with the lower instance striving to imitate and reach the higher one, but a pluralistic structure in which each being including both the gods and material things, has its own proper function.

Yet this pluralistic structure implies a unitarian basis. Each being can realize itself and reach its own plentitude because each plays its part in the one harmonious and perfect pattern that admits no final incompatibilities. It is the privilege of Man to discover this pattern and thus to be able to realize the ideal described in the Isa Upanisad: to see all beings in his own self and his own self in all things.[2] This constitutes true human plenitude and an absence of delusion and sorrow. The thirst for perfection, the striving for an ever better human situation, are inherent in Man. All depends however, upon one's nation for Man?

The texts of this subsection illustrate a certain fundamental trait of the Vedic tradition and at the same time show its evolution and pluralism. The fundamantal trait is deliberately suggested by teh title: *Cosmic Splendor in Man.* Human plentitude is not attained by isolation from the rest of the world, nor does it consist in the development of one part of the human being. Man integrates in himself all the realms of the world and he radiates the splendor of the entire universe. Man is not the victim of blind cosmic forces nor is he a mere cog in the cosmic wheel; his situation is neither that of an absolute monarch nor of a slave cursed with the burden of responsibility. All such ideas are foreign and inappropriate here. The underlying idea is one of wholeness, of integration. The perfect Man is not he who merely possesses a pure mind or a healthy body, for perfection implies a certain integration of all existing human values. At the same time our texts show a variation in emphasis and even a wide pluralism in their understanding of this wholeness.

The first text, from the Atharva Veda (XIX, 51), sees human perfection as an undivided, integrated life not only embracing the entire human realm but also daring to embrace the divine.

The second hymn, taken from the Rg Veda (X, 158), evidences the same desire to embrace the whole of reality, but seems to be more concerned with encompassing the whole of the cosmic creation. Man does not want to be excommunicated from the world; he longs to embrace it by a signle glance, both as a whole and in all its details. The happy life is here not to look at God, but to see the reality of the world face to face, in its entirety and in all its concrete particulars.

The follwoign prayer, from the Yajur Veda (XXXVI), constitues part of a ceremony and has a cultic character. The wholeness is here seen as harmony and peace, with Man having his own place in the framework of the universe. Disorder is the curse and the sin. Human perfection consists in being integrated in an orderly manner into the whole scheme of things.

The same atmosphere is breathed in another prayer, also from the Yajur Veda. It is addressed to Agni and asks for well-being of body, life, and mind and for whatever else may be needed for our perfection.

The two, other excerpts from the Atharva Veda (III, 22; VI, 38) portray Man's longing to reach the sumit of creation. Man cannot tolerate the thought of any splendor outside himself, that is to say, which he also may not possess. He wants the majesty of the elephant, the strength of the lion, the swiftness of the waters, the power of thunder, the might of the winds, and all the attributes of nature. He aspires even to the glory of the Gods and longs to be invested with it; he yearns to be king of the universe and thus candidly prays to the Gods to be endowed with unlimited power

Metaphysical Concept of Rigveda – Soul, God

The one that ignites the unseen particles, inexhaustible shining identical to one another, which procreate, give birth to all creatures in the universe by extending stretching expanding to become whatever designs, longings and desires of the implicate order, that must be the weaver moving and carrying this flying-failing treasure of galactic worlds, the sacrificial ladle reflecting sound in the tongue-flame within us.

The Rigveda really is all about the ultimate 'power' – the power that pervades the universe as soma (plasma), Indra (the force of

Kinetic energy) that ignites (kindles), Agni (fire, thermo nuclear and electric) surya radiation, not the sun, and Rudra (primal sound) – because metaphysics is the underlying substructure of any true science of physics.

The universe is teaming with life and earth is but one colony among thousands, a process which as Bruce Cathie said has no doubt been repeated countless numbers of times to produce system very similar to ours, which in turn have been populated by beings much the same as ourselves.

The groups of being who colonized our planet earth could only have traversed space in the knowledge of a very advanced physics and because that physics would have involved the collapse of space-time, their physics would have by necessity been metaphysics.

"The only way to traverse the vast distance of space is to possess the means of manipulating or altering the space time geometric matrix which provides to us the illusion of forms and distance."

Plasma physics, as understood by the electric universe folks is an evolving science, which is quite natural. The best Indian scholars seem to all agree that the early sacred Sanskrit text were more of the nature of enquire, in other words these great once were reflecting the one in the mirror of their won understanding. The Rishi prajapat paramesthi asks if the one can ever be known in Rigveda we know not if it can be held, the continuum-indeed if it can be known at all.

The inscrutable riddles that so often perplex any one who attempt to make sense of the Rigveda become clear by substituting the various meanings of words, especially the names of the old Rig-Vedic gods (deities, with terms that come from plasma physics and the electric universe school of thinking. It like and relate to the electric-universe ideas because their concepts fit so readily and indeed perfectly into eternal primordial metaphysics.

In ancient times metaphysics was physics because wisdom-knowledge was not separate from science. The wise, the seers in those eras were not cut-off from the now invisible aims that re truth (satya) and the substratum of all the manifested existence in this universe. Astronomers were also astrologers patterns in the micro-cosm are reproduced as repeating reflections in the microcosm. The phrase as above, so below is found in the text of Hermeticism, although these texts originated in the Vedas as did most western esotericism.

Therefore one of the multiple layers of meaning in Rigveda can be interpreted as primordial metaphysics seen through the lenses of an electric universe and plasma physics, which in the more advanced form is the key to space travel and free energy. It may be that Rigveda mantras are some what comparable to metaphysical formulas and plasma physics. The seers of Vedic age were equal to astrophysicists. The mantras were in existence long before either Brahmi or Sanskrit (1700–1200 BCE). The origin of Brahmi is disputed and unknown. Sanskrit is thought to have developed out of Brahmi although several Sanskrit sounds cannot be written in Brahmi (wikipedia).

The Vedic mantras are imperishable, existing in the highest ethers, where reside all gods (deities, those forces centipede and centrifugal that create, sustain, and destroy the universe.)[4]

The metaphysical concept of every deity in Rigveda.

Agni: Vital energy of life the fire of life a spark of universal intelligence bearing all the attributes of the supreme force.

Anu: An atom, a vibrating particle (van-to resonate).

Arya: Sky, space, medium of sound.

Indra: Intelligence (vind-to be powerful), the legendary 'god of gods' who rules over the other gods (lights) identified as sense-organ in man.

Tapas: Warmth heat, fire also one of the seven regions above the earth.

Divam: Day, heaven, the sky (vdiv – to shine, to play, rejoice, squander).

Bhuva: The atmosphere, ether.

Hiranya: Indicates the electric quality of forces; electro magnetism, (vhri – to capture, take away +van-a particle).

Svah: The sky, ether, radiance, the soul.

Soma as plasma: The Sanskrit word soma was my first revelatory insight for interpreting the older Vedic Sanskrit in the Rig veda as plasma physics. Sanskrit scholars have explained the word. Soma is so many ways. Soma is currently taken to mean a type of intoxicating 'creeper' plant.

Plasma is a 'sea' of electrically charged particles. Consciousness is often described a san ocean. All wisdom metaphysical schools teach that every thing is ultimately interconnected. The motion of charged particles a self-magnetic field that can act on other collections of particles as plasma provide sources of energy for driving electric currents over large distances.

"According to the principle of diffraction, when a wave passes through an obstruction, it spreads out into the shadowed space. A creeping wave in electromagnetism or acoustics is the wave that is diffracted around the shadowed surface of a smooth body such as a sphere."

In Rigveda, soma is said to be the procreator of Surya (the sun's energy, rays and radiation). Soma sees inside hidden things and knows all rays (ix.96.7), is the sun world (ix.96.18), giving birth to the luminous world of heaven, birth to the sun in the waters, clothes himself with the waters and the Rays (ix.42.1); has generated the light in the sun (ix.86.29); [soma] is the procreator of Agni [fire in all forms], protector of surya (the sun's energy) [ix.96.5]; no earthly person can taste (or enjoy) you (soma) (ix.85.4).

Indra: Indra is a very predominant god in the Rigveda and is described as a human man, strong, with a golden beard, and of golden color. Indra was said to be the leader of five tribes: the Yadus, Turvashes Druhyus, Anus, and Parus (1.108.8); Indra was 58 friends and 70 enemies; he seizes great wealth and is a donor of wealth and food. Indra released the waters in ninety-nine rivers, perhaps Indra is also a station, a position of command

and leadership like (humor me...) the Master Engineer of Hyper luminal plasma physics and international space travel time.

Rigveda II.15.2; who fixed the heaven in unsupported (space), and filled the spacious firmament, and heaven and earth (with light): he is who upheld and has made the earth renowned; in the exhilaration of the soma Indra has done these deeds.

The root etymology of the Sanskrit word India is 'kindling &' 'lighting;' an evolutes of Indra, from Indh "to kindle." Indra also has the meaning one who tears this (idom) from this (idom), and dr(i) 'to tear.' This one who tears; Indra who runs or rushes forth for soma.

NASA: The solar wind is an electrically conduce ting gas called plasma where matter has been torn apart into electrons, which are relatively light, and positively charged ions which are thousands of times more massive, whiled areas in shadow get a strong neattre charge when electrons in the solar wind rush in ahead of heavier ions to fill voids created as the solar wind.[6]

Soma [plasma] is intimately connected with Indra. Indra drinks lakes of soma, and soma is often said to flow for Indra's sake. Soma is Indra Soul [RV IX.85.3] and even his generator [IX 96.5] Indra is connected to Norse odin and Greek Uranus, and associated with an eagle.

Soul: Individual soul and supreme soul.

Brahma is the cosmic principal. Atamn is the psychic principal. It is the inner self in man. Brahma is Atman. The cosmic principal is the psychic principle. The universal spirit is the self in him. It is his inner guide (antaryamin). Brahma is the soul (Atman) of all. "The eternal knower is the soul, inner guide the immortal. It is the knower, but it is not known. It is the foundational consciousness which is the ground of the universe. It is the ground of our empirical consciousness. The eternal, universal light of consciousness resides in our heart and illumines all objects of our knowledge. It is the soul that is within all. 'That of which the whole universe is composed, that is, the real, that is the soul, that art then, O 'svetketu,' 'Tat tvam asi,' 'I am Brahma,' 'Aham Brahmasmi.' This soul is Brahman. 'Ayam atma Brahma.' Shankara emphasized the identity of individual soul with the universal soul."

Mandukya upnishad speaks of four stages of the individual soul and the universal soul. The individual soul in walking condition is called the vishva, which knows and enjoys gross external objects. The individual soul in the condition of dream is called the 'Taijasa,' which knows and enjoys subtle internal objects or cognition. The individual soul in the condition of dreamless sleep is called the prajna which is one homogenous mass of consciousness and bliss (prajnanaghana). It does not apprehend external objects or internal cognitions. The individual soul in the fourth ecstatic (turiya) condition is called the Atman which is one universal consciousness (ekatmapratyayasara) which knows neither external objects nor internal cognitions, which is not a mass of consciousness, which is neither consciousness (Prajana) nor non-consciousness (aprajna). It is one, non dual, non empirical super consciousness. The entire universe of gross objects constitutes the body of virat or vaisvanara. The totality of subtle bodies constitutes the body of Sutratma.

The God, deity, deva, Lord, is different name of supreme power which has been described differently in different shastras. It is very comprehensive term used not only for the different names of the divinities and of God in different religious traditions, but also for many other forms of preeminence in the human world. In Rigveda, powerful natural phenomena, which is super spirit and superhuman, is personified and deified, considered, "Lord," deities. When you use proper name, by saying varuna-mitra, Agni, Shiva or Yahweh, you are not only personifying but also limiting our reference to that one culture where the word is at home.

The Vedic revelation does not reveal one God. It just unveils a little the mystery of life by assuring us that the reality is concealed in the universe which has pervade everywhere and exists in all cosmic bodies strotra of Rigveda.

i.	O most youthful God!	RV I, 44,6
ii.	God of the sacrifice, O Lord, and envoy of men are you.	RV I, 44.9
iii.	O most radiant one, all visible!	RV I, 45.9
iv.	Good and bountiful, source of gigori	RV I, 45.9
v.	May our songs glorify God, the mightiest!	

Savitr: The unique Lordship of Savitra, the resplendent Sun, the vivifier, is so much a part of everyday life that no one will contest his supremacy.

Atman (a:tman/; Sanskrit: (आत्मन) is a Sanskrit word that means "inner-self" or 'soul.' According to the Rig Vedic concept Atman is the first principle, the true self of an individual beyond identification with phenomena, the essence of an individual. In order to attain liberation, a human-being must acquire self-knowledge (atma-jnana), which is to realize that one's true self (Atman) is identical with the transcendent self-Brahma. 'Atman' means "essence" breath, soul related to PIE atmen (a root found in Sanskrit and German and which means 'breath-and in ancient 'Greek' a tuoc' – atmos 'vapor' like in atmosphere.

The earliest use of the word 'Atman' in an Indian text is found in Rigveda (RV x 97.II). Yaska, the ancient Indian grammarian commenting on this Rigvedic vese, accepts the following meaning of Atman, the pervading principle, the organism in which other element are united and the ultimate sentient principle. In Rigvedic hymn 1.115.1, VII.87.2, VII 101.6, VIII.3.24, IX,2.10, IX6.8 and X 168.4.

"The Atman soul is indeed Brahma." It (Atman) is also identified with the intellect, the Manas (mind), and the vital breath, with the eyes and ears, with earth water air and akasha, with fire and what is other than fire, with desire and absence of desire, with anger and absence of anger, with righteousness and unrighteousness, with everything – it is identified as is well known, with this and with that.

"There is no higher object than the attainment of Atman. Shall quote the verses from veda which refer to the attainment of the knowledge of the Atman. All living creatures are the dwelling of him who lies enveloped in matter, who is immortal, who is spotless. A wise man shall strive after the knowledge of the Atman. It is he (self) who is the eternal part of in all creatures, whose essence is wisdom, who is immortal, unchangeable pure, he is the highest goal."

Freedom from anger, from excitement from rage, from greed, from perplexity, form hypocrisy from hurtfulness (from injury to others); speaking the truth, moderate eating, refraining from colony gifts, uprightness, forgiveness, gentleness, tranquility, temperance, amity with all living creatures, yoga honorable conduct, benevolence, contentedness. These virtues have been agreed upon for all the ashrams; he who, according to the precepts of the sacred law, practices these, becomes united with the universal self – 1.8.23.6.

वस्तु सर्वाणि भूतान्यात्मन्येवानुपष्यति। सर्वभूतेषु चात्मनं ततो न विजुगुप्सते।।6।।

यास्मिन्सर्वाणि भूतान्यात्मैवाभूद्विजानतः। तत्र को मोहः कः षोक एकत्वमनुपष्यतः।7।

स पर्यगाच्छक्रमकायमव्रणम् अस्न्नाविरं षुद्धमपापविद्धय। कविर्मनीषी परिभूः

स्वम्यूः यायातथ्यतोर्थात् त्यदद्याच्छाष्व तीष्यः स्याष्यः।।8।।

And he who sees everything in his Atman, and his Atman in everything, does not seek to hide himself from that.

> In whom all beings have become one with own Atman, what
> Perplexity, what sorrow, is there, when he sees this oneness?
> He [the self] pervades all, resplendent,
> Bodiless, woundless, without muscles, pure
> Untouched by evil. Far seeing, transcendent,
> self-being, disposing ends through perpetual ages.

All orthodox schools of Hinduism hold the premise, Atman exists, as self evident truth. Buddhism in contrast, holds the premise, 'Atman does not exist as self evident.'

Buddhist do not believe that at the core of all human beings and living creatures, there is any "eternal, essential and absolute something called a soul self or Atman Buddhist reject the concept and all doctrines associated with atman, call atman as illusion (maya), asserting instead the theory of "no self" soul in its core philosophical and conological text. In its stereological themes, Buddhism has defined nirvana as that blissful state when a person realizes that he or se has 'no-self, no soul.'67

> Hindus believe in Atman. They hold that at the core of all human beings and living creatures there is "eternal, inner most essential and absolute something called a soul, self that is atman." Within the diverse school of Hinduism, there are difference of perspective on whether souls are distinct, whether supreme soul or God exists, whether the nature of Atman is dual or non-dual, how to reach moksha-the knowledge of self that liberates one to blissful content state of existence, and whether moksha is achievable in this life or achievable only in after life. If one obtained the knowledge of 'self-soul,' (the Atman) and Brahma, and keep this knowledge in his mind that Atman is a part of Brahman; similar in quality and only different in quantity and lead the The only "divinity" that is not overcome by the powers of evil is the principle of life, the central life breath, prana, which is frequently identified with the atman.[3] Here again we have the strong conviction that life itself is invincible, that the Self is untainted and untouched by evil. Only evil or fall victim to the asuras can overpower the external organs, only the nonessential part of reality, and not the very core of life, the atman. Sin affects Man only in his manifestations, not ultimately in his very Being, uniess; of course, he is an atmahan, as Isa upanisad says, that is one who slays his own Self.[4] Thus it is only this selfsame core of our existence which will ultimately overcome evil.
>
> Even when it is overcome, evil is not totally annihilated. In the Language of this Upanisad, it is onluy expelled or sent to the very ends of the earth (or, historically speaking, to the limits of one's won "civilized" world); hence it is dangerous to go beyond certain limits, even geographically, because on may be affected by evil.

In Hindu tradition moksha is the central concept and included as one of the four aspects and goals of human life; the other three goals are drama (virtuous, proper, moral life) artha (material prosperity, income security means of life) and Kama (pleasure, sensuality, emotional fulfillment). Together, these four aims are called purushartha in Hinduism.

The Concept of Moksha Is Found in Jainism, Buddhism and Hinduism

Atharva Veda tells us when Soul (Atma) was provided to human being Vedic knowledge was revealed. Thus human soul contains all the knowledge of VEDAS. Rig Veda says that PURPOSE of Human Birth as already known to human soul is to assist the Grand Designer (Vishwa Karma) in the maintenance of His Grand wondrous Design. Rig Veda further enlightens us when soul administer the gross body a person moves towards self realization and he/she starts following cosmic laws of necessity (Vedic Rta) relating to iddm nan mam (nothing for self all for society), path of moderation, humility, love for the entire animate and inanimate life/things and many other such cosmic laws. However, Vedas categorically say "Alma can not be cognized by any of the senses and say sense organs."

It is the Soul which makes a person separate and distinct individual. The Spirit is the cause of his/her social being and along with mahabhuta – five main elements and three gunas of purity, activity and stupor, is the cause of good or bad actions of the individuals. The right and virtuous path is only known to the manifested soul (jivatma), which is nearest on self-realization and farthest when phenomenal and the material worlds become the closest (A.V. X-8-8). The individuals who know and understand the Spirit as the powerhouse of creativity in them create subtle waves of nobility, love, and harmony even if they sit silently in any gathering or assembly. Chhandogya Upanishad describes Spirit as the Creative force, which hides behind all animate and inmate life/things, moves us, moves the planets, and moves the universe.

Yajur Veda 34–43 refers to human beings as tri-ani pada i.e. having three bodies in one – divine (causal body where soul resides near the heart), spiritual (subtle body energized by spirit residing in shuniya (cosmic void) and gross body where senses and sense organs reside). The soul makes a person divine animal, spirit makes a person social animal and senses and sense organs make a person material and economic man. Hence in the Vedas a man is divine, social and material animal. Many hymns in Rig-Veda 1-70-2, 1-65-1 and others mention that God lives in our souls as a true preceptor (Guru). The Both the Supreme Lord and the living entity are known as atma. The Supreme Lord is called Paramatma, and the living entity is called the atma, the brahma or the the jiva.

Both the Paramatma and the jivatma, being transcendental to the material energy, are called atma. Generally people have many wrong conceptions about both of them. The wrong conception of the jivatma is to identify the material body with the pure soul, and the wrong conception of Paramatma is to think Him on an equal level with the living entity.

In the Upanisads it is explained that there are two types of souls which are technically known as jiva-atma and param-atma. ***Jiva-atma, or the individual soul**, is the living entity and* ***param-atma refers to the Supreme Lord** who expands Himself as the Supersoul, who enters into the hearts of all living entities as well as all atoms.*

This is also confirmed in Bhagavad-gita [13.23] where it is stated that besides the living entity, who tries to enjoy in his physical body, there is another, a transcendental enjoyer who is the Lord, the supreme proprietor, who exists as the overseer and guide, and who is known as the Supersoul. He is not an ordinary living entity, but the plenary expansion of the Supreme Lord. Because monist philosophers and impersonalists take the soul and supersoul to be one, they think that there is no difference between the Supersoul and the individual soul. To clarify this the Lord says that He is the representation of Param-atma in every body. He is different from the individual soul; He is parah, transcendental.

The individual soul, deluded by material energy, tries to enjoy the activities of particular types of bodies offered by material nature, but the Supersoul is present not as finite enjoyer nor as one taking part in bodily activities, but as the witness and permission giver. He is present within to sanction the individual soul's desires for material enjoyment.

The Supersoul fulfils the desire of the atomic soul as one friend fulfils the desire of another. The Upanisads compare the soul and Supersoul to two friendly birds sitting within the same tree. One of the birds (the individual atomic soul) is eating the fruit of the tree, and the other bird (the Supersoul) is simply watching His friend. Of these two birds – although they are similar in their characteristic natures – one is captivated by the fruits of the material tree, while the other, who is self satisfied, is simply witnessing the activities of His friend.

The Supreme Lord, who enters the hearts of all living entities in the form of the Supersoul, is compared to the witnessing bird. The other bird, the fruit-eater (living entity), who is enchanted by the fruits of material enjoyment, has forgotten his relationship with his friend. Forgetfulness of this relationship by the atomic soul is the cause of one's changing his position from one tree to another or from one body to another. Thus the jiva soul is struggling very hard within the tree of the material body, but as soon as he turns his attention to his friend, the Supersoul, the subordinate bird immediately becomes free from all lamentation.

The Katha-Upanisad states that although the two birds are in the same tree, the eating bird, which has to face the reactions of his activities, is fully engrossed with anxiety and moroseness as the enjoyer of the fruits of the tree, while the other bird, who is the witnessing Lord, maintains His transcendental position without being affected by the material atmosphere. If somehow the individual soul turns his face to his friend the Supersoul, the suffering living entity becomes free from all anxieties.

The fact is that individual living entities are eternally part and parcel of the Supreme Lord, and both of them are very intimately related as friends. But the living entity has the tendency to reject the sanction of the Supreme Lord and act independently in an attempt to dominate the supreme nature, and because he has this tendency, he is called the marginal energy of the Supreme Lord. The living entity can be situated either in the material energy or the spiritual energy. As long as he is conditioned by the material energy, the Supreme Lord, as his friend, the Supersoul, stays with him just to get him to return to the spiritual energy. The Lord is always eager to take him back to the spiritual energy, but due to his minute independence, the individual entity is continually rejecting the association of spiritual atmosphere.

This misuse of independence is the cause of his material strife in the conditioned nature. The Lord, therefore, is giving advice and instruction from within and from without. From without He gives instructions through such Vedic scriptures as the Bhagavad-gita, and from within He acts as the Supersoul to enlighten the conditioned soul about his spiritual nature. ***Thus the intelligent person, who understands the difference between the Soul and Supersoul, can advance toward a blissful eternal life of knowledge.***

Clear understanding of material nature, the Supersoul, the individual soul and their interrelation makes one eligible to become liberated and turn to the spiritual atmosphere without being forced to return to this material nature. This is the result of knowledge. The purpose of knowledge is to understand distinctly that the living entity has by chance fallen into this material existence. By his personal endeavor in association with authorities, saintly persons and a spiritual master, he has to understand his position and then revert to spiritual consciousness or Krishna consciousness by understanding Bhagavad-gita as it is explained by the Personality of Godhead. Then it is certain that he will never come again into this material existence; he will be transferred into the spiritual world for a blissful eternal life of knowledge.

Term Guru in Vedas is from Gu-darkness and Ru – to dispel. Thus Guru is dispeller of both inner and outer darkeness.

The souls of human beings remain immortal. Based on accumulation of past and present karma – thoughts, deeds and actions, it becomes fierce, calm, terrible, fearless, ignorant and enlightened, trembling and steadfast, forbearing and nonbearing, passionate and ascetic and a prey to bewilderment (Y.V. 39–7). Thus the quality of manifested soul is different for each individual. The purity of the manifested soul and keeping it free from the effect of bad, corrupt and evil deeds, thoughts and desires make it as our philosopher, guide and friend.

The soul has been addressed by various names and epithets in the Vedas. Samrat (the ruler of the body), Vaishva Deva, Teja, Vak, Agneye, Prajapati in chapter 39 of Yajur Veda. Each name or epithet indicates its attributes, like the controlling lord, the nourisher of human beings, the just ruler etc., It is also called Twashta – subtle soul. In Bhagavad-Gita apart from atma, jivatma, words like sah (self), dehin, deha, sharirin, shariri are used (B.G.3–42, 14–11 and 12, 2–18). All these later epithets generally mean lord of the body.

The Spirit which is the life force has also its intermediaries, mind, will, intellect and ego, which are much higher and powerful than the body self i.e. gross body consisting of senses, sense organs etc. However, the Spirit becomes more or less effective in the gross body, not so much with age but kind of activities towards perfection or otherwise. With evil activities, thoughts and desires the gross body can start degenerating even at young age and the spirit gets weaker. Many of the physical sicknesses are related to your activities and thoughts and get further aggravated with idleness that Bhagavad-Gita describes as sin. Since God is perfect, the spirit always aims at perfection and in this movement towards perfection; it helps the gross body to remain healthy.

R.V 6-47-9 mentions soul as twashta – the subtle soul shines when senses are under control and sattavic guna of purity and truthfulness is predominant. According to Atharva Veda XI-8-30, the manifested soul (jiva atma) in the body administers it. The gross body of human beings is the soul holding body. Those individuals, who do not allow the soul to administer the body, normally are devoted to the letters of the scriptures and not the spirit behind their teachings. They camouflage their materialistic outlook in the form of fake spiritualism. According to Bhagavad-Gita, such persons cannot attain Vivek (determinate intellect B.G. 2–42 to 44). However, where the body is administered by the manifested soul, even the human beings become Brahma and can say "Aham Brhaman Asi" – I am Brahman. This stage of perfect control of the body by manifested soul is described as "Chhavo" or "Shava." According to Atharva Veda XI-8-34, at this stage the soul in the human body becomes the highest force and vigour.

For more details on the subject along with the relevant Vedic hymn/mantra/rik about soul (atma), manifested soul (jivatma) and spirit (jiva) kindly see chapter 7 of Glimpses of Vedic Metaphysics on Website http://www.sabhlokcity.com/metaphysics/

The book is also available through search engines of and.

Kindly render divine and noble social service and forward this e-mail to other seekers of Vedic knowledge and get the blessings of rsis and munnies of yore who found the Vedic permanent truths for the benefit of mankind of all ages.

Atman is Sat. That which exists in the past, present and future, which has no beginning, middle and end, which is unchanging, which is not conditioned in time, space and causation, which exists during Jagrat, Svapna and Sushupti, which is of the nature of one homogeneous essence (Sada Ekarasa, Sada Ekarupa) is Sat. This is found in Atman. Srutis emphatically declare: Sat only was prior to the evolution of this universe.

Our common experience, rather innate inherent feeling, that we never were not and that we never will cease to be, even though our physical bodies may disappear, clearly proves that Atman always exists. In reply to the question whether we are in this world or not, it is said by all men: We are here. Do we possess body or not? Yes, we have bodies. Whence came this body? There must be some cause for our getting these bodies, for otherwise it cannot be a cause. That cause is Karma. It is only our Karma that gives birth to this body. The Karma, which generated this body in the previous birth, ought to have been performed in a birth anterior to that and so on backwards ad infinitum. Thus, on enquiry, we find that Karma and body are beginningless, of the nature of an unceasing flood, the source of which is unknown. Karma and body form an ever-receding chain. Therefore it is certain that Atman, which subsists and forms the substratum for this chain must also be beginningless by virtue of its nature. Thus it is proved now through inference that Atman is Sat during the past and present periods.

Why can we not say that the works performed in this birth generates this body? Just as the seed, which can generate a tree, cannot generate that tree which is the cause for its own birth, so also the works performed by this body will produce a new body in the next birth but cannot generate this body. Therefore we cannot say that works done in this birth has produced this body.

Then another point is, does that Karma which generates the body belong to us or to others? Certainly it is ours. We cannot enjoy in heaven through the Karma of another. If Mr. Krishna does an evil act, he will have to suffer. It cannot affect Mr. Sadasiva. Virtue brings its own reward for the person who does the virtuous action. That is the immutable law of Nature. If one were to go to heaven through the Karma of another man, a servant also should attain heaven through the performance of a sacrifice by a learned Brahmin. All should have attained liberation through the Nirvikalpa Samadhi of Sri Sankara or Dattatreya. But this is not the case. Therefore it is quite obvious that it is only one's own Karma which generates one's own body.

The Karma that we perform now in this birth will not go in vain. Actions are indestructible. They will generate fresh bodies in the future. We will do fresh Karmas with these new bodies, which will form the seed for still future bodies and so on forwards ad infinitum. The current of Karma and body will never have an end in the future, but there is an end to Karma through Knowledge of the Self. Karma is completely annihilated by the dawn of Brahma-Jnana. Then comes a cessation of body. Even if Karma is destroyed and future births come to an end, the Atman does not perish. It is ever existent. It is eternal. Karma is of the nature of Avidya. When Karma is destroyed, all causes of pain vanish. Jivahood disappears. The Jiva enjoys the supreme bliss of the Self. Atman always is. It exists in the three periods of time. The world may come and go, but Atman always remains. Pralaya or dissolution is only for this phenomenal universe but not for the changeless, self-existent Atman. The deluge and fire may destroy the illusory names and forms but they cannot touch the imperishable Atman. You can thus clearly understand that Atman is Sat.

Atman is Chit Atman is Chit for it shines by itself unaided by any other light and illumines the whole universe by its own light. It may be asked, how can we be said to illumine the whole universe when we are ignorant? The universe is of two kinds, viz., the external and the internal. The external universe embraces the five elements and their properties, sound, touch, form, taste and odour and their combinations of various sorts, various names and forms, qualities, properties, the quintuplicated elements, Brahma's egg, the four kinds of beings, viz., the oviparous or egg-born, the sweat-born, the seed-born and the womb-born. The external universe, however varied and big it may be, is after all only inert matter. It cannot be the object of our perception unless we throw upon it the flood of our consciousness light; it can never know us. It is illuminated by us only. It can never illuminate us.

The internal universe embraces the five Koshas; the three bodies, viz., gross, subtle and causal; the six changes, the six waves, viz., birth, death, hunger, thirst, grief and delusion; the five organs of knowledge; the five organs of actions; the five Pranas; the fourfold Antahkarana, Sankalpa-vikalpa, determination, self-arrogation and enquiry; the three states of consciousness, Jagrat, Svapna and Sushupti; the activities of the Avasthas, Visva, Taijasa, Prajna; Samadhi and fainting; mind, speech and body; friendliness, mercy, complacency and indifference; Yama, Niyama, Asana, Pranayama, Pratyahara, Dharana, Dhyana and Samadhi; the eight kinds of proofs; hatred, jealousy, lust, anger, pride, hypocrisy; Sattva, Rajas and Tamas; pleasure and pain; the four means of salvation; the three kinds of pain; thoughts, feelings, emotions, sentiments. This entire inside world is also inert and cannot be the object of our perception unless we turn upon it our consciousness. We only can know it; it can never know us. The mind is finite and inert. It has no independent intelligence. It is not self-luminous. It shines by borrowing the Light from the source. It is subject to various limitations and changes. It is only an inert product of subtle matter. Atman only is the source of Chit. Mind also is perceived by the Chit. Mind has a beginning and an end.

Gold shines with splendour when molten by fire in a crucible. Whence is this lustre? The fire does not impart this glitter in the gold. It is only an instrument in removing the dross from the gold. When the impurities in the gold are removed by fire, the gold shines in its real state. Even so when the purified mind dispels Ajnana, the Atman shines in its native glory and pristine splendour. The dispelling power of the mind is borrowed from the Atman. It does not belong to the inert mind. It is generally said that a lamp dispels the darkness of a room but the mere lamp-vessel, the oil or the wick have no power in themselves to remove darkness. Nor is Agni (fire) able in itself without the help of the wick, oil and lamp-vessel to dispel darkness. It is only when the fire and the three other materials join together that there arises the name, The light of the lamp, which light destroys darkness. Even so in this lamp of body filled with oil of Karma, the fire of Atman igniting the wick called mind acquires the name of Jiva and removes the darkness of Ajnana. This power is really in Atman and not in others. It is thus clearly proved that Atman is of the nature of Chit.

Atman is Ananda

Ananda is that bliss which is eternal, uncaused and unexcelled. It is the real nature of Atman. The pleasure derived from objects such as flowers, scents, woman, fruits, sweetmeats, and others is temporary and subject to Upadhi or vehicle and degree and so it cannot be called the bliss of Atman. We experience the bliss of Atman every day in deep sleep. It is not mere absence of pain that we experience there. It is undoubtedly positive happiness, for we remember on waking up that we slept happily. This indicates the fact of the existence of bliss to Atman in that state. Other objects, which make us happy in waking state and in dream, are entirely absent in deep sleep. The bliss in deep sleep state is Upadhiless. The bliss of deep sleep is unexcelled; because we eagerly long for it above all pleasures and we dislike those people who stand in the way of our enjoying the happiness from sleep. We prepare soft beds, soft pillows to enjoy this happiness. There are eleven degrees of bliss from that of man to that of Hiranyagarbha. Each of these degrees of bliss is a hundredfold greater than that which precedes it. But the Supreme

Bliss of Brahman is degreeless. It is infinite or illimitable as there is nothing superior to it. The bliss of deep sleep is degreeless.

It must not be argued that the bliss of deep sleep cannot be eternal as we do not feel it in waking state or dream. There is that bliss existing in the waking and the dreaming states also. But it is not enjoyed clearly in these states, being veiled by the actions of the internal organs. The experience of the passing, finite sensual pleasures obscures the ever-shining bliss of the Self. Although the smoke produced by the fire obscures the fire, though the fog veils the sun behind it, yet the wise do know that they can never obscure the fire or the sun. They see beyond the ashes and the fog, the fire and the sun. Similarly the knower of the Self fully knows that though the finite sensual pleasures caused by flowers, fruits, women and the like seem to veil the inherent infinite bliss of the Atman, they really owe their origin to the latter. They are fully aware that the infinite bliss of Atman shines unobscured and unlimited during all the three periods of time and all the three states of experience. The bliss of Brahman cannot be adequately expressed in words. It has to be felt and realised through direct Self-realisation. Though we experience it, it is not an experience like the enjoyment of an object, because you are then an embodiment of bliss itself. Therefore it is clear that the bliss of the Atman and that of deep sleep, which is no other than the former, are eternal.

The love, which the father shows towards the friend of his son, is on account of his love towards his own son. The love, which the father has for the son, is not on account of the friend of his son. Therefore son is dearer than the friend of his son. Similarly wealth and son are dear on account of one's own self. The love, which one has for his own Atman, is not on account of wealth or son. Therefore Atman is dearer than a son or wealth.

Man loves his wealth immensely. He crosses the seas and goes to the far off climes to earn money. But a son is dearer than the wealth; the father spends a lot of money to get his son out of the jail when he is locked up there for some crime. Therefore, son is dearer than money. Body is dearer than the son; the father even sells his son during famine for the sake of protecting his body. The Indriyas or senses are dearer than the body, because man protects his eyes, ears, nose, etc., when another comes to attack him. Prana or life is dearer than the senses. If the king orders to take away the life of a criminal, the criminal rather prefers to have one of his senses removed rather than give up his life. Therefore life is dearer than the senses. Atman is dearer than the life. When one is suffering from a serious incurable disease, he says: Let my Prana depart from the body. I will be happy. Therefore Atman is dearer than the life itself because it is an embodiment of bliss.

Satchidananda is only a provisional definition of Atman. We see in this phenomenal universe untruth, insentience, and pain. The Atman, which is distinct from Anatman, is therefore characterised for the purpose of easy understanding by us as Sat (real) as opposed to Asat or Anrita (unreal), Chit (consciousness) as opposed to Jada (insentience or unconsciousness) and Ananda (bliss) as opposed to Duhkha (pain). Even these terms, therefore, do not define Atman, but only distinguish it, which is beyond definition by words. To define Brahman is to deny Brahman only.

Sat, Chit and Ananda are not three distinct entities. They are not different from one another. They are coeval and coexistent with Atman. Just as water, Jal, Pani signify one and the same thing, so also Sat-Chit-Ananda signifies the one Atman. Sat is Chit. Sat is Ananda. Chit is Sat. Chit is Ananda. Ananda is Sat. Ananda is Chit. You cannot split up Sat-Chit-Ananda into three separate entities, just as you cannot separate light, heat, and luminosity from fire.

Limitation (Parichheda) is of three kinds: (1) by space (Desa), (2) by time (Kala) and (3) by things (Vastu). Body is limited by space. Atman cannot have any limitation by space, because it is all pervading and all-full. It transcends space. Atman is eternal. It cannot be limited by time. This body is conditioned in time and so it is perishable. The third kind of limitation, by things (Vastu Parichheda), is of three kinds: (1) Sajatiya, i.e., limitation by the existence of a similar thing, e. g., a tree is limited as a similar tree exists. (2) Vijatiya, e. g., a tree is limited, as a dissimilar stone exists. (3) Svagata limitation by the existence of differentiation in itself, e.g., a tree is limited as it is differentiated into the trunk, leaves, branches, flowers, root, fruits, etc., or a man is limited as he is differentiated into face, trunk, hands, legs, etc. Isvara is Abhinna-nimittopadana Karana. He created this universe out of His own body (Maya), just as the spider creates its web out of its own saliva, and entered Himself into these names and forms. Therefore there cannot be any Sajatiya Bheda such as Jiva-Isvara Bheda. There is no second Atman. There are no two Sats.

This phenomenal universe is not real. It is a mere appearance like snake in the rope or silver in the mother-of-pearl. It has no independent existence. Therefore there cannot be any Vijatiya Bheda.

Sat, Chit and Ananda are one. Atman is partless and homogeneous. The three characteristics Sat, Chit and Ananda are not distinct from one another. The tree can be differentiated into branches, flowers, twigs, etc., for they are finite things limited to particular part, of the tree, but Atman has no parts. Sat is present wherever there are Chit and Ananda. Sat cannot be limited by another Sat for there are no two Sats, nor by Asat for Asat cannot exist. If it is said that Chit is different from Sat, then it will be Asat like the horn of a hare. This sort of assumption will land you in a serious dilemma and confusion. All miseries come to a termination when one realises Atman. Therefore Atman must be an embodiment of bliss. Sat is Chit. Sat is Ananda also.

He who has realised this Sat-Chit-Ananda Atman is a liberated sage. He has nothing more to learn, has nothing more to do, has nothing more to gain. All his desires are gratified.

He has obtained all worlds. He is freed from the jaws of death. He attains immortality.

Concept of God in Rigveda

In the period of Indo-European unity, there arisen a concept of anthromorphism. The conception of anthromorphic deities of the sky, such as Agni, Dyaus, Mitra or varun, Surya, usha, Indra, Ashvins (Acvins), and it is therefore only natural that in the main the high gods of the Rigveda should be essentially conceived as human, as men of supernatural power, and free from death, but still as subject to birth and akin in their family relation to men. Though, the degree of anthropomorphism exhibited by the Vedic deities is extremely variable. In some cases the active element is constantly present, and the view taken may be set down as almost animalistic. The waters are indeed goddesses, but they are also wholesome to drink the goddess dawn bares her bosom like a beautiful maiden but there is comparison on here rather identity, and, if in some cases the goddess seems to be considered as one who appears morn after morn to men, means dawn is a fresh divinity.

Surya, the sun by his rising is born as the child of the sky, the constant presence of the actual deity prevents any real development of anthromorphism. The same consideration affects Agni, who never appears, as a god disconnected from his element of fire: when he is hidden in the waters or in the clouds it is as fire as messenger of man he is fire of sacrifice flaming up to heaven to bring gods and men together. But the difficulties of this view were clearly felt in connection with the question of the innumerable fires of earth and their relation t the God.

Indra on the other hand, is a god who has in considerable measures been emancipated from his connection with the phenomena which produced the conception primarily in all probability the thunder storm, which brings down the rain to earth, one of the greatest of India's natural phenomena. The identity of Mitra with the sun is strongly supported, but, whereas the personality of Surya remains, like that the Greek Helias, of the most shadowy character, and surya is always the material sun, mitra even in the Avesta is far from Chaired to his natural basis; he comes into view over the maintain of sunrise, it is said, before the sun, and in the Rigveda his connection with the sun can only be made certain by the parallelism of the Avesta, where he has distinct solar features: like varuna he is a celestial god who wathes over men and stires them with his speech to activity, while he supports heaven and earth.

Varuna is even more free from traces of nature, so that is remains yet doubtful whether that nature was really as is most probable the sky: he is lord of holy order, the watcher of men, whose vigilance nothing can escape. Soma in the Rigveda and later is never fully anthropomorphic, though in the Avesta he appears to the priest in the form of a man of extreme beauty, but an interesting myth of the Rigveda recounts the bringing down of soma from the sky to Indra the bird which bears down the drink is detected by the archer ksany who guards the soma, and who shoots an arrow at it.

Beside the concrete figures of the great nature gods with their extended sphere of action, there stand deities with definitely limited functions, though also nature powers of such deities. We have good example in the ksetrasyapati and vastaspati, who appear in the Rigveda itself. There are of course no abstract deities; they are, the one, the spirit who dwells in the field the other, the spirit who has his abode in the house, and neither conception can be asserted with any plausibility to be later than the period of growth of belief in the great God. More concrete still are such cases as sita, the furrow, and urvara, the field. It is significant of the great development of personification later that in the Ramayana Sita is predominately a mortal woman, wife of Rama, and daughter of Janaka. Traces indeed, remain of her former divinity for the legend tells that thers was no normal birth, but she sprang to life from the furrow when her father was ploughing, and at the end, when she determiners by a conclusive proof of show to Rama and his court that her purity had suffered nothing at the hands of Ravana during her enforced abode in the palace of her captor, her prayer to the goddess Earth is answered by the appearance of the deity, who takes her into the bosom.

The Struggle for Immortality

Daivāsura

The quest for immortality is one of Man's deepest instincts. At the same time he is aware that immortality is not his "natural" lot; immortality belongs, if at all, to the Gods, Thus a yearning to become a God springs up spontaneously within Man. We have already heard the chant of victory:

> We have drunk the Soma and become immortal!
> We have attained the light, we have found the Gods!

Man can become immortal only if he is divinized or, rather, divininzation amounts to immortality.

In connection with this theme the Vedic experience contributes two intuitions, the first of which is considered here and the second in the next text. The Brāhmanas tell us explicitly that not even the Gods were originally immortal, that immortality is not natural to the Gods, that they also had to struggle for it. Sacrifice is the way to immortality, because sacrifice is the one original and originating act, as we have already sen.

It would be merely a farce if the Gods were to achieve their immortality without a struggle, without the risk of not getting it-and so we have the scene set for the *asuras,* those beings that are unsually referred to as demons, for lack of a better term. One should recall in this connection that angels and demons have the same origin and that their good and evil features are themselves the fruits of a struggle and a test.

The fact that the Gods are obliged to win their immortality has two important implications for Men. First, the Gods are real and inspiring examples, for they have gone through the same fundamental experience as Men that of having to gain their real freedom. To attain freedom means to become immortal, to be free from the clutches of time, for as long as one is tied to time one is not really free. The Gods are really Men's fellow travelers on the journey toward immortality. Men's relation withthem is one of companionship, for Gods and Men share a common destiny in spite of their differing positions in an acknowledged hierarchy. The other implication, the recognition of which gives peace and serenity to Man, is that the Gods cannot be whimsical creatures, for there is a *rta*, an Order, whose dynamism is Sacrifice, which transcends both Men and Gods and which can in no way be manipulated or considered as being activated by an anthropomorphic will.

Let us now take a closer look at the texts themselves. Prajāpati, the Lord of all creatures, whose name is scarcely mentioned in the Rg Veda, holds in the Brāhmanas a position of capital importance. According to a lengthy narrative in the Brāhmanas, Prajāpati is the primordial being before whom nothing whatever was in existence. The Satapatha Brāhmana tells us over and over again that "Prajāpati is sacrifice;" that is, Prajāpati performed an act of self-immolation, self-sacrifice, in order that creatures might come to be. Thus creation is regarded as the sacrifice of Prajāpati, as teh ontological self-despoliation of the supreme principle in order to bring into existence the intermediate order of things which consists of the cosmos, which has come forth from the Father of all beings and is neither the Father nor sheer nothingness. This intermediate order, being neither stable nor self-existent, is by constitution transitory, or, in other words, dynamic. The reature is powerless in itself to sustain itself or to complete its full span of destin, but must attempt by means of sacrifice to recover its true status, to return to its source, retrieve its unity, that is, to become immortal, divinized.

Prajāpati, we may remember, created two types of superior beings, the *devas* (Gods) and the *asuras* (demons). In the beginning neitther the Gods nor the *asuras* were immortal. Both tried to become immortal and fought each other in order to achieve immortality. They discovered that only by means of sacrifice could they become immortal. Both performed sacrifice[5] and both strove to conquer the world.[6] The Satapatha Brahmana abounds in anecdotes about this struggle for immortality, a struggle of a unique kind, a veritable ritual battle in which the combatants are priests and the weapons sacrifices. Sacrifice is the sole means by which the gods may win the victory. Because the *devas* perform the sacrifice better than the *asuras* they win.[7] Beforwe the final vectory there are recurring conflicts and victories of a temporary nature, for the *asuras* try again and again to mount fresh assaults.

The rivalry between the Gods and the demons, the so-called *daivāsura* struggle, is the subject of one of the richest myths extant concerning the conflict constantly being waged between the two forces harbored in Man. The conflict here, however, is not ulimate. Both *devas* and *asuras* are offspring of the supreme God and it is not even certain which of the two are the firstborn.[8] The *asuras* are the enemies of the Gods but very seldom appear as enemies of Men. Both strive for immortality, but they also know that there is an incompatibility between them so that only one side can win the victory. The rituals of sacrifice, which is considered the sole total and all-inclusive act, consitute the rules of the game. The first instrument of sacrifice is the firstborn of Prājapati, *vāc,* the word. They will have to fight with it and untrue. The word is always right and wrong, true and untrue. The word is always ambivalent. The satapatha Brāhmana goes on to say that truth took refuge among the Gods and untruth among the *asuras* and that for this reason the *devas* become feeble and poor, while the demons become rich; but in the long run he who abides in truth reaches fullness of existence, while he who remains in untruth loses everything. It is by means of this sacrifice to truth that the Gods finally attained victory. The symbolism needs no further interpretation.

Daivāsura

SB I, 5, 3, 6

i). The Sacrifice ran awary from the Gods. The Gods called out after it, "Listen to us! Come back here." It replied, "Let it be so," and went back to the Gods. Now with what had thus come back to them, with that the Gods worshiped, and by this worship they became the Gods that they are to this very day.

ii). It is through Sacrifice that the Gods preceded to the heavenly realm.

iii). 1. [Once upon a time] the Gods and the *asuras,* both of who were offspring of Prajāpati, wre striving between themselves. Both sides were destitute of spirit because they were mortal and he who is mortal has no spirit. Among these two groups of mortal beings one, Agni, was immortal and it was through him, the immortal, that they both had their being. Now, whichever of the Gods was slain by the *asuras* was in very truth slain irrevocably.

2. And so the God became inferior. They continued worshiping and practicing fervent concentration, however, in the hope of overcoming their enemies who were likewise mortal. Their gaze, then, fell upon the immortal sacred Agni.
3. "Come," they said, "let us establish this immortality in our inmost self and have become immortal and unconquerable, we shall defeat our enemies who are neither immortal nor unconquerable."
4. They Said: "The Fire is with both of us; let us then speak openly with the asuras."
5. They said: "Let us establish the two fires, but then what will you do?"
6. The asuras replied: "Then we shall set it in place, saying: eat grass here, eat wood here, cook rice here, cook meat here." The fire that the asuras set in place, it is by this that mcn eat [cooked food].
7. So the Gods established that Fire in their inmost self and, having established that immortality in their inmost self and become immortal adn unconquerable, they defeated their mortal and conquerable enemies. And so he [the sacrificer] now establishes immortality in his inmost self, and though he has no hope of immortality, he attains a full lifetime. He becomes unconquerable, and when his enemy tries to overpower him, he is not overpowered. Therefore, when one who has established the Fire and one who has not are fighting, the one who has established the Fire overcomes. For by this (Fire) he becomes unconquerable, immortal.

SB II, 4, 2, 1

iv). 1. The beings came in a respectful manner to find Prājapati; by "beings" is meant the creatures he had made.
"Arrange," they said to him, "how we are to live." First the Gods drew near, ritually invested with the sacred cord [of sacrifice] and bending the right knee.
He said to them: "Receive Sacrifice as your food, immortality as your life-force, and the Sun as your ligth-sphere."

2. Then drew near the ancestors, bearing over the right shoulder the cord of sacrifice and bending the left knee. To them he said: "Receive the funeral offerings of each month as yoru food, the suadhā libation as your mind-swiftness and the moon as your light-sphere."

3. Then drew near the race of men, clothed and bnowing low. To them he said: "Night and morning shall you eat, your offspring shall be your death and fire your light-sphere."

4. Then drew near the animals. He allowed them to eat according to their fancy, saying: "Eat as chance allows, how, when, and where you will."

5. Then, finally, drew near the asuras. To them he assigned darkness and power. The power of the *asuras* does indeed exist.

SB II, 4, 3, 3

v) It is by dint of sacrifice that the Gods have brought to completion all their proper undertakings, and the same did the sages also.

SB V, 1,1,1–2

vi) 1. The Gods and the asuras, both having Prajāpati as their origin, were rivals of each other. So the asuras, swallen with pride, said, "In what, pray, should we place our oblation?" And they proceeded to place their oblations in their own mouths.

2. The Gods then proceeded to place their oblations each in the mouth of one of his fellows. And Prajāpati gave himself over to them. In this way they became owners of sacrifice, for sacrifice is really the food of the Gods.

vii) All that the Gods effect they effect by intoned recitation. Now intoned recitation is sacrifice; it is throught sacrifice therefore that they do whatever they do.

SB X, 2, 2, 1

viii) And when he had emitted the creatures, he [Prājapati] rose up on high and departed to that world where that [sun] shines; for up to then there existed no other that was worthy of sacrifice. The Gods began then to offer him in sacrifice.

ix) Prajāpati donated himself to the Gods. The sacrifice became verily theirs. Sacrifice is therefore the food of the Gods. When he donated Himself to the Gods he emitted an image of himself, which is sacrifice… By sacrifice he purchased himself back from the Gods.

TS I 6, 10, 2

x) It was by the perfect accomplishment of the sacrifice that the Gods proceeded to the heavenly realm, and it was by reason of heir defective performance of the same that the asuras were conquered.

i) Listen to us: *ā-sru-.*
Let it be so: *so' stu tathā iti.*
Sacrifice is the Gods' dynamic force.

ii) The verb *ups-ut-kram-*suggests an ascent by degrees.

iii) Destitute of spirit: anātman, without *ātman,* seems here to have a personal meaning of "with-out a personal spirit." Cf. v. 10, where the Gods desire to insert this immortality is always a second gift, the fruit of a second birth, the result of the sacrifice.

The sacrificer cannot attain immortality like the Gods, but he attains his own fullness as his complete dyus or lifetime.

One who has established the Fire: *āhitāgni,* the one who performs the *agnihotra* regularly. This sacrificial conclusion of a mythical text is typical of the B.

iv) Prajāpati gives sacrifice, immortality, and the sun to the *devas; māsi-srāddha* (cf. thought-swift: *manojavin*), and the moon to the ancestors (Fathers); alternation of day and night, offspring (*prajā*), and fire to men. To animals he gave no rite (and therefore no life-force) and no light, but only bodily sustenancy; to the asuras, only darkness (*tamas*) and pwoer (*māyā*). Some translate *māyā* as "illusion;" the power, however, is a shrewd and deceptive one, cunning might, which again related māyā, probably connoting magic. Noteworthy also are the different ways of approach: the devas are retually invested with the sacred cord (*yajňopavītin*) on teh left; the pitarah (Fathers) are prācīndvitin.

v) By sacrifice the Gods and the *rsis* have accomplished everything that is proper for them to do, or have composed their rite.

Brought to completion: the root *klp-*, to make possible, ti bring about, accomplish, perform, arrange, etc., is here used in the causative.

Proper undertakings: *kalpa,* fit; as a noun, rule, sacred ordinance.[48]

Asura in Rigveda

The Asuras are more probably to be taken as the powers of darkness than as men, though individual. Asuras may be quite well nothing but men, thus pipru is called a Dasa, and also an Asura, and the Asura Varcin, whose hundred and thousand men are slain by Indra and Vishnu when they overthrow Canberra, may fall in the same category. As studied, the Asuras appear but selfdom as foe in the Rigveda; in one hymn, however, we learn that Agni abandons the Asuras, and joins the Gods, that Indra slays Vrtra, and that the wiles of Asuras depart from them. In the Brahmana literature Indra of course, like, the other gods, fights against the Asuras, and after the usual period of defeat succeeds in defeating them in turn by the adoption of some ritual device.[49]

* * * * *

References

1. J.N. Sinha Indian philosophy vol.ii pg 428
2. Pannikar Mantramanjari.
3. RTHGriffith rigveda the oldest divine book.
4. Raimundo pannikar the Vedic Experiencepg 68
5. Raimundo pannikar The Vedic experience.pg 6
6. RTHGriffith rigveda the oldest divine book, Ask me everything first published in gr Britain 2009
7. ibid
8. J.N. Sinha Indian philosophy vol.ii pg 423.
9. The origen of the Universe The Big bang john Mills
10. Raimundo Pannikar Te vedic experience.
11. The sis systems of Indian philosophy ch.ii s k das; A study of Vedanta, ch ii; BN seal; syllabus of Indian philosophy pg 2
12. APU4 29 [saccidanandarupam tadavanmanasagocaram]
13. Tuii [satyam jnanamam tam bramha.
14. RVii 1.1
15. RV I 59,2,1,1/41
16. Rigveda iv 53.6
17. ibid
18. RVI 154.1.5
19. J.N. Sinha Indian philosophy vol II pg 420.
20. J.N. Sinha Indian Phylosophy vol.II 420 421
21. Rigveda viii 41.7
22. Rigveda vii 86.1
23. RIGVEDA vii 81.1
24. Rigveda I 48–5.6 Bergain religion vedique
25. Taitiriya samhitavii 2.7.2

26. Maxmuller ancient Sanskrit literature pg 343.
27. Rigveda samhita part 4 mandal 9–10 sriram Sharma Acharya pg 223
28. RTHGriffith rigveda the oldest divine book
29. ibid
30. ibid
31. vedic experience pannikar
32. An introduction to matter and force.
33. ekamsat vipra vahuda vadanti
34. pannikar vedic experience pannikar pg 660
35. vedic experience pannikar pg 666.
36. ibid
37. ibid
38. ibid
39. manu vi 32
40. Bu iii 6.1
41. ibid
42. ibid
43. ibid
44. ibid
45. ibid
46. ibid
47. ibid
48. vedic experience pannikar pg 80\816
49. Mantramanjari Panniker

Chapter - IV

Religious Belief of Rigveda

The Vedas represent different phases of religious thought. There are manifest sign of polytheism, organized polytheism, henotheism, monotheism, and monism. The grand, sublime, beautiful, and useful aspects of nature are personified and defied. They are regarded as ***SUPERNATURAL*** and ***superhuman*** spirits akin to human spirits. They are the deities presiding over the diverse phenomena of nature. They are not natural phenomena. They are pervasive supernatural entities, which govern the phenomena of nature, and which are benevolent to their worshippers, but terrific to their haters. They are mighty, invincible, wise, merciful, omniscient, pervasive, righteous, truthful, and benevolent. Hymns, prayer, oblations, offerings, and sacrifices easily propitiate them. They provide worldly prosperity, wisdom and moral qualities. They give victory in battles, wealth, long life, sons, grandsons and happiness1.

The Vedas are collection of hymns, seen by sages during contemplation that is why the sages are called "Mantradrasta." The Rigveda is the most ancient record of Indo-Aryan Religious thought. The word 'Rig' is derived from 'Ric' which means 'to praise.' To praise deities by means of hymns.

The Vedic poets believed to praise cosmic deities. The Agni (fire), the Sun (Surya), the dawn (Usha), the earth (Prithvi), the rain cloud (parjanya), the Maruts (storms), the Vayu, Vata (the wind), the Dyaus (Sky), the bright sky and day) the Mitra, the dark sky and evening Varuna means the *"Mitra"* and *"Varuna,"* the Savitra morning sun and the like. They are not distinct personalities like the gods of puranas. They are personified natural forces. They are endowed with great physical power, beauty, fierceness, intelligence, wisdom, omniscience, mercifulness, benevolence, justice of phenomena.

The Vedic poets intensively felt that the knowledge of the ultimate power can be obtained by receiving the knowledge of the whole universe by meditating on the Agni, the Sun, the Usha, the Mitra and Varuna and all the cosmic deities as mentioned before. They meditated and contemplated on the natural deities and derived the power and spirit of the cosmic intelligence through their intuition. And it is well-known fact that the human mind possesses infinite power to obtain knowledge; the knowledge of that world and knowledge of beyond the world i.e. the universe. It is also proved by Maharashi Patanjali in his "Yog Sutra" that through the practice of yoga; Yama (restrains); Niyama (observances); Asana (bodily posture); Prayanama (breath-control); withdrawal of the senses (Pratyahara); dharna, fiction of attention, Dhyana (meditation) and Samadhi (absorptive concentration) – one can obtain knowledge of the God, the supreme-reality, the ultimate power of the Universe.

During their meditation and contemplation the Vedic poets obtained knowledge that when the human-mind pays whole attention to cosmic entities, it gains the same spirit and power and become able to obtain the hidden knowledge of the universe. How did this universe begin? Who created the cosmic bodies? How do the galaxies work?

The 'ric' of the Rigveda is Verse or Prose that was to be chanted at the ritual. The Vedic seers got knowledge to compose the obtained knowledge of cosmic entitites, in the form of hymns, the suktas, and mantras because of the logic of the fact that vocal organ of the speaker produces letters (varna) and the pronunciation generates a sound wave which moves in air and contact the auditory organs, it produces an audible sound (dhvani). The auditory organ of the hearers apprehends only modification of the audible sound neither vocal sounds (varna) nor audible (dhavani) signify objects, but a succession of letters and audible sound appearing and disappearing in a definite temporal order produce one than gut – from (padasphota) which signifies an object. All letters and audible sounds have the power of manifesting endless meanings. But they cannot do so singly. When they combine with other letter in a definite order of sequence, they produce one word image and manifest one object determined by convention one word is the object of one thought (ekabuddhi visaya). A word is a thought – form (bauddha) produced by the perception of the last letter aided by the subconscious impressions of the cognitions of the previous letters. The produced word established in the chitta (the mind) as a meaningful concept and this concept create an image of an object with spirit, the power, the energy of that object.

When a person prays to Sun God with the prayer-

ऊँ भूर्भवः स्वः तत्सवितुर्वरेण्यं। भर्गो देवस्य धीमहि धियो यो नः प्रचोदयात्।।

The meaning of this mantra derives the power of the Sun to the mind (chitta) and the human mind unites with the consciousness of God 'Sun.'

The mind is known object (drashya), it cannot mangiest itself, it is manifested by the self, which is self luminous.[2] The self is immutable. The word Rig derived from the root word, "Ric," which means "to praise." Praise the Brahma by Shabda Brahman Vac, word, which are formed by arranging letters "varna." Letters cannot be formed without vowels and consonants. Nothing can be made without 'breath,' breath is soul, pran. Words (shabda) are arranged to form meaningful verses to praise the God to derive knowledge of Brahma, the ultimate power. Every word expresses a meaning, and meaning has knowledge. This knowledge acts with soul, breath, pran and convert into action (Karma). The perfect balance between knowledge and action is happiest stage of life. Knowledge is gross form of Brahma and action is of intention.

Sound is associated with the word. And, vibrations are produced with sound breath produce motion to sounds. The mobility of word has Rajoguna (Gunas, qualities of nature). Knowledge is prominent of satva Guna. Naad resides in vibration of sound in very subtle form, this is the Tanmantra of space (Akash, sky). Thus "shabda" word is eternal and meaningful, they can be destroyed. These are invincible. The ric of Regveda produced by

Shabda Brahma, and forms verse that have to be chanted during rituals and yajna to invoke Gods.

The soul (Atman) of the whole universe is "Shiva." Shiva (Parmatma) degenerate Kalagni (the absolute fire) from which all the other substances derived. Shiva is indefinite absolute (Para Brahma). He is supreme reality. He is self-existent and self-luminous. He is characterized by being, consciousness, and bliss (sat-chit-ananda). He is formless, nontemporal, non-special and non-causal. Supreme power (Shiva) is one, infinite, eternal, partless, subtle, and taintless. He is impersishable supreme self. He is full of eternal consciousness. He is devoid of Homogeneous, heterogeneous and internal differences. This is the monotheism of Rigveda.

The supreme power (Shiva) is omniscient and omnipresent. He is endowed with all powers. He creates the world with his power "Prikiti," and controls it from within. Prakriti is the conscious power of Brahman, which can create the multiform world in proximity to him. Parashakti is the self-luminous creative power born of Brahman. Shakti is called maya. The empirical world is an appearance of Brahman associated with infinite power. He is Brahma. He is Vishnu. Shiva is the heart of Vishnu. Vishnu is the heart of Shiva. There is no difference between them.

Shiva is the knower and creator of Vedas. He is known through them. The Vedas are Shiva[1], the Supre Substance (Power). All causes and effects are God Shiva is the cause Vishnu is the effect. Brahma is causal action. Shiva is one. But he becomes Trinity to fulfil this purpose.

Shiva is one, but he appears to be many jivas owing to avidhya or super imposition of nescience. This is monism of Rigveda. When the limiting adjunct (avidhya) is destroyed the jiva (individual self) becomes distinctless Brahma. This knowledge can be attained by renunciation (tyaga) of desires. Renunciation is not giving up of action. It is the conquest of egoistic desires. It is detachment. Detachment can be attained by purity of mind. Purity of mind can be brought about by the performance of duties (karma). Righteous action purify the mind, and unrighteous action pollute it. This is law of Rita of Rigveda. One, who performs ones specific duties, reaps the fruits of ones action in the shape of happiness and misery. This is religious belief of Rigveda. One should renounce the desire for fruits (as said in Bhagwad Gita[3]).

The eightfold Yoga is conductive to right knowledge. Knowledge (vid) aided by Yoga is a means to release. Penance produces purity of mind (sattva). The knowledge of Vedas can be realized through supreme mind and supreme knowledge (Para Vidhya). Truthfulness, austerities, sex restraint, and moral observances are ethical values of Rigveda. The body is a temple and self (soul) is Brahma, the part and parcel of ultimate, supreme power, the absolute. Atman, the Shiva. The worshipper of the universal power; the Agni, the Surya, the Usha, the Parjanya, the Mitra and Varun, the Vayu and like, think of himself as Shiva "I am He" (अहं ब्रह्मस्मि) "यथा पिण्डे तया ब्रह्मण्डे"4 ।

Belief, faith produces detachment and knowledge. The Vedic seers had absolute faith on the power of the universe that is the Lord, the Shiva and made efforts to reveal, to discover the knowledge of the mysterious power of the universe. They worshipped the natural power (natural deities) and obtain supreme knowledge of Brahma. Meditate on the Atman alone and be absorbed in and identified with pure-consciousness. Identity-consciousness with absolute desirelessness is the highest state.[5]

Rigveda teaches absolute monism or absolutism. There is one infininite eternal being, consciousness and bliss. The Gods of fire (Agni); the Sun (Surya), the dawn (Ushas) the earth (Prithivi), the Sky (Dyaus), the bright sky and day (Mitra), the dark sky and evening (Varuna), the rain-cloud (Parjanya), the storms (Maruts) the wind (vayu, Vata), the morning Sun (Savita) and the like are personifications of the different powers of nature. They are sometimes worshipped individually. This phase of religious thought is not naturalism, but anthropomorphic polytheism.

The gods are supernatural and superhuman power and endowed with spiritual qualities. They preside over particular phenomena of nature, but they are not confined to them. This is the element of polytheism in Rigveda. Gods pervade the whole nature and beyond, or a considerable part of it, and are endowed with some qualities of the supreme God. Sometimes the gods are involved and worshipped in groups. Sometimes two gods, sometimes three, four or more gods are invoked. Sometimes all gods (Vishve devah) are worshipped together, who are implicitly believed to be partial aspects of one supreme God. This phase of religious thought is called organized polytheism is one of the prominent religious belief of Rigveda.

The world – burns with misery so long as the mind burns with desires. The world becomes cool or full of joy, when the mind becomes cool or free from desires. When all objects are renounced and desires for them are destroyed, the Atman shines forth. When the mind is withdrawn from all objects and merged in Brahma, supreme Brahma (Para Prjna) dawns. It is called trance (Samadhi) [6]. Trance is the identification of the human-mind with supreme consciousness.

The vaishnavism called the supreme power "Mahavishnu." Mahavishnu is the root sound "Om." He is the origin of all mantras. He is to be brought through the Vedam. The whole world is manifestation of sound. All natural deities are manifestation of one sound. All the natural deities are gradually related to one-another as the major and the minor, as dependent on one another, and as generating one mother. Heaven and earth are mothers of Agni. Rudra is the father of the Maruts. Aditi is the mother of the Adityas. The Asvins are the brothers. Indra maintains the earth and the sky in their places. He is a major god. They are minor deities. The Maruts maintain the Sun, the wind, the fire gods in the sky. They are superior to the three gods. Varuna, Mitra and Aryamana kindle Agni, and are glorious through him. They are interdependent on one another. This phase of religion is organized polytheism.

Penance, celibacy, faith, in God and the Vedas, and learning in the Vedas and knowledge ought to be practiced for many years? A person experiences the glory of God by penance, celibacy, and faith, and achieving perfection in them. God creates the world of manifold forms, the natural personified and defied phenomena· Any one is related as the supreme God for the time being when he is worshipped. Maxmuller calls this religion henotheism. 'O' Agni, thou art mighty Indra, the wide ruling Vishnu, the king Varuna, the wondrous Mitra, Aryaman, the lord of beings. Thou art Rudra, the Maruts, the winds, and Pushan. Thou art Savitra, a bestower of treasure, Bhoga, the lord of wealth, Rbhu, Aditi, Bharata, Ida and Sarasvati. Thau art united with all gods, equal to them in strength. May, thau surpassed them, when thy power has expanded over heaven and earth.[7]

त्वमंग्र इन्द्रौ वृषभः सतामॉसि त्वं विष्णुरूरूगायोनंप्स्मे।

त्वं ब्रह्म रयिविद् ब्रंह्स्पते त्वं विद्यर्तः सचसे, पुरेन्ध्या।।

Here Agni is identified with many gods, and treated as superior to them. as previously described – This phase of religious thought is called henotheism. It is a step from polytheism to monotheism.

It is indispensable for every individual self to achieve Vidhya the right knowledge, given in Rigveda. Knowledge of reality, or Atman or Brahma.

The empirical world of duality and difference is known and transcended by avidhya. Avidhya is the knowledge of duality, relativity, difference, and plurality. Ignorant person runs after desires. Bonds of death are full of desires. An individual self intuits the supreme self-hidden in the heart-cavitics of all embodied souls, and neither hates nor loves anyone. A soul that abides in the Brahma can achieve knowledge of Vedas and that of "law of Rit." Rita is the social law. It is the law of truth, right and justice. It is the moral law. Varuna is the custodian of moral law of Rita. He adheres to the right, and punish sins.[7] Even the gods follow the law of Rita otherwise the whole world will be destroyed in a fraction of second. In other words the ¼ part of supreme self (Shiva) return to ¾ eternal part of it. It points to the existence of one supreme God, whose law is unalterable and in violable, though it is an impersonal order, which upholds, the gods and the world.

Hiranyagarbha or Prajapati, Vishvakarma, and Param Purusha gradually take the place of one supreme God. Hiranyagarbh is prajapati, the Lord of all creature.

> As given in the 'Hiranyagarbha' Sukta of Rigveda x mandla 121 hymn.
> In the beginning arose the Golden germ:
> he was, as soon as born, the Lord of Being
> Sustainer of the Earth and of this heaven
> what God shall we adore with our oblation.[8]
> He established the earth and heaven. He is the sole king of entire universe.

Whatever exists, existed, and will exist is this supreme person. He is the Param Purusha, the lord of immortality. The entire universe is only one fourth of his being. The remaining 3/4 remain in celestial immortality. The Param-Purusha is both transcendental and immanent. He is immanent in the whole world. The Purusha Sukta teaches Panentheism. These are monotheistic tendencies in Rigveda.

The Surya (Sun) rises and sets at the command of God. It rays all called 'Gau' (गौ). Gods of Heaven abides in Him and sustained by him. Heaven, earth and hell are maintained by him. He is immanent in them. He is the one inner self (antaratma) in all individual souls. Worship the Atman, supreme self-alone. The Atman is dearer than husband, dearer than wife, dearer than son, dearer than wealth, dearer than all. Atman means meditation on Atma. Intuitive vision is spiritual illumination, which makes the individual able to obtain the knowledge of monotheism. Monotheism leads to monism. One Reality is conceived, which is manifested in diverse ways. "There is one Reality; sages call it by various names; they call it Agni, Yama, Matarishvan"[9] 'That' one (Tad ekam) is not personal. It is neither male not female; it is neuter. It is an impersonal principle. There was nothing other than it. The Nasadiya Sukta clearly brings out monism of the Rigveda. 'That one' (tad ekam) was later identified with atman or Brahma in the Upanishads."

The monism adumbrated in the Rigveda is developed into idealistic monism in the Upanishads which regard Brahma, the infinite, eternal, omnipresent, omniscient and pure spirit as the ultimate reality.

The temporal special and causality bound world is mere manifestation of this infinite reality which is sometimes known as "name-and forms"[9].

The self is indeed a seer, toucher, hearer, some taster, doubter, determiner, and doer, a person in the nature of intelligence. It resides in the transcendental, Akasara, supreme self. The Vedic seers become drasta of the vision of supreme self, which they had known in their intuition. They achieved knowledge of the supreme self by praising him by Ric. Ric means to praise by their own names and qualities. The law of rit (Rita) provided the seers to see mantras in the supreme reality. Sages to compose hymn to praise the supreme lord and achieved knowledge to create various hymns devoted to various gods.

Sometimes known and sometimes unknown by the self. They are known by it. So the mind is mutable and the self is immutable. That is why the Vedic seers compose hymns to praise and pray to gods to derive their power to make their life prosperous, healthy, and successful.

The hymns of Veda have particular style of chanting, whose vibrations are believed to alter the very atmosphere surrounding them. One type of recitation is called prakrit path or musical composition of poems and the other is called vikriti or the imperfect type. This recitation includes suktas or hymns from samhita path (पाठ) Shanti sukta, Swasti sukta, Brahmamaspati Sukta, Saraswati sukta, manyu sukta, Rashtra sukta and sangyan sukta.

"The sound modulation in the chanting of Vedic words are carefully reproduced in the traditional recitation of the Veda and indicated in printing by special marks. Three accents are shown vadita (raised) svarita (sounded), and anudatta (not raised). They are respectively the high middle and law pitch represented in printing or writing by placing the figures 1, 2, 3 respectively above the accented syllables."

In the Vedic language every word has its main accent, and words with the same spelling have different meanings, owing to the differences in accent eg. 'Brahman' with the accent on the first syllable means 'prayer' and with the accent on the second; one who prays (Brahman).

The Vedic meters form final musical pattern in which variations of sound and rhythm produce the impression of high strong poetic eloquence. Syllables grouped into the verse division called pada constitute the metrical base.

Mandala and Hymns

In Rigveda there are 10 mandalas. Mandala 2–7 is the oldest part of Rigveda and called "family books," they are arranged by length (increasing in number of hymns). Each mandala consists of hymns called sukta (su-ukta) means well recited which are intended for various rituals). The suktas in term consist of individual stanzas as called rk (praise ricas) which are further analyzed into units of verses called pada (foot).

The religious belief behind the verses or mantras is that mantra or verse is so call the real nature of one self is known through reflection on it as non different from the supreme self. Reflection is on the deity represented by mantras results in the knowledge of identity of a soul with the deity. The mind of a worshipper reflecting on the deity embodied in a mantra becomes identical with him. So vasugupta calls a Yogin's mind a mantra. It experiences atman, and becomes the supreme knows unlimited by time, space and endowed with omniscience and the like. A mantra is so called for it released a soul from bondage through reflection on it. Reflection is meditation on the manifestation of atman of the nature of perfect. 'I-consciousness.' It unites a soul with divine power. A mantra is a mystic syllable (Om i.e. Aum), a word, or a group of words charged with mystic, divine, spiritual power. The secret of a mantra lies in its power of manifesting pure knowledge because of a soul's immersion in pure, undifferentiated, supra mental, transcendental consciousness. A mantra consists of sounds and embodies pure knowledge. It is composed of letters, and all letters are of the nature of Shiva. Vowels are like seeds, and consonants are like womp, they are in their real nature, one universal consciousness, and power. Agama says, "Mantras ought not to be discussed or disputed by person of small intelligence, "wise person ought to put faith in them on the authority of "Agama."

The seers and Rishis of Rigvedic time with their complete mental energy and instuition contemplate on the cosmic deities; like Agni, Surya, Vayu, Mitra-Varuna, Dyaus, Purjanya, etc. and mutter the obtained knowledge of these deities repeatedly and compose the divine words with meter. The nature and power of mantras are incomprehensible by the intellect. It can be comprehend by developing intuition. One can experience its real nature by continuous meditation on the deity enshrined in it, and by constant repetition of it for certain periods. Its power is revealed to yogin of limited power of meditation, who strives for trifling supernatural powers produced by nada bindu and the like, vasugupta says, "The experience of the power of mantra is acquired through meditation on the great lake."

The supreme divine power permeating the universe unlimited by time and space, the essence of mantras, transparent and proffered and replete with perfect 'I' consciousness, is called the great lake.

The knowledge and belief inherent in the hymns.

The Vedic poets conceived one reality which is manifested in diverse ways. There is only one reality sages intuited in it different names eg. Agni, Yama, Matarshvan. That one (Tad ekam) is not 'personal.' There is a cosmic person (param purusha) whose body is the whole universe. He has a thousand heads, a thousand eyes, a thousand feet.

He pervades the whole terrestrial space and transcends it. Whatever was or whatever will be – all that is purusha. He is lord of immortality. He is untouched by the fruits of action (Karma). All creation is his grandeur, but he is every superior to the entire creation. The whole of the universe is only one-fourth of his being; the remaining three fourth remain in celestial immortality[10]. The inner nature of param purusha is transentental though he is immanent in the whole universe. He is both immanent and transcendental. The Purusha Sukta teaches panentheism. These are the monotheistic ten dencies in Rigveda.[11]

Purusha Suktam, पुरूष सुक्तम्

The word 'purusha' means God Almighty. This Suktam is in praise of the glory of God. Reciting this confers blessing on one's life. This mantra is chanted by Rishis before performing Yagna so that these are no obstacles of intermissions during Yagna.

The religious belief hidden in this hymn is…

Purusha Sukta

Purusha Sukta is one of the five suktam of the Sri Vaishnava Sampradaya tradition. The other four are narayan Suktam, Sri Suktam, Bhu Suktam and Nila Suktam.

The Purusha Suktam is seen earliest in the Rigveda as the 90th Suktam of its 10th Mandlam, with 16 mantras. Later, it is seen in the Vajasameyi Samhita of the Shukla Yajurveda, the taitiriys aryanyaka of wishing Yajur Vedam, the Sama Veda and Atharva Veda, with some modification and reactions.

The Purusha referes to Param Pursha, Purushottam, and Narayan in the first tier at the base of the Vishaaka Yoopa, asked him. "Why do you do nothing?" Because of not knowing. Brahma replied "perform a Yajna, your senses, the devas, shall be the ritvij. Your body shall be havis. Your heart the altar, I shall be he, who enjoys the havis, the offering. From your body sacrificed, shall you create bodies for all living creatures, as you have done in kalpas before this."[12]

The Yajna was called "Sarvhul" the offering of all. The act of creation itself grew out of Yajna, the rite of sacrifice who was worshipped at this sacrifice? It was the Purusha, who performed it? Brahma, the creative aspect of the Purusha, who were the ritvik priests? The devas who are the purusha's senses. Who was tied as the beast of the sacrifice? What was brahis, the altar of sacrifice? All of nature, who was the fire? The heart of Purusha.

The religious thought and message of Purusha Sukta is love of God, that the supreme power, param purusha himself in the fire of creations, to create all the worlds. From this sacrifice did all of creation emanate? The religious belief of purasha sukta is-

> "This great purusha, brilliant as the Sun, who
> is beyond all darkness, I know him in only
> heart. Who knows the purusha thus,
> attains, immortality in this very birth.
> I know of no other way of salvation."

Purusha Sukta of Rigveda is a powerful him of the insight of the great seer, Rishi Narayan, on the Cosmic Divine Being as envisaged through the multitudinous variety of creation. Through this Sukta one can enter into the state of super consciousness. The sukta begin with the affirmation that all the heads, eyes, and feet in creation are of the purusha. It is the belief that, "we do not see many things, bodies, objects, persons, forms or colours, or hear sound, but rather only the part of one supreme power param-purusha. If all the souls of the world emmanents from one supreme than why do people think themselves different from each other? Why this discrimination on the basis of religion, cast etc. We are all single whole of consciousness. This the God himself sung in the hymn by Rishi Narayana. Purusha Sukta is most frequently quoted and most important hymns of the Regveda. It reveals to us thc character of the creation-sacrifice: Its all – embracing function in which the entire universe is involved. It is cosmothendric God, man and universe are correlated."

God without man is nothing, literally "no-thing." Man without God is exclusively a "thing" not a person, while the cosmos man and God is "any-thing." Chaos. The three are constitutively connected.

First Mantra

> सहस्त्रषीर्षा पुरूषः सहस्राक्षः सहस्रपात्।
>
> स भूमिं विष्वतो वृत्वात्यंतिष्ठदषांगूलम[13]

Purusha (The Universal Being) has thousand heads, thousand eyes and thousand feet (thousand signifies innumerable which points to

the omnipresence of the universal being. This is the appearance of incredible purusha. There was no movement, no mobility. Only pure consciousness was there, the breath, Rishi (Prem) soul, supreme soul. That was swayambhiloka. The pure-consciousness was in the form of truth-existence-bliss, (sat chit, Ananda). The desire to become many was originated in the mind of universal being (ऐकोऽहं बहुस्याम्). This is the primordial, the first truth of the universe.

Sayanachary a states that purush is "virat." Meaning of which is infinite.

सहस्त्रषीर्षा पुरूषः सहस्राक्षः सहस्रपात्।

स भूमिं विष्वतो वृत्वात्यंतिष्ठदषांगूलम्

After pervading throughout the world, it remains ten fingers above it. The meaning of which is The Universal being in its pure form resides above, above of this whole universe. Rishi Narayan opines that purush has thousand heads, in the womb of incredible and indescribable person, mutable and immutable person resides. "मयैवांषो श्रीवलोके" Shri Krishna says in Bhagwad Gita. Purusha is distinct from its material testament, the body, manas, buddhi, and ahamikara. It is devoid of Satva, rajas, and tamas. It is knower. It is eternal and immutable (a parinamnitya), while prikriti is eternal and mutable (parinaminitya). Purusha is beyond the time and space. Purusha is seer (drishta) and the Rishi's mind fixed their consciousness on the eternal pure consciousness then it becomes drista the knower of supre self. Agni, Vayu, Surya, Surya generates through Vedatmak' Agni, the eternal Agni and becomes "विराट्–हिरण्यगर्भ–सर्वज्ञ" Hiranygarbh, raishanar are thousands, infinite. "गयो वा इमे त्रिवृत्तो लोकाः" "त्रिवृदाग्निः" Agni, Vayu and Aditya).[14]

Second Mantra:

पुरूष्र एवेदं सर्व यभदूतं यज्ञ् भव्यंम्।

अतामृतत्वस्येज्ञानो यदन्नेंतातिरोहेति1।

The Purusha is indeed all this (creation) is essence; that which existed in the past, and that which will exist in the future. Everything (the whole creation) is woven by the immortal essence of the great Lord (Purusha); by becoming food of which (by getting consumed in whose immortal essence through surrender) one transcends the gross world and becomes immortal. Sayanacharya describes the meaning of this mantra, as in this creation the body of all of the human-being and living-being are part of the param purusha as such the body of all the creation in future will also be the part of param purusha.

Fourth Mantra:

त्रिपादृहर्व उदैत्पुरूषः पादौस्येहाभवत्पुर्नः।

तत्ो विध्वङ॰ व्येक्रामत्साशनानष्ने अ्भि। 15

The Three feet of the purusha is raised high above (in the transcendental Realm), and his one foot becomes the creation again and again. There in the creation. He pervades all the living (who eats) and non-living (who does not eat) beings. The fourth feet of the Brahma (Param-Purusha), immutable (अक्षर, देव) creates (mutable-purush-prikriti). The parsionary of hypothesis demands that the self itself be of the essence of consciousness, which manifest all things in the world.

Sixth Mantra:

यत्पुंरूषेण ह्विणो द्ेवा य्ज्ञमतेन्वत।

व्स्न्तो अेस्यास्ीदाज्यं ग्रीष्म दध्यः शहद्धविः।16

With the purusha as the (sacrificial) fire, the deva performs and continued Yajna (sacrifice), spring was the clarified Butter and summer was the fuel, Autumn was Haris (sacrificial offerings) of that Yajna.

आठवा मंत्रः

तस्मोघ् ज्ञात्सेर्वहुतः संभेृतं पृषदाज्यम्।

पषून्तौष्वके वायव्यो नारण्यान्ग्राम्याश्र य।।

From the complete offerings of his (Virat's) Yajna (यज्ञ) (sacrifice of creation) the Rigveda, and Samaveda was born. The chhamdas (Vedic meters) were born from him, and the Yajurveda was born from Him.

Twentieth Mantra:

ब्रह्मणोस्य मुखेमासीबाहू रोजन्यैः कृतः।

उरू तदेस्य् यद्वैश्येः पद्म्यो षूद्रो आजामत।।

The Brahmanas were His mouth; the Kshatryas became His Arms, the Vaishyas were His Thighs, and from His Pair of feet were born the Shudras.

In preceding Mantras it is stated that The Moon was born from His mind and The Sun was born from His Eyes, Indra and Agni (fire) were born from His Mouth, and Vayu (wind) was born from his breath.

The Devas performed the external Yajna by meditating on the real Yajna (contemplating on the purusha who is shining behind everything;) and thus they first obtained the Dharma. (Oneness of Purusha), by meditating on the greatness of the Chidakasha (blissful sky) during those earlier times the spiritual Aspirants become the shining one itself. Today this type of efforts and meditation is required to make the world free of crime, pollution, and destruction. Every soul is the part and parcel of the supreme soul so it possesses the ability to obtain knowledge and spirit of the supreme soul to bring the global peace.

Om peace, peace, peace.

Meaning of Religion Belief

The person possesses the supersensuous ability to see certain facts of supernatural power and in Vedas these types of persons are called Rishis means "drishatas of mantra" or seers of mantras. The human mind, at certain moments, transcends not only the limitations of sense, but also the power of reasoning. In that way they come to face to facts beyond these physical world. These facts are the basic of all the religion of the world.

Religious belief refers to attitudes towards mythological supernatural, or spiritual aspects of metaphysical facts, that is a religion, religious belief is distinct from common religious practice or religious behaviors with some believers not practicing religion and some practioners not believing religion. Religions belief, being derived from ideas that are exclusive to religion often relate to the existence characteristics and worship of a deity or deities, divine intervention in the universe and human life and gain logical explanations for the values and practices centered on the teaching of a spiritual leader or group.

Law of life is the law of belief. Habitual thinking of human being's conscious mind is establishes deep grooves in their subconscious mind. The conscious mind of human being is referred to as 'objective' mind because it deals with external objects.

There are two levels of human-mind; the conscious or rational mind and the subconscious or irrational level. An individual thinks with conscious mind, and whatever he habitually think with conscious mind sinks down into the subconscious mind, which creates according to the nature of thoughts. The subconscious mind is often referred to as subjective mind. Human beings subjective mind perceived by intuition. The subconscious mind manifests itself when person is in deep state of meditation and contemplation. And the knowledge obtained through intuition. The thoughts, experiences, knowledge, and learning of human-conscious mind deposited in subconscious mind and converted into belief.

Law of mind is law of belief. The person believes in the way as the mind perceives and works. The belief of human mind is the thought of the mind. As the person thinks about, it becomes his belief. When a person observes the objects around him and engage his/her mind with kind of thoughts his subconscious mind forms 'belief.'

If human-beings mind involve in worldly thought, he forms worldly belief or empirical belief. When human-minds try to think beyond they limitations of senses; thinks about the working of the universe, the sun, the moon, the stars, the fire, the air and think about metaphysical objects, he has to contemplate with his inner-intelligence, that is called intuition, and this belief is called religious belief.[16]

Human-mind has to know the realtiy. The real nature of himself, nature of nature, the surrounding, about real world; working and discipline of it. The real knowledge builds real belief and false knowledge forms false belief.[17]

Knowledge is a quality of the self, which inheres in it. It is in the nature of manifestation there are innumerable cognitions apprehending an infinite number of objects. But knowledge is mainly of two kinds, valid knowledge (vidhya) and invalid knowledge (avidhya). Valid knowledge is what apprehends an objects different from it.[18]

It is of four kinds: 1. Doubt (samshya) 2. Illusion (viparyaya) 3. Indefinite (perception), and 4. Dream (Swapna).

Doubt is indefinite knowledge. It is internal and external. Internal doubt is produced by attributes of the knowing self. Will the lunar eclipse predicted by astrologers happen or not? This doubt is caused by the expectation of the occurrence or non-occurrence of an event external. A person unfamiliar with a jackfruit tree has an indefinite perception of it.

Valid knowledge forms true belief invalid knowledge forms false belief. Human mind must cease to believe in false belief, opinions, saperstitutions, and fears of mankind. It has to begin to believe in the external varieties and truth of life, which never change.

What Is Religious Belief?

Religions belief is a strong belief in a supernatural power or powers that control human destiny; Religious belief require, faith, faith on the working of universal power the supernatural power working behind the whole world. It requires the mental attributes like perception vigil, watch consecration, hastily, toleration, traditionalism-orthodoxy, supernatural virtue or theological virtue, meditation. In other words – religious belief refers to attitudes towards mythological, supernatural, or spiritual aspects of a religion.

The individual or empirical self has empirical cognition, pleasure, pain, desire, aversion, violation, merit, demerit, and disposition. The empirical self is Karta (actor) enjoyer (bhokta) and guide (abuidrastr). To see, to perceive, and to understand is nature of the consciousness of an individual self. The external objects are known when they come in contact with intelligence of an individual, the intellect reflects on them. The reflection is the cause of the knowledge of all objects. The individual self thinks about his own inner self and reflects, "I am a knower." "I am an actor." "I am happy to see it" etc. the acquired knowledge becomes his "belief."

Vyasa says that the self can have an intuition (Prajna) of itself by concentrating attention on its reflection in intellect (buddhi). His pure self knows its reflection in intellect. Vyasa further holds that the mind (Chitta, Buddhi) becomes the objects of knowledge of the self; mere proximity like a magnet. The intellect attracts the self and self generates the intellects to know more about the self its consciousness, unconsciousness, abilities, conscience and memories. The inner self of a person posses the power of supreme self (यथा पिण्डे तथा ब्रह्मण्डें) "(Individual being has the qualities of cosmic being)." The pure self can intuit itself only through the empirical self determined by the modes of intelligence in which it is reflected by concentrating its attention on its own reflection apart from the mode in which it is reflected.

Intellect, ahamkara, manas, and external senses constitute the psychical apparatus. It is the instrument of knowledge and action. The empirical self-acquired knowledge of the world through the individual acts upon through it and makes 'belief' about it.

The empirical self possesses a body and sense organs by which it can know, see, and enjoy. An individual self is determined by a body and mind and has determined sensor and intellect. Activity of the self is illusory. As said before an empirical self has merit, demerit, knowledge, ignorance, pleasure, pain, and like are modes of intellect in conjunction with the external objects. When due to ignorance, an individual experiences pains and want to overcome it by its intellect.

He experiences that when he perform right action he gain pleasure, and when wrong action he gain pain. He wants to overcome the pain fear and sorrow and wants to like a happy and prosperous life. Gradually, his intellect become transparent owning to the excess of sattva Guna in it. His inner self becomes active and knows about "Atman" the pure-self. The individual becomes identical with Atman and try to obtain. Supreme knowledge and power of the universe. Thus his belief becomes Religious belief.

He knows about transcendental self, parmatama, Brahma the ultimate power of the world.

Form of Religions Belief

Each and every religious sect has their own religions belief. Each have identifiable and exclusive sets of belief or creeds, surveys of religious belief have often found that the official doctrine and description of the belief offered by religious authorities do not always agree with the privately held belief of those who identify as members of a particular religion.

Religions belief has broad classification. Universalism: Some believe that religion cannot be separated from other aspects of life, or believe that certain cultures did not or do not separate their religious activities from other activities in the same way that same people in modern western. Culture do other with this world view resist the influence of science, and believe that all political decisions and laws should be guided by religion. Still other with this world view, believe that all political decision and laws should be religion.

Orthodoxy

First used in the context of early Christianity, orthodoxy is a religions belief that closely follows the edicts, apologies, and hermeneutics of a prevailing religions authority. The term orthodox was applied almost as an epithet to a group of jesiwh oblieves who held to pre-enlightenment understanding of Judaism and now known as Orthodox Judaism.

Fundamentalism

Fundamentalism as a religious belief which associated with theologically conservative positions or traditional understanding of a text and are distrust of innovative reading, new revelation, or alternate interpretations.[19]

Modernism/Reform

The renaissance and later the enlightenment in Europe were associated with verifying degrees of religious tolerance and intolerance towards new religious ideas. Modernism took particular exception to many of the more fantastical claims of religions and directly challenged religions authority and the prevailing beliefs associated with the established churches. In response to liberalizing political and social movements some religions groups attempted to integrate enlightenment ideals of rationality, equality and individual liberty into their belief system.

It is more important to note that from an early period the utmost stress is laid on the secret character of the instruction contained in these works; the rule is that they are the highest mysterious, and that their doctrines should not be imparted to any pupil other than a son, who has not already studied with the teachers for a year and who does not intend himself to become a teacher.

The wise sages realized by the blessings of cosmic mind in their heart the bond of what is the in what is not. The religious belief of Rigveda is absolute one it is most highest, most significant belief. Meaning of the word 'Religion' is unique in the mind of wise sages "the ved-vyasa," i.e. composer of cosmic knowledge.

Religion Means

A set of beliefs concerning the cause, nature, and purpose of the universe, especially when considered as the creation of superhuman agency or agencies, usually involving devotional and ritual observances, and often containing a moral code governing the conduct of human affairs.

The word 'religion' originated in 1150–1200 AD, origin of the word lies in Latin word 'ligare,' which means bond with universal power to which prefix re (added) "State of life-bond by monastic vows" also conduct indicating a belief in divine power. In angle French-religion (IIC) and old French, religion means 'devotion' Latin 'religion means (nominative religion) means 'respect for what is sacred,' reverence for the God.

Thus the Vedic sages conceived monism through their contemplation and intuition.

The Vedic religion traverses the whole gamut of polytheism, organized polytheism, henotheism, monotheism and monism which are elaborated in previous chapters. The Vedic gods are easily propagated by hymns, adoration, prayer, oblation, offerings and sacrifices. They are givers of wealth, strength, happiness, sons and grandsons, victory in battles, and a life of hundred years. They are also givers of wisdom and moral qualities. They are born of father and mother, and yet immortal. Mortals are elevated to the same immortals.[20]

The Vedic seers (sages) got the knowledge of the beginning of the universe as given in the Nasadiya Sukta that "Then there was neither existence nor non-existence, there was no sky, nor heaven beyond. Then there was neither death nor immortality. There was neither day or night nor distinction between them. There was the sole one (tad ekam) that breathed by itself without breath; there was no other than one. Then there was darkness without light. All was engulfed in the primeval cause. That one was born by the power of austerity (tapas). Their firs arose desire or will in the cosmic mind and from the first one sprang the seed of creation. The wise sages realized in their heart the bond of what is in what is not. From whom this creation arose, the highest seer in the highest heaven knows.[21] This is pure spiritualistic monism. That one (Tad Ekam) was later identified with Brahma or atma."

Religious Belief in Rigveda

Importance of hymns: Chanting for adoration prayer hymns to propitiate god was one of the vital religious beliefs of Rigveda. The hymns of Rigveda are addressed to the elements of nature, personified as deities, and are prayers for protection from calamities and for alignment of prosperity, longevity, wealth, strength, happiness, sons, and grandsons. Also for obtaining wisdom and moral qualities. The Rishis, to whom the hymns of the Vedas manifested as revelations, are the authors of those hymns. The seven Rishis are (Saptrishis) referred to in the shatapatha Brahmans as Gautam, Bhardwaja, Vishamitra, Jamadgani, Vashishtha, Kashyapa, and Atri. The seven Rishis are represented in the sky by the seven stars of 'the great Bear'[21]. Vedic religion was based on performing sacrifices in order to propitiate the gods; music formed an important part of the rituals, which structured the sacrifice. In fact singing, instrumental music, and dance were described as divine in Vedic literature; it was believed that they propitiate deities.

Chanting of Vedic hymns is the earliest instance of the deep relationship between religion and awakening of senses to gain knowledge. The Rigveda relied on recited hymns (richa). The musical chanting of the Samaveda employed more notes (finally setting on seven notes) and is said to be the source of the later secular and classical music. Infact, the word sama itself is a compound expression and includes two entities: the first component 'sa' refer to hymns i.e., richa, and the second component 'ma' refers to the musical notes.[22]

Vedic music also included instrumental music of various types. Music was used mainly for two functions; to propitiate deities and to accompany sacrificial offerings. Both solo and choral music were in vogue for major forms of music were prevented in samagyan, takes as a whole. Each kind of music effected different changes in Vedic mantras as were perceived to be necessary by the concerned musician. The veena, tunav, dundhubi, hommi-dindhubhi and tanav were the prominent instrument representing the four major instrumental categories, auto phones, membraphones, aerophones and chordophones.

It is found that humans can only absorbed 20% of what they hear from sermons. By companying with a combination of the words and melody a hymn singing is a stronger edifying tool. Hymns are repeated frequently, which is an important factor of memorizing adding together the music and rhymed verses making the hymns much more digestible and stick to the mind longer.

Besides, hymns singing is an act of thank giving to God. The book of psalm filed with thanks giving. In Rigveda "Richa (ऋता) means to praise and glorying God. If you praise God and glorify him and do not sing. You utter no hymn. Your worship remains incomplete. Hymn singing is a representative of how your heart feelings. As your heart feels God provides and strengthen the same feelings and knowledge."

Sacrifice (Yajna)

Another religious belief of Rigveda is sacrifice (Yajna). Sacrifices were made in which milk; butter, honey, the soma juice, and food were offered to the Gods. Prayers and sacrifices were intended for obtaining cattle, wealth, sons and grandsons, a life of hundred years, victory in battles, and happiness and bliss. Health, wealth, and happiness were the goal of prayers and sacrifice.

Vedic scriptures point out the sacrifice was essential from the very beginning of creation. Prajapati (the Lord of creatures) a god having a major position in the early veda, was described as the embodiment of sacrifices. In Prajpati identifying himself with the universal desires: "May this body of mine be fit for sacrifice." For the purpose of creating the world. Gradually the early Vedic pantheon emerged dominated by the fourfold godhead namely Indra, Agni, Soma and Surya. Extensive hymns were consecrated to these gods as is written in the Rigveda.

During the early Vedic period there were five great kinds of sacrifices namely Bharmayajna, Devayajna, Pitrayajna, Manushyayajna and Bhulyajna as sacrifices to Brahmin (the highest reality, to devas, to ancestors, to human being and to all living creatures respectively. They apply to the two manners of performing sacrifice, either the Shrauta rite that was done by Vedic priest according to Shruti (i.e. sacred literature of divine revelation).

Yajna in itself is to be seen as the very essence of Veda. From the early times, the ritual was understood to be the link between the human and the divine and a vehicle towards liberation. By such a link the human could access the divine and fulfill the very purpose of the human existence. Yet, in its incipient from Yajna practice was in connection with the cyclical natural phenomena particularly the session (ritu) and the overall order or things perceived in nature. The place of human beings within the whole system of things was attentively taken into account. In this manner, from empirical observations, the concept of cosmic order or Divine order (rita) developed and the practice of Yajna became gradually a rite. The Shrauta rite was particularly attentive to what were the necessary objects and how they have to be used within the sacrificial arena. Particular attention was given to how the actions were to be peformed or how the participants had to behave during the time of ritualistic activities.

The enclosure (vedi) of the sacrificial ground was systematically arranged in an arena suitable for that specific purpose according to what the ritualistic literature recommended. Some objects used were the sticks (arani and idhan) in order to help kindling the sacred fire by friction. Other objects were logs of wood (samidhah) as fuel, the offering spoon as sacrificial instrument/utensil (sru or aghihotra havani) the pressing stone of soma stalks (graven), the sacrificial verse (camasa) holding soma and food offering, the list of objects being quite long within the vedi there was an area known as antarvedi surroundings the fire pit (kunda) in which the sacrificial (agni) has to burn various offerings. The antarvedi area has to be strewed with sacred grass (kusha) on which water was sprinkled according to specific rules. The sacrifice/offering/oblation (agnihotra) was patronized by the Vedic priests (ritvija) in charge with putting into the sacrificial fire articles consisting of nourishments (annaloma) like milk, clarified butter, cereals, fruits, various powders, vegetables and flowers etc.

Science of Yajna

Gayatri and Yajna (यज्ञ) are described as the pillars of Indian philosophy and culture. The eternal course of universal knowledge comprised in their Gayatri Mantra is deciphered and the cosmic energy of sound contained in Mantra is activated and expanded with the help of Yajna.

The four Vedas signify the philosophy of eternity and absolute complementary role of Gayatri and Yajna in divine creation. Atharveda also deals with sound therapy aspects of Mantras for the treatment of the ailing human system at the physical, psychological, and spiritual levels. The samveda forces on the musical chanting patterns of the mantras and the subtle form of Yajna by defining the later as the process of mental oblation on the surface of internal emotions thought the cosmic radiation of the omnipresent subtle energy of sound. The Yajurveda contains the knowledge of principles and methods of performing Yajnas as spiritual and scientific experiments for global welfare[23].

Literally speaking, Yajna means selfless sacrifice for noble purposes. Sacrificing of the ego self abbesses and material attachments and adopting rational thinking, human compassion and dedicated creativity for the welfare of all is indeed the best Yajna which should be performed by all human beings.

For a daily agnihotra (Baliaisva) a small copper pot is used. The inverted pyramid shaped Agnihotra pot receives, generates and decentralizes electro sphere. It acts as an effective bacteriostatic and antimicrobial reactor. Copper is universally acknowledged for is excellent conduction of electricity and heat. The Agnihotra has an obvious link with fire, heat, electromagnetic force and because of its inverted pyramid shaped kunda, it does have connection with the cosmic energy fields.

The dimensions of the copper pot used for the daily Agnihotra are: 14.5 cm × 14.5 cm at the top. 5.25 cm × 5.25 cm at the bottom 6.5 cm in height with three steps. For large Yajna, the dimensions are increased proportionately and the kundas are also made up of specific combination of clays.[24]

Chanting of Sanskrit Mantras

The power of sound vibrations are considered effective since ancient time in the field of science also. These vibrations can penetrate the energy spheres at the subtle and cosmic levels. All the alphabets of the Sanskrit language are endowed with special vibrational powers, which set out harmonious wave patterns when pronounced. It is interesting to note that Dr. Howard Steingull, an American Scientists has established that recitation of Gayatri Mantra Produces 110,000 sound waves per second. In fact recitation of the Gayatri Mantra during the fire worship (Yajna) acts supplementary. The patterns of chanting of Mantra are so designed that latently contain the essence of the music or the quite essential sound of the torrent of life sustaining energies emanating from the cosmic energy centre of the corresponding mantras (The cosmic energy of the Sun is associated with Gayatri Mantra).

Purification of Environment by Yajna

The industrial wastes, rapid urbanization, air and water pollution, disturbances in the ozone layer – formation, radioactive waves etc. have established the human, animal, plant life cycles. The ecological imbalance caused by these acts of 'civilized men' has resulted into disastrous threat not only the human survival but to the life as a whole of our planet.

Agnihotra is basically a healing process. "Heal the atmosphere and the healed atmosphere will heal you – is the modus operandi."

Purification of environment through the constituent electrons of the substences fumigated in the Yajna is an obvious effect of this process.

Dr. Hatkine has mentioned that – mixing ghee and sugar and burning them creates smoke, which kills the germs of certain diseases, and secretion takes place from some glands related to the windpipe, which fills our heart and mind with pleasure.[25]

Sugar crystles present in 'Havishya' have great power to purify the atmosphere. It kills the germs of T.B. measles, smallpox and cowpox, remarks Prof. Tilward.

According to Dr. Shirowich, a Russian scientist-

1. Cow's milk contains great power of protection from atomic radiation.
2. Houses having cow-dung covered floors enjoy complete protection from atomic radiation.
3. If cow's ghee is put into Yajna fire, its fumes lessen the effect of atomic radiation to a great extent.

These eradicate bacteria and other microorganisms, which are the root cause of illness and diseases. This must be the reason why the incidence of physical ailments, sickness, and diseases becomes less in the household, where Agnihotra is regularly performed.[26]

Purification of Air

1. Removal of odors: Under steam vitalization, the various volatile oils get diffused in the surrounding atmosphere along with steam and smoke. Since these oils have distinct good smell, the foul odors are automatically replaced. This aroma can be experienced easily in the surroundings when Yajna is performed due to diffusion of substances like thymol, engmol, pine, terpinol and oils of sandal-wood, camphor and clove.
2. Removal of Bacteria: As stated, products of combustion, the partial oxidation of hydrocarbons and decomposition of complex organic substances produce formal aldehydes which is powerful antiseptic. It is also interesting to note that germicidal action of formaldehyde is only effective in the presence of water vapor, which is also produced, in large quantities in Yajna. The use of formaldehyde spray for disinfecting of walls, ceiling etc.

is common and such as pray is automatically produced when Yajna is performed.[25]

3. Effect on plants and Vegetation: The disinfection of air is not only useful to animal life also helps plants life through the bacteria responsible for diseases in both may be different. The aromatic substances during Yajna get diffused in the air and offer protection to plant life against harmful organisms. This ensures healthy plant growth. Agnihotri atmosphere and ash can be used as adjustant in the Natural methods. It is a holistic concept of growing plants in healthy atmosphere and maintaining ecological balance by performing Agnihotra (Yajna) in the middle of farm and using Yajna ash as a fertilizer[26]
4. Role of CO_2 generated in Yajna: Consignment of the wood and other organic materials to flames has been always controversial because of generation of CO and CO_2 and increase in consequent greenhouse effect. It had been argued that performance of Yajna also produces CO and CO_2. It should be noted the way in which the samhidhas and Havishya are burnt in Yajna is process of slow combustion at higher temperature while the burning of coal in factories or in house hold fire involves rapid combustion where oxygen is sucked in large quantities and enormous CO_2 is emitted. In the slow combustion-taking place in the process of Yajna, small quantity of O_2 is utilized; meager CO_2 is emitted that poses no threat to the environment. In fact whatever CO_2 is generated it is readily absorbed by surrounding vegetation and CO_2 cycle is strengthened.

   The other important aspect of the fact that CO_2 produced during the yajna. The CO_2 produced during thYajna is not bad for health because produced CO_2 remains mixed with other aromatic oils and antiseptic products. It therefore acts as a vehicle in transporting such products to distant surroundings. The use of CO_2 as a cerebral stimulant to assist the patients suffering from lack of ventilation is common is medical world. Its use to control and cure many mental disorders are also known to medical science.

Small amounts of CO_2 inhaled by the persons performing Yajna acts as a stimulant and more and more aromatic fumes are inhaled which help in curing mental disorders.

5. A group of scientists led by Dr. Manoj Garg, Director, Environmental, and technical consultant and the Uttar Pradesh pollution control board conducted experiments during the Ashwamedha Yajna at Gorakhpur, U.P. These experiments were set-up at about 20 meters east the Yajnashala. The sample of 100 ml each of water and air collected from the surroundings were analyzed using high volume envirotech APM-45 and other sensitive instruments. A summary of their results-

In air sample (Unit mg per average sample)[27]

Instant	Level of Sulphur dioxide	Level of Nitrous Oxide
Before Yajna	3.36	1.16
During Yajna	2.82	1.14
After Yajna	0.80	1.02

Bacteria count in Average water sample[28]

Before Yajna	4500
During Yajna	2470
After Yajna	1250

Minerals in the Ash (Bhasma) of Yajna

Phosphoreus 40% mg per kg. Potassium 3407 mg per kg, calcium 7822 mg per kg. Magnasium 6424 mg per kg Nitrogen 32 mg per kg Quispar 21 w/w.

These results clearly support the claims made about the role of Yajna in control of air pollution. The Deupty Director, Agriculture had submitted technical report based on such results, recommending the use of Yajna's ash as a effective fertilizer.[29]

Importance of Mantras during Yajna

Mantras are pronounced in Yajna in accordance with the prescribed methods and rules. It benefits the person concerned and stimulates useful vibrations and causes beneficial excitements in the environments. Besides, it makes possible the stimulation of causal energy of materials used in Yajna to such an extent that the hidden potentialities underlying them are greatly enhanced.

When Mantra chanted collectively during Yajna, its sonic power increases exponently due to-

a. The collision of sound waves generated by the mantra chanting with the thinnest screen. Flame screen of quivering fire of Yajna and high frequency vibrations generated thereby;
b. The subtle interaction of sound waves of the mantras with cosmic energy centre (Devta) associated with their specific configurations as carry shabdas.
c. The fundamental thermodynamic effects associated with the fumigation of the sacrificed havishya in the Yajna fire.
d. The compound effect of the vital mental and causal energies of the people, who are in performing the Yajna.

The sound-waves of the mantras, instead of proceeding it in their natural circular motion, are carried upward in a spiral form by the force of the electrons generated by fumigation of the Havisha after sublation of Yajna fire. The collective chanting of mantra in specific rhythm in front of the Yajna flames gives rise to unique sound-wages which have infinite effects in the outer space.[29]

The most important religious belief of Rigveda is that every one must keep optimistic outlook in life.

अभ्दयः सम्भूतः पुथिव्यै रसौच्च। विष्वकर्मणः समवर्तताही।

तस्य त्वष्ठी विदधेद्रूपमोति। तत्पुरूषेस्य विष्वमाजान्मग्रे।[30]

1. Dawn on us with prosperity, O ushas, daughter of the sky, Dawn with great glory, Goddess, lady of light, dawn thou with riches, Bounteous one.
2. They, bringing steeds and kine, boongivers of all wealth, have oft spedforth to lighten us. O ushas, waken up for me the sounds of joy: send us the richest of the great

Earth, water, fire, air and sky (ether). These are basic elements from which the world came into existence. Vishvakarma created this world. The Sun rises with enormous light and heat and creates auro. The Sun possesses the glory of the Adi (original) purusha.

The Vedas speak of the Divinity in various ways. It speaks of the absolute, undiscriminated essence, in neuter terms like Aksharam the indestructible, the Eternal, (That which the veda knowers speak of as Aksharam, as the Bhagwad Gita says) Ekam, the one, sat of Tat sat, the ultimate reality and Brahma, the Divine essence, and also as om (an indeclinable word, the ultimate Being, and Atma (the supreme self or over soul). The Divine Manifestations, the Vedas have definitely stated that the manifested Deva is only an aspect of the ultimate Being The Rigveda says:

The one Being sages call by many names as they speak of

Indra, Yama, Matasrishvan,

The wise poets with their words shape the one Being in many ways:[31]

As Yajurveda says

Agni is that, Aditya is that,
Vayu is that, Candramas is that,
The Bright one is that, Bharmana is that,
Apas are that, Prajapati is that[32]

The Rigveda says that they are free from hate (adraha) and that none among the Devas is ever remise, and addresses them as: Ye furtheress of Rita, pure in spirit, infallible. This make an essential difference between the Devas found in the Vedic samhitas, and those found in later literature for instance, unlike the puranic Indra, the Vedic Indra is always pure:

Indra, pure, come thou in our midst, come, pure, with they pure aids, pure one.

Bring affluence for us and pure and adorable be then pleased...

Pure, thou slayest power of darkness.

All Vedic Gods and Goddesses are followers of Rita and represent 'satya.' In the very first hymn of the Rigveda Agni is spoken of as Gardian of Rita and as satya. Indra too is described as satya (Truth) and equated with Rita. Similarly, Surya (Dhadhiura) is spoken of as Rita. Ushas in Ritavari, the observer of Rita. Aaditi is rtasya patni, Queen over Rita, Mitra and Varuna are specially in charge of working Rita (ritvana). To one who doubts his existence. Indra says: 'I exists O singer, look upon me here, all that exist' I surprises in splendor. The Eternal law's (Rita) commandments make me mighty.[33]

The Devas also represent the finest of human qualities: they are the strongest, the kindest and most noble, loving, tender, beneficent, and helpful. A Deva is the best of sages, the best of poets, the best of heroes, most father like (most mother like in the case of Devi, the best friends, and the best comforter).

And the Deva are all beautiful, Agni is most wonderful usha is the perfect combination of beauty and holiness. Day and night are twin beauties, Maruts are wondrous – looking like kings decked in splendor Varuna is the poet who cherishes manifold forms (rupa) by his poet's power (Kavya) and Indra has been the Model for every form (rupa) and if is his form that is to be seen everywhere. To contemplate the Devas is to contemplate beauty (Sri), glory (bhagra) and spendour (mahan, mahas) as well as brilliance varcas power (Vjas), Valour (Sahas), benevolence (sam) and love (sumati). The Devas open out a world of light jyotis, and life (jivas) before us. Divine love says the Veda, lies behind and creation of the beauty of the world:

In love though mudest ushas (the dawn) glow,
In love though mudest surya (the sun) shine,
Then Indra, knowing, thinking, Lord of tawny steeds,
Above all glories waxest great.[34]

The Devas bring bliss, blessed is all that the Devas regard with favor.

It is usual for religious cults to attach themselves to particular concepts of the Divinity, e.g. as father or mother, but it is part of the Vedic poets liberty of mind to be bound down to one single idea in expressing what lies beyond thought. So, while there are people who contemplate the Diety only as father, the Vedic poet says:

RV II 35.15 Tv. By Grifith

"I Deem Agni my father deem him my
Kinsman, deem his my brother and friends for ever,
Thou bounteous one, art our father,
And our mother, lord, than last been

Vedic worship has been described as nature worship. But the term applies only to a section of the Deities worshipped. Even there ideal human virtues are attributed to them to such an extent that it will be inaccurate to take them as more symbols of natural phenomena. It will be more correct to describe the worship as vibhuti-yoga (the path of splendor) in the sense in which the Bhagvad Gita has used the expression a contemplation of the Divinity in term of the beauty and glory of creation.[35]

Abinash Chandra Bose Opines – The term polytheism is a misnomer for the vedic religion. Polytheism is ruled out by the definite and systematic identification of the vedic deities with the ultimate reality, and their consequent indentification with one another, can polytheism ever worship one. Deity by another name as the Veda does (eg. Apollo as Zeusor Athena) Again, the vedic Devas, even when based on natural phenomena, do not get thoroughly anthropomorphised like polytheistic gods. For example, Homar in his Iliad tells us of a goddess who came to the battlefield of troy, he helps a man and had her hand slashed by his opponent. Out of the wound came a celestial substitute for human blood. The Goddess borrowed her brother chariot, and drove through the sky to her Olympic home. She went to meet her mother while the horses fed on ambrosial hay. Compare with it vedic portrayal of a Deva. Let us take Varun. He he is divine king watching over eveyman. His envoys move about on the earth from heaven and, thousand-eyed, they look upon everybody. King Varuna sees everything lying between heaven and he has counted earth-the twinkling of man's eyes. When two sitting together take secret counsel, king Varuna knows, being there the third. His fatal snares are stretched for the man who tells a lie. But when though this description Varuna develops into a person, and we are told that heaven and earth belong to king Varuna. It can be described.

> Both the oceans are the lions of Varuna
> And he is merged within the small water drop.[36]

He is no longer a person; he is one (ekam) eternal being beyond time and space.

Whereas Jadunath Sinha in his Indian Philosophy opines that the different gods are the personifications of the different powers of nature. They are sometimes worshipped individually. This is not naturalism, but anthropomorphic polytheism. The Vedic poets were not worshippers of nature. They worshipped the whole or considerable part of nature and beyond and endowed with some qualities of supreme godhead.

Sometimes the gods were invoked in groups of number of dual gods such as Mitra and Varana, Indra and Agni. Agni and soma were invoked. Sometimes three gods working together such as Aryanman, Mitra and Varuna, or Agni, Soma and Gandharva were paired sometimes four deities such as Bharti, Ida, Saraswati, and Mahi were worshipped.[37] Sometimes many gods were praised. May Mitra and Varuna Aditi the Sindhu, the earth, and the Sky grant us happiness and long life. sometimes all the gods together, Vishwa Devas, were praised and invoked, 'sit down on the sacrificial altar, O Vasus, O Vishe Devas, O Adityas, worthy of worship,' may all gods protect us for our welfare.[38] Thus gods were inter-related to one another. When all gods were worshipped together, they were implicitly conceived as practical aspects of one supreme God. A collection of gods working in harmony payed the way for one God. This stage may be called organized polytheism.

The fire god Agni is the domestic God. He is the Lord of the house. He is the Youngest, respondent and beautiful god. He is mighty, great, invincible, and destructive. He is wise righteous, omniscient and benevolent. He is the mediator between men and gods. He is the messenger of gods, he carries the oblation to the gods. He brings them to the sacrifice. He is the steward of both worlds. He shines on heaven and earth[39]. He has twofold birth, celestial and terrestrial. Agni is fire and also Priest, Sage, Father, Brother, Friends, Guest and finally the light of lights, the soul within our soul,[40] and the Deva who is identified with every other Deva or Devi and with the ultimate reality. The Vedic sages poetic mind most enthusiastically contemplates on every aspects of Agni. As simple fire, Agni is the child of two mothers (the two sticks that produces it by rubbing each other) and is lifted up by ten young virgins (the priest fingers, anguli, being in the feminine gender), and by another analogy he is the banner (ketu) of the people. His physical beauty is ecstatically described, making him appear divinely marvelous.

> Thou wondrous one! Lord of wonders, who makes us
> Perceive the wonder that's most splendid life giving
> Give treasures, beautiful and great, including many sons,
> With brightness, O beautiful one to they singer.[41]

Here we start with the beauty of the simple flame but soon find ourselves facing Divine Effulgence – the Mystic fire.[42] which is contemplate by the sage poet as the supreme source of light and life.

It is the context of a mystic vision that we can understand the vedic sage when he says about Agni universal (vaisvanara).

> A steady light, swifter than thought, is stationed
> Among the moving things to show the way;

All the Devas, of one mind and like wisdom
Proceed devoutly to that one intelligence.
My ears strain to hear, my eyes to see
This all spreading light lodged within my spirit;
My mind roams after beyond its confines;
What shall I speak, and what indeed, shall I think.[43]

We need also to know the style of mystic expression to understand what significance the vedic sage intends to convey by describing the domestic fire (grahapatya Agni) as the Lord of the household friend (damunas).

The most appropriate Vedic Symbol for the Lordship of the Lord is perhaps the figure of Agni, the friend of man, the mediator, the sacred and sacrificial fire, and at the same time the fire that is the sun, in burning things, and in the heart of man everywhere the same yet every where different having varied and even almost contrary effects. The devotion to Agni does not represent nature worship, much less pantheism it is the recognization of an underlying polymorphic reality that softens wax and honey but hardens mud, dries up plants may bring life of death, and always transcends all our powers, mental as well as physica.[44]

The very first Mantra of Rigveda
Om agnim lie purohitam
Yajnasya devam Ytvijam (Ritvijam)
Hotaram ratnadatamam
Means
I magnify God, the divine fire,
The priest, Minister of the sacrifice,
The officer of oblation, supreme giver of treasure

The word ratviji is explained by Yaksha (Nirukta 3,19) as rituyaji and by Sayana as rauyajati in his comm…on 1,1,2: Bohtlingk-Roth too explain it as: nach vorschrift and zeit folge operand, regdmassing operand (offering oblations according to prescription and season); Yitvij is (he who offers oblations in sacrifices rta);

The vedic karmyogi is essentially a man inspired by kshatriya ideals. He affirms and accepts life fully, and bends his energy to its proper direction according to Dharma. He lives his physical life intense thrilled by the glorious sunshine loving the beautiful earth, and his fellow beings, and his family and fighting to death when Dharma demands it is epic view of life and not tragic view because he believes in the immortality of the soul, and in the heavenly abode that a waits one after death of one has lived and died according to Dharma.

Yam opo adrayo Vana
Garbham rtasya piprati I
Sahasa yo mathito jayate nrbhih
Pythivya adhi sanavilI

'Agni the child of satyalok whom the waters, stones, trees, nourish; who being produced by altrition with force by men, is born on the ridge of the earth.

Agni is here called ritya garbha child of satya (loka) because he is born in satya loka.'

Agni is Rajata (observer) because Agni's birth is due as much to the singing of hymn (in which truth is embodied as to attrition: compare the epithets sanojar, sahaskrta, sahasah, sanu, urjo napat, urjah putra and also savaso napat. Vedic idiom expresses by the idea of "offspring" that the Gods essential nature is savas since, being in possession of truth, is one of the essential qualities of Gods, is apt.

It is clear that Rtajala is stronger expression for Rtavan and the epithet rtjala can be used

Vardhan Yam Purvih ksaks virupan
Sthatus ca ratham rtapravitamII

"Whom (Agni) conceived in satya-loka, nourish for many nights (day) the multi formed (waters) and what is mobile and what is immobile."

Tvam yajnesv rtvijan
Agne hotaram t late'
Gopa Ytasya didhi sve dameII

O Agni they praise thee that art the priest, the hotly, is sacrifice. Shine in they abode, thou that art the guardian of satys loka.

Ababhyena sousa
Gne Toksas tvani daha I
Gopa Ytasya didhi II

O Agni, consume the demon with (thy) flame that cannot be imparted shine thou that art the guardian of satya-loka.

Adha hy agne
Krator bhadra sya
Daksa sya sudhotr I
Rathir Ytasya brhoota bubhutha II

For thou host becomes the charioteer of auspicious resolve, of splendid ability of the might hest of god's.

"Agni has been established among the tribes of men, the embryo of the waters, mitro, the Friends coming from satya-loka (i.e. heaven) the worshipful one, desired has bestraddle the ridge, the wise one is to be invoked with hymns[45]."

Agni pervades all spaces of the atmosphere. "Thou, O Agni the Flaming one, art born from the heaven, thou art born from the waters and the flint; thou art born from the forests and the herbs; thou art born brint, O lord of men, to men[46]."

Agni is the divine ladder of the divine tribes, the guardian of the seasons. He is fallible. His blessings are flawless. He is intent upon right (Yta) and true. In him all commands all wishes dwell. He adheres to his own power of mind. He knows all rules. He has proclaimed his rules to the mortals. He knows everything that leads us astray. He protects us from sin that defiles us. He is friend and protects of his worshippers. They live in his companionship protected by him. He is self dependent god, he promotes prayer of worshippers. He releases men from all sins committed in thoughtlessness. He reigns over immortality.[47]

SOMA

The same mode of imagination and expression we find in the case of soma, primarily the juice of plant of the name, offered as libation, but also contemplate as a Deva in his beauty and grace, and as the ultimate being. In the physical sense soma (given the name of Indu)[48] is made to flow towards Indra as libation (Indray endo parisrva). The moral idea appears when soma flowing in streams of Rita is asked to glorify Indra and make all noble (arya)[49]. Erotic mysticism comes in when the poet says that some is pleased with the holy waters (used in the worship) as a young gallant with graceful maidens.[50]

The Soma is the beneficent deity. He clothes the naked, he doctors (Bhishakti) the sick; by his grace, the blind sees, the lame walk. And soma is king over all. King soma is invoked to clothe the fighting soldier in immortality.[51]

Priests in the Yajurveda declare that some, and not their earthly ruler, is king over them. The sage has a transcendental vision when he addresses soma.

Thou art vast (lit the sea), then revealast everything O poet! Under they law are the five regions of the world.

Thou transcendent heaven and earth,

O purifier ! thine are the lights (jyotis) and the sun.[52]

Anticipating the Bhagwad Gita style of describing vibhuti Yoga (The path of splendour) the Rigveda speaks of soma as Brahman among Devas, the leader among poets, the sage among the falcon amid valtures, the svadititi (tree) in the woods but says that 'soma goes singing over the cleansing sleeve.' It appears that the poet, thinking of soma as the Supreme

Being, does not wish to withdraw his eyes from the juice of the plant that was being offered in worship.

Soma asrgram indvah
Sula rta sya sadane I
Indraya madhu matiamah II

"The soma juices most sweet have been pressed and let loose (to flow) into the abode of satya-loka for Indra;"

Sam daksena manasa jay ate kavir
ritasya garbho nihita yama parah I
runa ha sania prathanam vi jajnatur
Guha hitam janima neman odyatamy

The wise one (soma) is born with an efficient mind; the offspring of satya-loka has been placed beyond the twins. Even in their youth did the two bring him forth, the being half is hidden and half has come up.

The torrent of soma, the observer of men, is purified; he calls the gods from heaven with a Brahman (hymn), he fulgurated with the shout of Brhaspati; the oceans encompassed the pressed juices, as it were.

Soma clothed himself with the rays of the sun, stretching the three-fold thread according to his knowledge carrying (out) the latest prescripts of the priest, the husband goes to the rendezvous of the wives.

The king of rivers, soma, Lord of heaven, is purified, roaring he goes on the paths of satya-loka. The yellow one, flowing in a thousands streams, is purified, he purified; he produced speech, proceeding towards wealth.

Indra

Indra was found in the Vedas, is not suggested like natural phenomenon, nor like Agni by the ritual of worship. He is the idealized epic hero. Through the idealization he rises far above the national hero, he becomes the national God. He is endowed with all the qualities which, when found in a man, are said to make a superman of him. In the usual Vedic way, superlative terms have been used for him as for other deities. He has been spoken of as the strongest (ojistha[53]), mightest (sushmintama), most vigorous (inatama[54]), most powerful (savishtha[55]), most heroic (nritama[56], most potent (shaishthas), greatest among a chariot-borne, worries (rathitama) and the conqueror (jetri). He differs from the primitive hero in that he is the champion of Rta, and is undaunted and unwearied in his fight against virta, the enemy of Tta, so he is the supreme virtra-slayer (vrta-hantana). He is the ideal Kshatriya unbending and firm, and unfailing in his resourcefulness. The poet says of him.

> He whom we worship bows not to the firm or to the stiff,
> Or to the challenger incited by the ruthless foe;
> To Indra the lofty mountains are the plains and the
> In the deeps there is a foothold for him.[57]

Indra is not only the most valiant (as compared to men) but also the most compassionate (avrikatama) the greatest among the good (satam-j yasthama), the noblest (varishlha), the best sage (vipratama), the most beneficent (sivatama), the most beloved (preshtha), the most fatherly of father (pitritama pitrianam), the nearest (antama), and the best of gladdens (mandintana); whenever the poet sings of Indra his heart is lifted, the spirit of courage and action fills the atmosphere, and the language brings the thrill of a new life, and the urge of an indomitable will, Hero of Heroes Indra helps man by rousing all that is heroic within him. In the exhortation of Indra to win his autonomy (by defeating vritra), there is also the exhortation to man to win spiritual svaragya by fighting to victory the power of evil. 'Beheroic,' brothers, following the example of Indra-imam sajata and virayadhvam – is the call of the sage[58]. Indra has eternal youth in him years do not age him, nor do months and days wear out Indira[59], and they are brave fighters and saviour (tarti), the protector (avitri) and sages pray to him for bliss (svasti), The poet goes into lyrical ecstasies singing and praying to him.[60]

> Mighty Indra, with the sweetest of songs
> I catch the garments him as a child the father's

The worshipper of Indra has the loyalty of soldier: 'I will not see three, Thunder-wielder, For the highest price – not for a thousand, nor for ten thousand nor for an infinite sum, O 'Lord of countless wealth.'[61] With his heroism, which sometimes terrifies us by its fury and terror, there also goes another aspect of Rita-beauty and glory-and these receive the poets ardent admiration, 'He moves with steeds yoked to Rita, making men happy by the chariot – nave that finds the light, Indras glory manifest his transcendental nature. Not even a hundred heavens or a hundred earths, or even a thousand suns could match his being. He is the model (pratimna) for al the world. He is clad in vesture beautiful as heaven to look on and (the siva of later literature) has been an active dancer.

> (Nritya) He is also pratirupa, the prototype, of all form of beauty.
> For each and every form he is the model,
> It is his form that is to be seen everywhere,
> Indra by his charm (maya) moves in many forms,
> Truly, his bay steeds are yoked a thousand times.

Here vedic realism merges in transcendentalism, and bring in Vedanta. Shankaracharya, commenting on the verse quoted in Brihad Aranyaka Upanishad says "why did he come in so many forms? were name and form not manifested, the transcendent nature of Atamn as pure intelligence would not have been known."

In Indra we find not only the poet's Mythopic imagination surrendering itself to his transcendent vision, as in the case of other Devas but a near approach to his human personality through in fairly detailed working of the formed and what is of greater consequences, Indira's personality is shown in two distinct aspects, the heroic and the beautiful, in the transcendental sense. Indra is the one (ekah) the single (kevalhah), the ultimate (parah), the supreme (parmah), the primal (prathamah), the great (mahan). As a Deva (manifested Divinity), he is co-existent with Rita and satya and he is the savor (trata), the Rescuer (pata) the purifier (pavaka) and the leader through the path of goodness (sunitah). As hero (surah), Indra is the destroyer of wicked power (virtraha ghanam virtrani), the conqueror unconquered (jeta aparajitah), Lord (patih) and king and Ruler over his own divine dominion, made free from vrtrads or the enemy's aggression (savrat), and the Lord of the people (genapatih), but he is also the beautiful (carah) the most cooderful/wonderful (citratamah), the marvelous (dam sana), beauty itself (vapuh), clad in loveliness (sriyam vasana) the loverly one (venah) and he is Lover (jirah) longing in love (usana), a friend (sakha) a household friend (damuna), the bourtiful/beautiful one (maghana), a poet (kavih), a dance (nytur), jo yous (mandrah) and gladdening (manda mahnhh). He is graceful through strength (savasa dakshinvavan). Inspite of the rudeness that has sometimes gone with his heroism, Indra is most wonderful as a person and illustrates on a grand scale the combination of valor and tenderness as well as of majesty and beauty in the ideal hero. It is not without significance that he has been addressed as both father and mother and worshipped with deep longings of love through ecstatic songs. The majestic figure of Indian literature, once of all, the prototype of the God man and the godly hero. As some orientlists have rightly thought, Indra returns in later literature in a thoroughly human form as valmiki's Rama who kills his vrita in Ravana aided, thoug not by maruts, 'the sinless gallants of the Rigveda,' by maruti (marutis son) or hanumat, who is equally sinless, Sita speaks of her husband as 'Indra-like,' The pace first revolt against kahatriyahood in post-vedic times has its impact on this ideal kshtriya, puranas have pictured Indra as a theatrical king with the vices of an earthly tyrant. The Buddha-however, though opposed to military heroism, spoke of Indra as 'one who by self-control, become the greatest among the Devas.'

Ushas

It is almost a literary miracle that he poets who spoke so vigorously and passionately about the mighty could again speak so tenderly and sweetly about he lovely youthful maiden, Ushas. As in Indra the vedic poet created the ideal hero of all times, so in Ushas, Goddess of dawn, he made his portrait of the ideal all times, so in Ushas, Goddess of Dawn, he made his portrait of the ideal women, radiant in her beauty and youth as well as her goodness and purity. She is the vision of the quiet, beaming beautiful dawn incarnated as young woman, with all the freshness, grace and glory that belong to it. Ushas has been the amima hidden in the secret recesses of the Indian mind, inspiring and enlivening it age after age with the exaltation of feminine beauty and charm. We also find the poet approaching the virgin Goddess Usha as sons of the mother Maturna. Sunavah[62] who knows if this worship of the virgin as mother was not a legacy of the Veda to the later ages.

Usha is 'true to Rita'[63], sublime by Rta "Lovely as a bride adorned by her mother sings the poet," then showest thy beautiful form for all to see. Blessed (bhadra) art then, Dawn' she does not break the law of order (dhaman) as she comes day by day to the appointed place: like a maiden in pride of beauty. Goddess to met to God (Surya, the Sun), who long for and smiling. Youthful and brightly shining, than discoverest thy bosom before him. As if knowing that her body is bright likes one who has bathed, she stands visible to us: dispelling all malignity and darkness. Usha daughter of heaven has come with light like virtuous women the daughter of Heaven bends her forehead, facing men. Like a dancer she enrobes herself with her embroidered garments, and bares her bosom, as a cow does her udder creating light of the world of life. Sister of Varuna (Guardian of Rita), sister of Bhaga (divine luster) she, joyous Dawn, is asked to subdue the strength of him who work evil, and disclose lovely treasures.

> सह वामन न उषो त्युच्छा दुहितार्दिवः
>
> सह द्युम्रेन वृहता विभावरि राया देवी सरस्वती।

This Dawn hath Yoked her steeds afar, beyond the rising of the sun. Borne on a hundred chariots she, auspicious Dawn, advances on her way to men.

> Bring us to wealth, abundant, sent in every shape, to plentiful refreshing food.
> To all subduing spendour, usas, might one to strength, thou rich in spoil and wealth.

As long as the Vedic poet speaks of the Devas, the Divinity manifested on the relative plane of existence, he retains his full liberty to imagine (kalpayanti) him or in terms of different natural and human forms. Beautiful word-images based on analogues from life have been built on the concept of Asvins as dual Deities, Maruts as multiple Deities and Apas as Divine Maidens, and even Ushas (Dawn) is sometimes spoken of in the plural. The two Asvins are 'like two hymn-singing Brahmanas; like two charioted heroes' like two idamsels beautifying themselves; 'like a wise married couple; like two chakrravka birds; like two lips that speak sweetly with the mouth; and like two breasts that give nature to our life. The many maruts are like, "Seers with rheir hymns; like kings bedecked with ornamemnts like spotless gallants, leaders of their people; like wise men most venerable; like warriors in thie coast of mail; like wise men most venerable; like warriors in their coast of mail; like youthful suitors and like playful children that have beauteous mothers. Apas have been compared to graceful maidens but also describes as the motherliests."

While the sage in the Vedic age contemplates the all-pervasive single Divinity, the poet in him delights in the pictures queue visions of Devas. The poet however, acknowledges the sage, and so, as a rule, the particular visions carry with them an underlying sense of the one divine essence. The Atharva veda, giving precise description of the unity of the Divine being, by saying that he can not be spoken of as second or third or fourth or fifth or sixth or seventh or eight or ninth of tenth, makes the following remarkable statements.

He is the one and one alone.

And in him all Devas become the one alone so, to worship a Deva is also to worship the one. The Vedas speak of Devas as immortal. But man's mortality refers only to his body and its limited, earthly existence; his soul is immortal. So there is prayer to Rudra; God of Death; Release us from mortal life and not from immortality. A sage addresses his fellow men as sons of immortality, who inherit the celestial regions. No wonder that the Vedic sage should claim brotherhood with the Devas: Boneteous ones, we have established now our brotherhood, equality in the mother's womb, or should say that 'the Devas are of one spirit with men.'

In the Rigvedic hymn with its call to the 'sons of immortality' mentioned above. It is said that physical immortality for man was found undesirable, and so the sage yama laid down his own dear body as a sacrifice (Yajna) and was the first man to have die. This is the Celestial region that they inherit, the heaven in which life the rishis of great tapas, the heroes who, in contested battles cast away their lives, and those who were steadfast in Rita.

Rigvedic deities by guiding men on the right path (supatha) lead them from mortal life to immortality (amritative dadhatana).

The spiritual essence in man has been called 'atman.' The Rigveda uses the word 'atman' in the same sense in 'Beyond the statute of the Devas no one even if he had a hundred souls (atman), can life.

The word atman has been used by a Rigvedic poet in paradox "Food is soul (atman pituh) dress is body (tanur Vasah), the unguent gives (spiritual)" power a recognition by the poet of the spiritual value of material things.

The word 'Jyotis as well as Atman has been used to employ the supreme spirit too.' The Rigveda speaks of the cosmic spirit as 'Atman in; Surya, the Atman, in all that moves and all that stands still.'

The description of purusha (ultimate Being) as thousand headed, thousand armed, thousand footed; has to reference to an imaginary monster; it just means that Deity immanent in innumerable men. Though very ancient, the Vedic language is the language of literature, and those who use it presumably count upon the acquaintance of their audience with the delicate hymns of their expression and the authentic and spiritual association of their words. For example, it was from audience fully conversant with the details of the Vedic ritual and the function of the different priests that the Vedic poet song.

Agni we adore, the purohita,
The Deva of our Yajna, the Ritvij,
The Hotri, the highest source of treasure.

Here Agni is at once fire for the offering; the priest and the Deity; and the treasure-ratna of which – he is the supreme source, is according to the Vedic conception never merely material. It is, as a Rigvedic poet says else where, 'both terrestrial and celestial wealth (parthivasya maharayao divyasya).

In fact, we are made to expect poetic and spiritual association of his words when the poet says in the next stanza: Agni, adored by poet of old, is adored by new poets too. In a later stanza Agni is called wise kavi (sage-significance to the Vedic people further on, Agni is called protector of eternal law, (gopa ritasya), using a most widely significant Vedic word, Rita. And the hymn closes with the prayer, "Like father to son, O Agni, be easy of access to us; for the Vedic poet and worshipper, it is a hymn of prayer that produces an atmosphere of holiness and sublimity and arouses intense feelings of devotion. And when the compiler placed the hymn at the beginning of his collection, he must have found it particularly elevating. It however, the suggestion as well as the meaning of the solemn words are ignored and anthropologically minded scholar tries to read into this noble hymn the native wonder of the primitive mind at the newly discovered fire, it will only be a primitive approach to literature. Unfortunately, in the interpretation of the Vedas one often finds such uniformed and unimaginative approach."

The Gods were considered to be friendly to the worshippers. They were regarded as father, brother, friend, companion, protector, and forgiver of sins. They were regarded as deadly and destructive to the enemies. They crushed haters of gods, sorceress, and cheats. They were custodians of the mortal law. They promoted the welfare of the virtuous and punished the vicious. They maintained to physical order and the moral order. Rita was the germ of law of Karma. The virtuous were transported to heaven, and vicious were condemned to hell, the nether region of darkness.

Transmigration was yet to come. Moksha was not conceived virtue was truth. Sin was untruth. The gods purged the worshippers of their sins. To be united with god and to attain immortality were also regarded as the goal of religion.

Suciro havya martuah sucianm
Sucim hinomy adhavaram sucibhyah I
Ytena satyam Ytasappa ayan
Chutianmanah sucaban pavakah II

O Maruts, pure are the offerings of you that you are pure; I prepare a pure sacrifice for you that are pure. The bright ones, pure, of pure birth, honoring Brahman, have attained satya loka by means of brahmana.

The maruts are the Gods of the winds and storms, the companions and friends of Indra. They are said in the veda to be the sons of Rudra and Prisni, the latter explained by sayana as the many colored earth, but regarded by professor Roth as a personification of the speckled clands.

They who, self-luminous, were born together with the spotted deer,

Spears, swards, and glittering ornaments

Strong is their birth: Vigour have they to issue from their mother; strength, yea, even twice energy is theirs. And these sons, the sons, the singers, in their racings have enlarged the bounds, so that the kine must walk knee-deep.

Pushan: Giver of prosperity, pushan is a God who protects and multiplies cattle and human possessions generally. In character he is a solar deity, beholds the entire universe, and is a guide on roads and journeys.

Bring us the wealth that men require, a mainy master of a house,

Freehanded with the liberal meed/need.

Thou, glowing pushan, carriest an awl that urges men to prayer.

They're with do than tear up and rend to shreds the heart of every one.

Savitra

The stimulating Sun: Savitra, the generator vivifier, is a name of the Sun, in the Veda sometimes identified with the sometimes distinguished from surya.

Uprisen is Savitra this God, to quicken, priest who neglects not this most constant duty.

To the Gods, verily, he gives rich treasure, and blesses him who calls them to the banquet.

Having gone up on high, the God broad handed spreads his arms widely forth that all may marks him.

Even the waters bend them to his services: Even this wind rests in the circling region.

Though born by swift steeds he will yet an yoke them: Even the fleet chariot hath he stayed from going.

Adityas Sons of Aditi

In the highest heaven dwell and reign those Gods who bear in common the name of Adityas. They are the inviolable, imperishable eternal beings Aditi, eternity or the eternal, is the element which sustains them and is sustained by them. The eternal and inviolable element in which the Adityas dwell, and which forms their essence is the celestial light.

May Mitra Aryaman and Bhaga hear us, the mighty Varuna, D aksa, and Amsa.

With one accord may Aryaman and Mitra and Varuna this day accept this praise song. Adityas bright and pure as streams of water, free from all guile and falsehood, blameless, perfect.

Aapris: Propitiatory Hymns

Vasushruta

"Aapris is the collective name of the Gods and deified objects addressed in the hymn."

To Agni, Jatvedas, to the flame, the well-enkindled God, other thick sacrificial oil and it is also told that-

"Adored, O Agni hither bring Indra the wonderful, the friend, on lightly-rolling car to aid."

"open yourselves, ye Doors, Divine, easy of access for our aid."

"fill, more and more, the sacrifice."

"Faid strengtheners of vital power young mothers of eternal law. Morning and night we supplicate."

Vishnu: The Pervader of All

This god "the all-pervadking or encompassing, is not placed in the veda in the foremost rank of deities, and, though frequently invoked with Indra, Varuna, the maruts Rudra, Vayu and the Adityas, his superiority to them is never stated, and he is given described in one place as celebrating the praise of Indra."

The secret of "shabda-brahma" is hidden in the Vedas.

ऋग्भ्यो जाता सर्वषो मूर्तियाहुः

सर्वा गतिर्याजुषी हैव षष्वत्।

सर्व तेजः सामरूप्यंह षष्वत

सर्व ह्रीव ब्रह्मणा हैव सृष्टम्।। 64

Means all the substances मूर्त पदार्थ of the world; idols, images, metal, stone, trees, planets and the whole cosmic bodies are formed from Riktatva and the scripture which provides the knowledge of this "Rik-Tatva" (ऋक तत्व) is called Rigveda. The whole mobile-substances (गति तत्व) of the universe. Movements of air, vibration, revolving of earth and planets around the sun. Sun's revolvements around the around the galaxy, moons revolvement around the earth, movements of the other satellites around their planets are called "यजु" (Yaju). The movements and static condition of the world is created by yajurved (यत्गति) yat (यत्) means movements and Ju (जू) means stability or space (vkdk'k). The air originated and blows on the basic of the stability of the space (आकाष). Each and every movement needs a static base, if we don't have earth to walk then how can we walk. In Vedas "Brahma" is called static "Akam," non-mobile God is the inactive efficient cause of the evolution of prakriti.

The Vedas are authoritative because they are creations of God, the perfect person (purusha). The ultimate power, which is called neither existent non non-existent as in Nasadiya sukta "Then there was neither existence nor non-existence there was no sky, nor heaven beyond. Then there was neither death nor immortality. There was neither day. Nor night nor distinction between them. There was the sole one (Tad-ekam) that breathed by itself without breath; there was nothing other than one. Then there was darkness without light. All was engulfed in the primal cause. That one was born by the power of austerity (tapas). There first arose desire or will in the Cosmic Mind and from the first one sprang the seed of creation. The wise sages realized in their heart and bond of creation, he from whom this creation arose the highest seer in the highest heavy know. This is pure spiritualistic monism. The one (tad ekam) was later identified with Brahma (Atma)."

In Purusha Sukta of Rigveda it is said that "The whole of the universe in only-fourth of his being. The remaining three-fourth remains in celestial immortality." This three-fourth is static (यज्) and the one-fourth (जत्) is the movement (गति) this is (Yajurveda) so as to say that the God exist because the veda bear testimony to his existence. The existence of Vedas depends upon Brahma the (tad-ekam). The existence of God depends upon the Vedas but Vyasa urges that there is a beginningless creation (anadi sambandha) between Veda and the pre-eminece of God. The Vedas may be said to be the ratio cognoscenti of the existence of God. We may know the existence of God through the Vedas, though God creates them and is prior to them in existence.

God (here the ultimate power) is the prime mover of prakriti. He upsets the equilibrium of prakriti and starts the evolution of the world.

This is the optimistic out look of universe, of the Vedic seers who obtain knowledge by brahma.

The whole (Tejas, tej tantra) light, fire, Agni is originated from Samveda Agni is 'samved.' Samveda is known as vitan-ved, vibhuti ved, mahima ved, etc. That's why shrikrishna told in Gita that (वेदाना सामवेदोस्मि). The substance (Tatva), which provides that knowledge of sam, tej, Agni is called samveda. The whole world is running by som (सोम) and Grain (अन्न) Rig, Yaju, and Sam the triad is called "Agni-Veda" (आग्नि वेद) and Som (सोम) is Aharva-Vedic. The root cause of the world is 'Agni and Som,' that's why it is said that:

"अग्निषोमात्मक जगत्"

In Vedas breath (प्राण) is called deity (देव) is called Dev Raj Indra (King of all Gods) Indra. Nex to this cosmos (Dev-lok sansthan), pitra loksansthan (पितृलोक संस्थान) begins and next to it Rishi Pran Sansthan (ऋषि प्राण संस्थान) exists. These three breath air (izk.k are in root of the world exist.

In India these three Pran (breath) sansthans are known as three Rins (ऋण) i.e. (ऋषि ऋण, देव प्राण) on the basis of these breath cosmos (प्राण संस्थान) our three sansthans forms: Adhibhauthik, Adhidevic and Adhyatmic.

Purusha, in the world (Sarashti) is formed as Vak (वाक) as Avaya Purush. This purush is reached as kshar, Akshar and Mahabhut (स्थूल). Due to vibrations, the breath transformed into Yshi, then pitra, then Dev, then gandharva, then Paramesthi. This lok is called Gau (गौ, विद्युत) Lok.

From the centre point (Nabhi) of Vishnu, Brahma was born. The Brahma was in the form of breath (प्राण). In the form of very subtle substance. In the mind of the Brahma, Desire of being was originated (एकोम–बहुस्याम्). Brahma is spaceless. It is devoid of spatial character. The Upanishad expresses it in like; Brahma is the subtlest of the subtle and greatest of the great. Brahma is non-causal. It is devoid of guna (attributes). Brahma is existence. Brahma is bliss. It is quaint essence of bliss (Yasa). Brahma is tajyalam, creator, preserver, and destroyer of the world.

All creatures sping-out of Brahma (tajja). They live in Brahma (tadan). They are reabsorbed in Brahma (talla). Brahma is cosmic principle.

Increase of Wealth

Rayisanvardhana

This prayer is for everyone, both those who are engaged in trade and business and those who cultivate their fields. It is a morning prayer, appropriate for a time when men are looking forward to the new day, full of hope and confidence. When the first rays of the Sun appear and the hour of sacrifice approaches, what will men requiest from the Gods, if not the treasures of health, wealth and, offspring? The innocence and candor trhat are found here, as well as in many other hymns of this type, derive precisely from the fact that human perfection and type, derive precisely from the fact that human perfection and happiness are always viewed from an integrated perspective, which embraces both material and spiritual values in one indivisible and harmonious unity.

In this hymn all the Gods are addressed; all are considered to be present and accessible to the worshiper's petitions: Agni, Indra, Soma, Varuna, Surya, Savitr, Brhaspati, Tvastr, Vāyu, Vāta, Visnu, Aryaman, Bhaga, even Sarasvati and the the Goddesses, are invoked in turn. The prayer starts with an address to Agni, the most friendly of the Gods, and concludes with an invocation to the Sun, the giver of life, who graciously grants the new day.

Not only are the the Gods besought to give abundantly so that there may be a sufficiency, but they are also requested to give "over and above" so that the worshiper may share and pass on wealth in his turn (v.5). The miser is not spared. He is urged not to resist the contagion of this liberal spirit, appropriate to both Gods and Men (v.8) and exemplified even in the magnitude of the expanses of heaven (v.9), but rather to give with a generous hand.

In its simple and realistic way this prayer expresses Man's search for plenitude and the infinite.[65]

Light, Fearlessness, and Bleassing

Jyotirabhayam svasti

This hymn brings to a climax the prayer of the preceding one. There is fear of things, of the unknown, of nothingness, and there is also the fear of fear, about which modern psychology has much to say.

This prayer expresses the confidence that there is a wide world of light and grace where all the shadows of fear are banned, and the external obstacles in the way to happiness can be overcome by taking refuge in the strength of the Lord (v. 4). It is, further, by making friends with the world at large that fear is overcome, for, if all beings become our friends, fear simply cannot arise.

This stress upon fearlessness as a human value of capital importance and a sign of personal self-realization is maintained not importance and a sign of personal self-realization is maintained not only in the field of martial courage but also, and mainly, in the realm of human perfection. We read, for instance, in one Upanisad

"Certainly, Janaka, you have achieved fearlessness"

– said Yājnavalkaya.

"May fearlessness be with you, Sir!"

– Replied Janaka of Videha,

while in another we find the vivid metaphor: "the further shore of fearlessness."[9] That shore is heaven which we only attain when we practice and are surrounded by universal friendship. "In the heavenly world there is no fear."

Jyotirabhayam svasti

AV XIX, 15

1. From that which we fear, O Lord, make us fearless.
O bounteous One, assist us with your aid.
Drive far the malevolent, the foeman.

2. Indra, is the Savior who kills the Demon,
our longed-for protector, coming from afar.
May he defend s from the farthest point,
from the middle, from behind, and from before!

3. Indra is the Savior who kills the Demon,
our longed-for protector, coming from afar.
May he defend us from the farthest point,
from the middle, from behind, and from before!

4. Lead us to a wide world, O wise one,
to heavenly light, fearlessness, and blessing.
Strong are your arms, O powerful Lord.
We resort to your infinite refuge.

5. May the atmosphere we breathe
breathe fearlessness into us:
fearlessness on earth
and fearlessness in heaven!
May fearlessness guard us
behind and before!
May fearlessness surround us
above and below!

6. May we be without fear
of friend and foe!
May we be without fear
of the known and the unknown!

May we be without fear
by night and by day!
Let all the world be my friend!

1. From that which we fear...: *yata Indra bhayamahe tato no abhayam krdhi.*
   Lord: Indra; also in v.4.
2. Evil spirits: *druh.*
3. Demon: Vrtra.
4. Blessing: *svasti,* grace, well-being.
   Infinite refuge: *sarana brhanta,* vast shelter.
6. Let all the world......: lit. may all the regions become my friends.

* * * * *

References

1. J.N. Sinha 'indian philosophy' vol.ii pg. 418.
2. J.N. Sinha 'indian philosophy' vol.ii pg 130.
3. Hymns from the vedas Abinash Chandra.
4. J.N. Sinha 'indian philosophy vol iii.
5. Ekam sat vipra vahuda vadanti agnim yamam matarishvan apah.
6. Griffith Rigveda the Oldest divine Book.
7. J.N. Sinha 'Indian philosophy vol ii 434.
8. Pannikar' The vedic experience.
9. J.N. sinha Indian philosophy vol ii 421–22.
10. Rv x 90
11. J.N. Sinha 'Indian philosophy volii pg 424.
12. Pannikar 'Vedic experience' Mantramanjari.
13. Rigveda Bhashya 'Swami Dayanand sarwarti.'
14. RTh Griffith. 'the oldest Divine Book.'
15. Rigveda Bhashya 'Swmidayanand Sraswati.'
16. ibid

17. Josef. Murphi 'The power of your subconscious mind.'
18. J.N. Sinha Vol.ii pg 312.
19. Wikkipedia free encyclopedia "Religious belief"
20. J.N. Indian philosophy voi.ii 423.
21. Rv x 1291–2
22. The six system of indian philosophy ch.ii S.k. Das
23. ITC Sangeet Academy.
24. Origin and philosophical foundation of yajna A brief introduction.
25. Literature.awgp.org.
26. The integrated science of Yoga' Sri Ram Sharma Acharya.
27. ibid.
28. Akhand jyoti pg 22 1997.
29. ibid
30. Literature. Org 'intedrated science of Yoga SriRam Sharma Acharya.
31. ibid.
32. Rv iii 55–1.
33. Rv x 114.5.
34. yajurvedava 32.1.
35. sv 442'Hymn from the Veda pg 21 Rv iv 40.5
36. Rv viii 100. 3–4.
37. Rv ii 35.15
38. Rv viii 98.11.
39. Homars Illiad Book v The The Goddess is
40. Rv I 36.
41. Rv ii 3–4
42. J.N. Sinha vol.ii Indian philosophy.
43. ibid.
44. Rv vi 6–7
45. Rv vi50–6
46. The vedic experience 'MantramanjariRaimundo pannikar pg 142.
47. vishvevaranand indological series 48 Satyaloka in Rigveda.
48. Rvii 1.1.
49. Rv 1 59.

50. Rv x 30.5
51. Rv viii 79.2
52. Rv vi 70618
53. Yv 8.40 Rv ix 8.29
54. Rv I 127.9.
55. Rv iii 9.2
56. Rv V 38.2
57. Rv x 108.6
58. Rv vi 224.7
59. Rv vii 53.2
60. Rv viii 1.5
61. Rv viii 81.4
62. Rv v 9.1.
63. SHABDA BHRANH Karpurchand kulish
64. Pannikar Mantramanjari

Chapter - V

Ethical Values of Rigveda

वेदोः खिलो धर्ममूलम्''

मनुस्मृति –जप 2–6

"Vedoakhilo Dharm Mulam" (Manu-Smriti 2–6). It means the vedas are the source of all knowledge i.e. religion, morality, righteousness and good conduct (Ethics of life).

According to Swami Dayanand Saraswati (1824–1883) "All the sciences meant for the good of mankind flow from the fountain head of the Vedas ever since the creation of the universe."

"The Vedas radiated that light which illuminated the world by teaching those universal and eternal truths and principles that help mankind to realize the nature and co-relation of God with the soul and the creation."[1]

Indeed, the Vedas are the first source of knowledge, ever come to mankind. As Maharishi Dayanand Saraswati "considered the Vedas as a rock of firm formation, talking them for his guiding view of life, his rule of inner-existence and his inspiration for external work, and even more, as the word of the eternal truth on which man's knowledge of God and his relation with the Divine being and with fellows can be rightly and securely founded. As he opines all the sciences meant for the good of making flow from the foundation head of the Vedas ever since the creation of the universe is true and you can feel it by developing your inner self and obtain some trutha of vedas... The various branches of knowledge and sciences were just the off shoots sprung from the first nucleus."

"Sarvaevedat Prasidhyati"

All knowledge flows from the Vedas.

According to Maharishi Aurobindo Ghosh (1872–1950) "Among all the materials of our past the Veda is the most venerable and has been directly and indirectly the most potent as authoritative revelation, and inspired Book of knowledge, Vedas are plenary revelation of religions, ethical and scientific truth. It's religious teaching is mono theistic and the Vedic gods are different descriptive names of the one Deity; they are at the same time indications of his powers as we see them working in Nature and by a true understanding of the sense of the Vedas we could arrive at the all the scientific truths which have been discovered by modern research."

Aurobindo Ghosh wrote in his famous essay on "Dayananda and the Veda" Among the great company of remarkable figures that will appear to one eye of posterity at the head of renaissance, one stands out by himself with peculiar and solitary distinctness, one unique in his type as he is unique in his work. Such is the impression created on my mind by Dayananda.

Dayananda asserts the presence of an ethical element in the Vedas, he finds in the Veda the law of life given by God to the human being. Dayananda asserts the presence of such a cosmic element, he finds in the Veda the secrets of creation and law of Nature by which the omniscient governs the world. Neither western scholarship nor ritualistic learning has succeeded in eliminating the religions and ethical values of the hymns.

Veda contains truth of science as well as truth of religion. Affirm that Vedas contain truth of creation, maintenance and destruction of the universe. The very depth and range of wisdom is hidden in Vedas. All the ethics of the world; the law of revolution of the earth and other planets which are revolving around the Sun from the very beginning. This revolution is based on principles of ethics. The Moral laws and physical laws of the universe call Rit (ऋत) forms the ethical principles of the world, nature, mankind and soul. Nirukta bears evidence to these laws and capacity and in the Brahmans and Upanishads we find knowledge of all rituals and customs which are derived from the suktas of Rigveda.

Vedic Ethics and Values

The word 'Ethics' means system of moral principles; the ethics of a culture or the rules of conduct recognized in respect to a particular class of human actions or a particular group, culture etc.[2]

Ethics means norms and ideals prevailing in a group or society. It may be referred to as standardized forms of conduct/behavior of individuals understood and accepted in a particular field of activity. The word ethic has been defined as "moral principles that govern or influence a person's behavior." Ethics are sets of values about what conduct ought to be. They give an idea what is right and what is wrong, true or false, fair or unfair, just or unjust, proper or improper, e.g. Honesty, obedience, equality, fairness, and then doing the right thing. Ethics is this, a fundamental personal trait which one adopts or follows as a guiding principle or basic Dharma in One's life.

There is a deep-rooted relationship between Ethics and values in the life of man. in ethics, value denotes something is degree of importance with the aim of determining what action of life is best to do or live, or to describe the significance of different actions. It may be described as treating actions themselves as abstract objects, putting value to them. it deals with right conduct and good life.

In the sense that a highly or at least relatively highly valuable action, putting may be regarded as ethically good and an action of law, or at least relatively law, value may be regarded as 'bad.'

Value can be defined as broad preferences concerning appropriate courses of action or outcomes. As such, value reflects a person's sense of right or wrong or what ought to be "Equal right for all, excellence deserves admiration." Value tend to influence attitudes and behaviors.

Salient Ethical Values of Rig-Veda

Rta is the moral law. It is truth and righteousness. The gods are the custodians and followers of the moral laws.[3] Varuna is of fixed, unswering right conduct (didhavrata) sin is untruth and unrighteousness. It is falsehood (anrta) and delinquency virtue is rewarded. Vice is punished. Virtue is not only external conduct in conformity with moral law. It is also the purity of inner life. the Gods descry the impure motives and intentions and punish them.[4] They know the pure thoughts of worshippers, and promote their prayer[5]. Duties to men and duties to God were recognized. Charity and hospitality to men and kindness to animals were enjoined. Falsehood treachery and fraudulence were condemned. Witchcraft, spells, sorcery, and black magic were despised. Gambling was denounced though it was prevalent. War was not condemned, ethics of non-violence was absent violence is to be met by violence. Strength bends 'before strength.' Let us stand straight that we may walk and live.[6] The Buddhist ethics of Ahinsa was unknown to Vedic age. Asceticism was foreign to the spirit of vedic people though it might be practiced by a few people. The world is said to have been created by the austerity (tapas) and self-abnegation of the cosmic spirit. There was no caste system, though Purusha Sukta refers to four classes. There was no child marriage. Woman enjoyed a high position in society. They did not observe 'purdah.' Same women were composer of mantra. "One in many, unity in variety, is the perennial message of the Vedic India. The last sukta of the Rigveda breathes this out unequivocally thus: Assemble speak together, let your mind be of one accord."

Let all priest's utter the mantras in a common way. Common be their assembly, common be their mind so be their thought united. United by the thoughts of all that all may live happily, that ye may be happily reside.[7]

Rita, Eternal older, Eternal law of nature in its cosmic sense law of eternal morality teaches us to "law of Karma." This is one of the important ethical values of Rig Veda. This is beauty of cosmos and beauty of nature. To work continuously. To go forward continuously, never stop to work in righteous way. This must be our goal of life. Rita in its social sense in the fundamental moral law which impose order and "symmetry on the life and character of man and produces ethical form of goodness. Both the Natural law and the moral law have been know as Dharma: for instane we find the Natural law in the following prayer."

यः पुष्पिणीश्च प्रस्वेश्च् धर्म्रणाधि दाने् व्यनेवनीरधारयः

यश्चासंम् अजंनो द्विद्युतो दि्व उरूरूवीं अथितः सायुक्ष्यः।। [8]

ऋतं शंतेन्त ऋतु दीध्याया दि्वस्पुत्रासो् अंसुरस्यतीराः

विप्रं पदम्डि॰रसो दर्धाना यज्ञस्य धर्म प्रथमं मंनन्तं।।2।।[11]

I sing a lofty song, for she is mighest, most divine of streams.

Saraswati will I exalt with with hymns and lauds, and, O vashisth, heaven and earth.

Thou who by the law (dharman) hast spread about flowering and seed-bearing planet and stream of water, thou who generates the matchless light in the sky.

Or in the mythopoeia picture of streams of water.

Indra let the unwedded young girl.

Skilled in Rita, flow bubbling fountain streaming forward.[9]

so may saraswati auspicious send good luck; she, rich in spoil, is never niggardly in thought,

when praised in jamadagni's way and lauded as vashishth lauds.

Rita as moral law is a dominant idea in the Vedas. Ideal sages are described as people who praise Rita and think straight.[10]

ऋतं शंतेन्त ऋतु दीध्याया दि्वस्पुत्रासो् अंसुरस्यतीराः

विप्रं पदम्डि॰रसो दर्धाना यज्ञस्य धर्म प्रथमं मंनन्तं।।2।।[11]

Men are asked to think of wealth and strive to win it by Rita and by worship.[12]

Mankind wishes to collect.

Money from all directions.

ऋतस्य पया नमसा विवातेत्

Intent to do righteous task from the inner-will by following righteous way (Rita) meditate and contemplate on God from inner and self-wisdom and obtain the pervasive form and omniscient form of God. Man and his wife asked in the Atharva Veda to enjoy good future by absorbing Rita and bearing themselves according to Rita. The veda says that those who live in terms of Rita as moral form also participate in Rita as aesthetic form-good life is made happy by nature's beauty and benignity.

Sweet blows the breeze for one who lives by Rita; rivers pour for him sweets.[13]

Under the light of human behavior was found to conform or not to conform to the vedic values. Hence it fell into two confecting categories. Sathys and Asathya (truth and untruth)[14], Rita and Anrita (justice and injustice, good and evil), for example, in the Rigveda the sinless (anagah), Devas are described as Yitas Pan (followers of Rita) and sathyah (true), and sinners (papasah are spoken of as anritah without Rita) and asathyah (without truth).[15]

In a general way the Prefix Su-stands for good and dus-stand for evil; eg.

Agni, make me have good conduct (su-charita)
Bar me against bad conduct (dus-charita)[16]

'vasH (Su asH),' good existence, implies goodness, bless. Many hymns contain a prayer for this eg. We will follow the path of goodness (svasti) like the Sun and the Mood/Moon (that follow and cosmic Rita most regularly).[17]

The terms 'suman,' 'sumati,' good heartedness, imply the spirit of friendship and love for fellow being. Eg. In the prayer may we be good hearted (सुमानसः) at our days.[18]

Interesting to note that the vedic prayer for wealth carries the qualification that it should be obtained the rough good means eg. – agni, lead us to wealth by the good path (supath):[19]

अग्ने गर्भ सुपथा राथे अस्मान्विष्वानि देव वयुनावि विद्वान्।

सुयाध्यम् स्मच्चुहमण मेनो भूमिकां ते नमअन्ति विधरे।।

स्वास्ति पन्थमनुचरमे सूर्याचन्द्र मसोविव।

पुन र्दद् तान्घतां जान्ना सं गैमेनही।।

What should be the attitude towards evil according to Vedas? First to non-cooperate with it, and follow the path of goodness, "leave here those who are opposed to goodness (Shiva) – those who are evil-minded is the paraphrase in the Atharva veda – and let us cross over to power that are beneficent"[20]. But when evil is aggressive and sends its challenges to good, the veda advocates the acceptance of the challenge and battle, with a will to victory "The races of mankind are great oppressors (purudruhah), says the Rigveda, and Prays to Agni: 'Burn up malignity that strives against us' huri on him your bolt to thunder who treats us 'the robber and oppressor.' "[21]

इन्द्रो युणं वेरूणा दिद्युमेस्मिन्नो जिष्ठयुग्रानि बंधिष्टं वज्रम।

यो नौ दुरेवौ वृकृतिई थीतिस्तस्यिान्नि मायाम् भिभृत्योजः

The Vedic poet has expressed great indignation against 'him who threatens us without offence of ours, the evil-minded arrogant, rapacious man. the opposition to Rita is symbolized in the person of the Demon vritra (or werpent Ahi) whom Indra, the champion of Rita, has constantly to fight and overpower. The exhortation to Indra is also exhortation to man.

Go forward, meet the foe, and conquer,
Thy thunderbolt can't be resisted;
Indra, manlinessi thy strength,

Destroy vrtira, win the waters,
Acclaiming self-dominion[22].

The Atharva Veda says that the earth chose Indra and not vritra. The Veda emphasizes that it is only against evil that man should fight. In the Yajurveda the newly crowed king, while being given a bow, is told that it will be 'Indra's vritra-slaying weapon. War is the final unpleasant welcome. Says the sage in Athrva Veda[23], 'That is what people living in the reign of the seven rivers had always to do' Indra gave freedom to man by slaying Vritra; says the Rigveda' so the Vedic warrior came to be known as Kshatriya, Protector or Rita, a term originally applied to Varuna and Mitra, Guardians of Rita.[24]

This is the stronger side of Vedic ethic. The Vedic sages try in the peaceful way through their ritualistic prayer to ennoble everybody. They with their offerings of soma juice in streams of Rita, to overflow and glorify Indra, making aryas of all and driving away the enemy. When this fails there is only one alternative left: to be led by Manyu, war fury, but will Varuna Guardian of Rita, as the companion and fight valiantly.[25]

Health and Strength

In addition to the spiritual and moral values the Veda thinks in terms of physical and material well-being. It speaks of the optimum duration of life as a hundred years. There are prayers for mental efficiency, physical health, sweet speech and fair days.

The Veda believes in full biological growth and finds a virtue in the normal coordination of means and ends in instinctive life.

It wants good nourishment, fine offspring, and brave men[26] fit to fight out life's battles. Vigour, virility and valour are interlinked by it. Give to men the strength of men, O hero! Is a Rigvedic prayers.[27] Indra in each and every fight, give mainly strength to our bodies and ever conquering valour; is a prayer in samveda. The vedic sage desires a combination of 'winning intelligency (medha) and un impaired and unsurpassable courage (sahas).'[28]

तं नो दात मरूतो वानिनं रथं आपानं ब्र चितयं द्विवे दिवे।

इषं स्तोतृभ्यों ब्रजनेषु कारवे स्निं मधामष्ठिं दुष्टरं सहः

He also wants union among brave and good men for collective welfare.

The rocky stream flows on. Move ye together,
Stand erect, and cross over, my comrades
Let us leave here those. Who are not good? (RV) [29]

Quit you like heroes and cross over, comrades
Leave here those who are evil minded.[30]

Education and Household Life

The Vedic control of the fighting insisting in man by bringing it under the discipline of Rita as moral law-or Dharma as the term came to be called in later times-has had a profound influence on the Indian system of welfare. Similar was the control over sex-life. it was two fold: a long preparatory period of Brahmacharya (education) for young men and women; leading to the healthy growth of the virile side of nature, accompanied by continue and sublimation of sex; and thereafter marriage based on mutual love and joint rulership of the household.

Monogamic marriage was one of the ethical value of Rigveda. In Monogamic marriage the partners are united into an abiding duality.[31]

The vedic ritual requires the presence of both husband and wife. The biological purpose of marriage, fulfilled through parenthood, is very clearly recognized. Conjugal love is held sacred[32].

The wife on the way to maternity is described as most blissful (Shivatama). The address of the; bridegroom to the bride in the Atharva Veda – "I am song, that art verse, I am heaven, than art Earth, we two are together shall live here becoming parents of children[33] has been used in the later Vedic literature, as a sacred formula lifting the biology of human-reproduction to a spiritual plane."

The veda thinks of the wife not only a joint ruler but also as a queen exercising her sovereignty over all the members of the household including her husband's parent's. she is desired to mother has husband in his advanced years. The wife, verily, is the home, says the veda else where[34].

Her intellectual personality is recognized and she is invited soon after her marriage to address the vidhata (religious assembly). [35]

In which it was the ambition of sages to speak eloquently.

The Veda distinguishes itself from all other Indian literature by the high regard in which it hold woman. The word of address for Goddess, subhage, O graceful one! (the masculine form subhaga being use for a god) has been used in the veda for a woman too.[36] The Veda has not only represented the Divinity as virgin or as mother, but also honored the wife by comparisons with the Deity; eg. In purity Agni has been compared to 'the chaste wife loved by her husband, the appearance of Vac (sacred speech) has been likened to that of the loving, finely robed wife before her husband. There are comparisons making graceful references to woman eg. Dawns are said to sing their songs 'as women active in their tasks do, and the Deity is described as clothed with the rites' like a women with her robe.[37]

The Veda also shows tenderness for children eg. Vena (the loving and beloved one) is caressed as a child by the poets with their hymns[38]. Children are the symbols of racial immortality. A sage prays: 'May I be immortal through my children.'[39]

The poet asks his friends to decorate the Yajna (rita) as they decorate a child to make it look beautiful.

The Vedic home with the sacred 'domestic fire' in it was a sort of temple in itself. The Atharva veda speaks of a modest thatched house 'rising on the pillar with Rita'; calls it, 'a queen and goddess and says it was first made by Devas.'[40]

The Rigveda compares an ideal house to a lotus take and to a divine mansion.[41]

'Hospitality, according to the Veda, is an essential domestic virtue. The house of an inhospitable man is no home, says a Rigvedic Sage.'[42] According to this ideal a good householder must share his food with the needy. 'He is all sin who eats all alone.'[43]

Cooperating Living

The Veda inculcates the ethics of collective living though mutual love and concord. The prefix sam (sym Greek sum-, Latin-cum and English come-with its Variants Con, as in concord, cor etc.) is used to express this Sam has its variants in Sa and Saha we find a systematic attempt to build up sam-hridaya (or sahridaya) literally concord i.e. the union of heart and sam-janam, unity through common understanding, at all social levels.

At the marriage rithal in the Rigveda man and wife pray that the Devas may unite their heart (sam-ajantu hyideyani nau) Believing in united collective life, the Veda upholds social virtues like fidelity and friendship. "For one deserting a friend who knows the truth there is no grace even in the holy word" says the Rigveda.[44]

There is the prayer for a friend: "Give us a home," give us a friend.[45]

Vedic ethics does not discriminate against the foreigner. There is a prayer in the Rigveda for the forgiveness of sins against the man who loves us, a friend, a comrade forever, a brother, a neighbour who is always with a stranger and us.[46]

Ritam Satyam Ritam Satyam

Chants the Yajarvedic age, uttering the two key words of Vedic religion and Vedic civilization.[47]

Satya and Rita are pursued through the social activities of Brahman and Kshtriya respectively the functionaries being known respectively as Brahmana and Kshatriya, Brahman is the pursuit of knowledge, particularly, spiritual knowledge; and it is the spiritual leadership of the people. Both these were guided by the Veda or Brahman in Atharva Veda:

> Step beyond what is human
> Take up the Divine word,
> And establish thy leadership
> Along with all the friends than host[48].

This was used as a initiation formula, spoken by Acharya (Spiritual-teacher) in the upanyana (initiation ceremony) when he invested the religious student with the veda and give him authority to teach.[49]

Kshatra is a protective power by which people are ruled and their safety and liberty defended, in the later case by fighting. It is the function of making Rita (moral law and order, justice) prevail on the earth. The Divine Gardinas of Rita, as stated in the Rigveda, are particularly.

The Devas mitra and Varuna who are described as 'great kshatra (kshatriya), the lofly Rita, identifying kshatra with Rita.'[50]

These Divine Kshatriya are said to be 'true, attached to Rita, upholder of Rita for all races, and to have attained their' active energy by tending Rita with Rita.[51] They rule all the world by Rita. The kingly worshippers and Priests pray to mitra, that they 'may strive for the most spacious and well-protected savarjya, self-dominion ruled over by Rita[52]. Indra, the model for the Khstriya is exhorted to fight vrita, the enemy of Rita, and proclaim his self-dominion. Mitra and Varuna are invoked in the Yajurveda to inspire the earthly king, the former for satya (truth) and the latter for Dharman or Rita[53].

The following according to the Yajurveda, is the preparation for satys (truth, in the ultimate sense).

By self-dedication (Vrala) one obtains consecration (diksha)

By consecration one obtains grace (dakshina),

By grace one obtains reverence (shraddha)

By reverence is truth (satya) obtained.[54]

The Vedic Ritual

The Vedic Ritual is the form as the Vedic poetry is the spirit of vedic worship. The hymn is the heart joints the milk libation; says a Rigvedic sage[55].

The Vedic cult is so to speak, externalized through the ritual. The text of the veda accepted by all as Divine revelation (within the soul of the sages) was recited before the people along with the ritualistics offerings on a fire kindled for the purpose and this brought the masses into contact with the holy word (vac) which, as we have said was believed to be purifying and ennobling by its very sound, even without, the aid of the meaning. The Theory of Sabda Brahma prayer through sound and its melody and rhythm (nada) was put forward in later times in support of this view. In the veda itself we find the tendency to accommodate the common man by insisting on only the word of prayer. In Samveda they're the call:

Come together, ye all, with power of spirit (ojasa) to the Lord of heaven.

The ritual had popular appeal, and generally there was the prayer for the people as a whole, or for all living beings eg.

May be live for a hundred years[56]
Carry us across, as by a boat
Across the sea, for our good.
Drive away our sin,
To Rudra, the powerful…we bring these
So it may be well with our four hymns,
Bipeds and quadrupeds,
And in this village all be well fed, all remain undiseased.

All worshippers individually and collectively were expected to come with pure bodies and heart: come let us praise Indra, the pure with pure saman hymns. The Soma juice is said to have been Praised by the invoking masses of men, who have freed themselves from taints to sin, and it is poured out with the word of Rita, with truth, with faith, with Tapas.[57]

The ritual is not only performed in all purity but is also believed to purify everything, "with sacrifice (the Yajna as Rita) I purify both earth and heaven, says a Rigvedic sage."[58]

The some juice poured according to Rita is also expected to ennoble men: Active they (somas) glorify Indra making Aryas (noble men) of all, and driving away the enemy. There are rituals of atonement which require the worshippers to ask forgiveness for his sins. There is a collective prayer to Agni ending with line-shining bright, drive away our sin-which comes at the end of every stanza as a refrain.

Ethical Values of Purusha Sukta

The Purusha Sukta of the Rigveda is not only a powerful hymn of the insight of the great seer, Rishi Narayan, on the cosmic divine. Being as envisaged through the multitudinous variety of creation, but also a short cut provided to the seeker of Reality for entering into the state of super conciseness. The Sukta is charged with a fivefold force potent enough to reuse god-experience in the seeker. Firstly, the seer (Richi) of the Sukta is Narayan, the greatest sages ever known, who is rightly proclaimed in the Bhagvata as the only person whose power not even, all the Gods, can ever imagine. Such is the Rishi to whom the Sukta was revealed and who gave expression to it, as the hymn on the supreme purusha.

Secondly the mantras of the Sukta are composed in a particular metre (chandas) which makes it contribution by generating special spiritual force during the recitation of the hymn. Thirdly, the intonation (svara) with which the mantras are recited adds to the production of the correct meaning intended to be conveyed through the mantras, and any error in the intonation may produce a different altogether. Fourthly, the Deity Devata, addressed in the hymn is not any externalized or projected form as content in space and time, but is the universal being which transcends space and time and is the invisible super-essential essence of experience. Fifthly, the Sukta suggests, apart from the universalized concept of the Purusha, an inwardness of this experience.

पुरूष एवेदं सर्वम्

This statement describes unity in diversity. The Rishi Narayana discovered during his contemplation that the whole universe is originated out of one supreme power. His desire to reveal the thought that the whole word is manifested by one ultimate and supreme power inspired him to reveal purusha-sukta. The process of manifesting the world out of one supreme power is included in 'Yajnavidhya; knowledge of Yajna, and that is science, spiritual science.'

विज्ञानं यज्ञे तनुते कर्मापिच (तैत्तिरीय अरण्यक 8.5.1

On the contrary, to obtain the knowledge of one supreme power by studying the worldly power is Jnana (ज्ञान).

In Srimad Bhagwad Gita, Lord Krishna described both the terms Jnana (knowledge) and science (विज्ञान).

ज्ञानं तेहं सविज्ञानमिदं वक्ष्याम्यषेषतः(Gita 7.2)

The root of this world is 'Brahma' and the form (part) of Brahma from which world manifested into being is 'Purusha.'

All gods spoken of by the Vedas subsist in Brahma. None can excel it. None can transcend it. They can not exist without it. Brahma is their essence. It is the ground of the order of Nature. Rita is grounded in Brahman[59], "Fire burns, the Sun rises, the wind blows, and death overtakes creatures at its command." The uniformities of nature are sustained by Brahman. The Vedic poets conceived the supernatural deities presiding over the forces of nature and the physical and moral order (rta) sustained by them. They had the glims of one Reality. The upnishadic seers conceived it as one Brahma or Atman. The unambiguously advocate spiritualistic monism or Absolute Idealism.

All creation is "purusha grandeur, but he is every superior to the entire Creation." The whole of the universe is only one-fourth of his being, the remaining three-fourth remain in celestial immortality.[60]

The Upanishad speaks of higher (pare) Brahman and lower (apara) Brahma. The former is formless (Amurta), unmenifest (ashabda), immortal (amrtya), abiding (sthita) and transcendental (tyat). The latter is formed (murta), manifest (sabda), mortal (martya), fleeting (yat) and empirical (sat). the former is impersishable and immutable (akshara). The latter is perishable and mutable (kshara). The former is transcendental (santa) or nor-phenomenal (nisprapancha), undecayng (ajara), immortal (amrtya), redeeming (abhaya), and unexcelled (para). There is no reality beyond it. It is devoid of all attributes and determination. It is unqualified indeterminate, and unconditioned. They are not two Brahma, but one Brahma viewed from the empirical stand point is determinate. This Atman is not this, not this (नेति–नेति)[61]. It is "summum Bonum" (Shiva).[62]

Virtue (dharma) and Vice (adharma) are independent of time, space, and causality. They are super-conscious. They can be known from the Vedas only. They can not be perceived by the sense. Nor can they be inferred. They cannot be known by reason. The scriptures are the only sources of knowing them. This is authoritarian. But the scriptures are embodiments of intuitions. They are not irrational, but supra rational. Dharma and adharma can be known by reason subordinate to the scriptures.

Ishvara reveals the Vedas. The injunctions (Vidhi) and prohibitions (nisedha) are creation of God. The individual selves (jiva) have relative freedom to perform enjoined acts of commit-prohibited act.

God awards good (artha) to those who perform right act (dharma), and evil (anartha) to those who perform wrong acts.

May I Attain the Span of a Hundred Winters

Rudr

The optimism of Vedic Man is so deeply rooted in his world view that even when he is obliged to face the terrible aspect of the terrible aspect of the divinity, represented here in Rudra, the destroyer, the thun-derer, the father of the Maruts or Storm-Gods, he is not taken aback and asks from this same God what his mercy can do. He approaches him with wily prudence, entreating him with due care so as to avoid arousing his anger. He enters boldly into his presence to request from him all the boons that, preciesely, the terrible adspect of the divine can grant. The destructive and punishing God is always and also the benevolent and merciful one. This hymn in praise of Rudra is an expression of the varied emotions that this God simultaneously inspires.

It is difficult to decide whether or not there is a certain conscious diplomacy or strategy in this Vedic prayer. It gives the impression question, though he cannot always understand, the power and whims of the divine. In any event, this masterpiece of entreaty of approaching the divine. It is Rudra to whom Man prays, whose destructive energy he desires to quiet. He begs him to be merciful, for he desires to escape his destructive might and to benefit from his healing power.

The Anthropocentric Sacrifice

Sārīrayajňa [63]

The "Conscientization" brought about by the Upanisads does not end with the integration of Man into the framework of sacrifice; it centers sacrifice on Man. If Man performs the sacrifice without the necessary knowledge, if he is unconsicious of its meaning, its will not be a true sacrifice. Man is an essential element magical interpretation we are led to recognize that sacrifice is not only-and one will soon be led to add, not even mainly-directed to the maintenance of the physical cosmos, but of the world of Man. A cosmic catastrophe may well occur if Man fails to perform sacrifice, but defection in this regard is difficult to check. Moreover, there are so many Men on earth and the mechanism of the whole procedure is so complex that one cannot be absolutely sure of the faction and importance of one particular thread. On the other hand, one thing is sure: that Man cannot lead an authentic human existence if he does not perform sacrifice. Sacrifice becomes more centered on Man. Human life is itself a sacrifice and there is an emphasis on both knowledge and Man.

The first text of this selection ends a long passage at the begninning of the Brhadaranyaka Upanisad which seems to indicate that all sacrifices culminate in the recognition that the all-embracing sacrifice is the sacrifice of, in, or to the Self, and that only by this kind of sacrifice is a worshiper saved from perishing. The dynamism of the whole text is worth pondering, for it gives another clue to this momentous Upanisadic mutation. This fourth brāhana gives a condensed explanation of the divine sacrifice by which the world came into being. it comes to the conclusion that all is the action of the ātman. It so, to worship the ātman is the way given to Man for collaborating in the world-making sacrifice. The text gives so far as "world," as the open space of which one can be aware, as the realm of onus's won experience, as the world that opens up to a Man. For this reason it is also stated in the same place that "if a Man departs from this world without having seen his won world, that if it is not recited, is of no anvil." It is then obvious that by meditating on such an ātman (in the active sense in which to meditate is to become what one meditate upon) each worshiper obtains the object under which the ātman appears to him. But this truth has to be known and discovered, otherwise the works are ineffectual. Sacrifice is the human act par excellence, but it entails also the risk of its misuse for personal profit or greed.

The second text from the Chāndogya Upanisasd takes up and develops the idea of human life as a sacrifice. All existent things are homologized to different sacrifices. By this means the full range of Man's life on earth is sanctified, for everything corresponds to some facet of the life-giving and world-saving sacrifice. In this process of correlation stress is laid on the human element. it is affirmed, for example, that the *daksina* or honorarium given to the priest at the time of sacrifice (which in ancient times was considerable and burdensome) cannot simply be reduced to dāna or almsgiving; it is not even specifically stated that the priests should be the beneficiaries. More important are the other four gifts mentioned: fervor, uprightness, harmlessness, sincerity. Another passage of the same Upanisad (iii) inreoduces an important act, which also demonstrates the man-centered character of sacrifice. The priest who knows the intricate cosmological origin of the different rites of sacrifice can undo certain mistakes that may have crept in, thus signifying the power Man has over the merely mechanical or blind forces of the sacrifice. The underlying idea is that of an ontological substitution by means of ritualistic identification. Prajāpati brooded over the worlds, and their "essences," their "juices," *rasah,* were extracted. from the earth came forth its essence, fire, and from the proceeded the Rg Veda. So any mistake in the RG-Vedic recitation can be rectified by means of the corresponding fire sacrifice. Knowledge here is power.

The importance of this new idea should not be overlooked. It is the beginning of Man's not for directing the forces of nature for or against other human beings, but kfor a restructuring of the same cosmos begins to fall into human hands. Man emerges now as more than simply a partner in the cosmic process produced by sacrifice; he appears the rectifying mind, as the spirit who by his knowledge can correct mistakes that false calculation may have allowed to creep in. One is tempted to say, extending the metaphor when the utilization of the energy condensed in matte has not been properly calculated.[64]

* * * * *

References

1. Vedic Ethics and values; Vedprakash Vedic: Ethics Values.blogspot. in.
2. Dicshnary.
3. Rv I 65.3:I 68.4

4. RVi 189,6iv 5.4
5. RV iv 6.1
6. Rv I 36.14
7. Jadunath Sinha Volume ii Indian philosophy pg 426
8. Rv 10.191 2–4
9. RV ii 13.7
10. Rv iv 19.7
11. RV x 67.2
12. Rv x 31.2
13. RV I 90.6
14. HYMNS from the Vedas Abinash Chandra pg 3
15. Rv iv 15.2
16. Yv.vs 4.28
17. RV V 51.15
18. Rv vi 52.5
19. RV I 189.1.19
20. Rv x 53.8
21. RV iv 41.4
22. Rv i80.3
23. AV xii 1.30 RV iv 21.10
24. RV iv 21.10
25. RV viii 25.8
26. Yv vs 8.53
27. RV x 148.4
28. Rv ii 34.7
29. rv x 53.8
30. Av xii 2.2 6.30
31. RV x 85.42
32. RV vii 31.9 Av xiv 2.71
33. AV xiv 53.4
34. RV iii 53.4
35. RV x 85.26 27,35
36. RV vii 26.13
37. Rv x 123.1

38. RV ix 104.1
39. RV v 4.10
40. Av ii 12.5
41. RV x 107.10
42. Rv x 117,4
43. Rv x 117.6
44. RV x 71.6
45. Rv ii 11.14
46. RV v 85.7
47. YV vs 11.47
48. AV vii 105.8
49. RTH Griffith ATharva Veda VOL. I pg 379
50. RV v 68.1
51. RV V 68.iv
52. Rv v 66.6
53. Yv vs 9.3.9
54. Yv vs 19.30
55. RV iii 55.8
56. RV vii 66.16
57. Rv ix 113.2
58. RV I 133.1
59. Kathopnishsd ii i.3
60. RV 10.90
61. Bramopnishd iv 4.22
62. Jadunath sinha Indian Philosophy vol.ii
63. panniker Mantramanjari
64. Mantramanjari Panniker

Chapter - VI

Relevance of Religious Belief and Ethical Values of Rigveda in Modern Era

Maharashi Dayanand Saraswati (1824–83) considered the Vedas as a rock of firm foundation taking them for his guiding view of life, his rule of inner existence and his inspiration for external work and even more, as the word of eternal truth on which man's knowledge of God and his relations with the divine being and with fellows can be rightly and securely formed. According to him, all the sciences meant for the good of making flow from the fountainhead of Vedas ever since creation of the universe. The Vedas radiated that light that illuminated the world by teaching those universal and eternal truths and principles that helps the mankind to realize the nature and coordination of God with the soul and the creation.

Indeed, the Vedas are the first source of knowledge ever comes to mankind. It is said in Manusmriti that "Vedokhilo Dharmamulam" means Vedas the source of all Dharma.

According to Maharashi Aurobindo Gosh (1872–1950) Among all the materials of our past the Vedas are the most venerable and has been directly and indirectly the most potent, an authoritative revelation and standard of all truth. In his book entitled 'secret of the Veda,' he has commended as follows:

'It is a remarkable attempt by Swami Dayanand the founder of Arya samaj to re-established the Veda the as a living religious scripture.

Dayananda took at his basis a free use of Indian Philosophy, which he found in the Nirukta.'

Vedas are the law of life by God to men. Vedas have the knowledge of secrets of creation and law of nature by which the omniscient governs the world. Neither western scholarship nor ritualistic learning has succeeded in eliminating the psychological and ethical value of the hymns. Dayananda affirms that the truths of modern physical sciences are discoverable in the Vedic hymns.

The ordinance of Manu is considered to be as efficacious as the prescription of Doctor (Yat Vai manur avadat tad bheshajam) Manu fixed Indian conduct for all time. "By seeing the self in all beings and all beings in the self, and practicing thus equality of vision, one attains absolute suzerainty or self-realization." In modern era, the Vedic values are very essential to be followed by each and every persons of the world specially because they need peace and self-realization and same to be provided for all students who are future of the world.

Religious belief of Rigveda is indispensable to know and utilize in modern era to develop attitudes towards spiritual and supernatural aspects of religion. Religious belief is distinct from religious practice or religious behavior. Law of life is the law of belief. The progress and peacefulness of life depends on what the person believes.

To make the modern person known about the Rig Vedic religious belief, this research will provide facts, reasons, and cause to the modern man to study, know and practice to form the new society in which all the persons may live happy, peaceful and prosperous life. The new society in which all the present problems like stress, degradation of personality of man, crime, corruption and worse attitudes and degradation of thought can be removed and a new mind which works for the benefit of the society must be developed.

Religious belief is a strong belief in a supernatural power or powers that control human-destiny. Every human being has faith; faith on God.

God, the supreme power that runs the whole universe. Faith on God generate mental attributes like, presentation, vigil, watch, consecration, chastity, toleration, traditionalism, supernatural virtue meditation and contemplation on supreme power. Religious belief of Rigveda are chanting of hymns, prayer and adoration to the cosmic deities like Agni, Indra, Surya, Mitra-Varun, Usha, Earth, Ashvins and like to propitiate the natural deities to achieve wisdom, prosperity, happiness, peace, ions and grandsons and victory in wars and longetivity of life.

Today, in modern-era the whole is being divided on the basis of religion, caste, and creed. Actually people forget the very meaning of religion, etymologically the word religion means, faith on such a supreme power which runs the universe the belief in the existence of God and activities that are connected to worship. The God is one, supreme power, one reality (Ekam Sat). It means religion of the people of the world is one because Supreme power working behind the whole universe is one. But due to ignorance people defines religion as "thought and concept of mind of different communism" and thus they are divided into various communities.

To inculcate the religious belief of Rigveda is to bring a drastic change in the society to alter their thought about religion and make them united. As in the Rigvedas last Suktas it is said that "Let they all be united and Let ye know the one reality." When the same thought resides in the mind of all the flow of energy increased and power of energy reaches to the universe in turn the universe give the same power to the world. So the Vedic hymns should be chanted together to increase wisdom and to prosper the world. To build the concept of "Satyam, Shivam, Sunderam" the religious belief of Rigveda becomes essential to know.

Creates the thought that Purusha (Param Purusha) is only one reality spreaded all-over the world. Chanting of hymn with proper stress and intonation is earliest practice to maintain relationship between religion and awakening of senses to gain supreme knowledge. While chanting mantras the power of sound vibrations are considered effective since ancient times and it is very scientific and Om (Aum) chanting produces a vibration in human-mind, which resonates with the universal vibration of Aum as Aum (ॐ) sound is pervaded all over the universe. By connecting with universal sound vibration, human mind connects with its true self where treasure of knowledge is hidden. Om is the solution of all kinds of problems. When a person concentrated on Om for a definite time period he becomes able to eliminate all kinds of problems and diseases from his body and life.

The industrial wastes, rapid organization, air and water pollution disturbances in the ozone layer – formation, radio active waves etc. have destabilized the human being, plants and animals life cycle. The crop is not growing healthy due to imbalance in climatic condition and sometime scanty rainfall a condition of drought is created.

शांति शांति।

To understand the practical aspect of the topic "The Religious Belief and ethical values of Rigveda." O Lord, Lead me from unreality to reality,

From darkness to light

From death to immortality.

The mantra clarifies that without keeping right coordination with the environment, the man can't lead a happy and prosperous life.

ॐ भद्रं कर्णेभिः श्रण्शुयाम् देवाः

भद्रं पश्चयेमाक्षभिर्यजत्राः

स्थिरैरगड़तुष्टुवान्ंसस्तनूभिः।

व्यषेम् देवाहितम् यदायूः।

Om, O' Lord, may we hear from our ear what is auspicious. May we see from our eyes what is true and auspicious and adorable able. May we pray with steadiness of mind? May we devote our life span for services of God?

Significance of Sacrifice Yajna in Modern Era

The industrial wastes, rapid organization, air and water pollution disturbances in the ozone layer – formation, radioactive waves etc. have destabilized the human being, plants and animals life cycle. The crop is not growing healthy due to imbalance in climatic condition and sometime scanty rainfall and sometimes floods. The manpower indulging in agricultural activities committing suicide, which is a great loss of the universe. How can we improve all these situations? In Rigveda the knowledge to build a pure and healthy society, is hidden today. To explore the knowledge of Rigveda to reform the modern society is prominent step in the field of research.

According to Modus Operands "Agnihotra (Yajna) is basically a healing process." 'Heal the atmosphere and healed atmosphere with heal you.' Purification of environment through constituent electrons of the substances fumigated in the Yajna is an obvious effect of sacrifices.

Dr. Hatkine has mentioned that 'Mixing ghee and sugar and burning them creates smoke which kills the germs of certain diseases and secretion takes place from some glands relate to the wind pipe which fills our heart and mind with pleasure.' According to Dr. Shrowich, Russian scientist cow milk contains great power of protection from atomic radiation. That is why cow milk and ghee (purified butter) are used in Yajna.

In Rigvedic period there was an optimistic outlook of life was prevailed. This is one of the prominent needs of present age. Everyone is getting distressed due to various problems of life, which are taking place due to ignorance, or lack of right knowledge of managing and leading life. in every situation if human mind remain stable and silent, the knowledge to solve the problem automatically comes in the mind and thus an optimistic outlook of life which is generated and developed by, chanting Aum, hymns, performing Yajna, Pranayam, Yoga and meditation is maintained to save and survive life.

Gods are considered to be friendly to the worshippers. The human mind which pays its whole attention to pray by chanting hymns and worship God to receive power and wisdom certainly obtains the godly wisdom to live the life. In this way the prosperity and happiness mixed with every breath of man. This ethical value of Rigveda is badly needed in the present age to make the man happy. If a person does this practice he becomes happy and make his family harmonious. If a family becomes harmonious a society runs in an order and. If every society runs in proper order the country and world get peace, prosperity happiness health and wealth. Today there is a need to regard the Vedic deities (Agni, Indra, Suryua, Jal (Water), Praithvi, Mitra and Varuna and like) as father, brother, friend, companion, protector, and forgiver of sins. They were regarded as deadly and destructive to the enemies. Enemies mean the persons who were not paying their proper attention to strengthen them, to save them, to make them healthy. It becomes obvious that who in modern era we are facing so much problems, because unknowingly and ignorantly human-beings are destroying the natural and supernatural power. The nature is commended by supreme principle, "Brahman" because it is the ubiquitous cosmic principle. It is called Atman because it is one eternal home principle. It is called Atman because it is one eternal home genius consciousness (ekatma pratyayasara)[1]

All gods spoken of by the Vedas subsist in Brahman. The most transcendental. Nothing can exist without it. It is the ground of the order of nature. As previously mentioned "Rita" is grounded in Brahman. The person breaths, eat, walk, and think every action is under "Rita's" command. Every person should follow the law of Rita. When we disobey it, our life destroys. The Earth is becoming warm; the depleting of ozone layer is causing "Global warming. The trees are cutting down; the water level of earth is decreasing. All the calamities are occurring due to disobeying the law of Rita. The God (the transcendental, supreme powers, the nature; 'fire burns, the sun rises, the wind blows, and death overtake creatures at its command." All the activities of the nature are obeying the law of Rita. The uniformities of nature are sustained at its command.[2]

यच्चिद्धि ते विशो यथा प्र देव वरूण व्रतम्। मिनीमसि द्यविद्यावि।

म नो वधाय हत्नवे जिहीकानस्य रीरधः। मा हृणानरग मन्यवे।।

Whatever law of thine, O God, O Varuna, as we are men,
Day after day we violate
Give us not a prey to Death, to be destroyed by thee
in worth, To thy fierce anger when displeased.

They crushed haters of gods, destructive to the enemies. They promoted the welfare of the virtues and punished the virtuous. The virtuous were transported to haven, and the vicious were condemned to hell, the nether, region of darkness. This value of Rigveda is 'must' to learn for everyone.

The prime important had been given to "Virtue," virtue was truth, sin was untruth (anrita). The gods purged the worshippers of their sin. 6 (RViii 7.10; iv 12.4). Virtue of Rewarded; Vice was punished 5. (RV iv. 5.4)

To learn the true lesson of life to know the true goal of life is very necessary in modern age. People forget their reality, their purpose of life; they are wandering here and there unnecessarily purposelessly because of ignorance, taking in knowledge of reason of their life. Why do I come here? What is my goal of life? What is God? And what is religion. They believe that there questions are only related to spiritual persons; they have to be devoted their life for the purpose to realize themselves and to know the God… In my opinion; "Every individual soul is a part of super soul (supreme power), without connecting to this supreme power how can he lead a peaceful life." So to realize himself or herself, and to know God is the prime duty of each and every person. Then only the person and the world become prosperous, healthy, and happy. So the goal of religion is, "To be united with the gods and to attain immortality were also regarded as the goal of religion (RV V 4.11)." The aim of religion is to obtain earthy happiness and heavenly bliss.

Rita is the moral law. It is truth and religiousness. (RV I 65.3)

As above stated man is part and parcel of the supreme power, his whole destiny is commanded by law of Rita (the prime principle of supreme power).

Thus everyone, including god, is bounded to the law of Rita. God's intentions and motives. The gods descry the impure motives and intentions and punish them (RV I 189). God knows the pure thoughts of the worshippers, and promote their prayer (RV iv 6.1). Duties to men and duties to gods were recognized. When a person directly connected to the God, he becomes very kind and possesses true heart, in which all the negative qualities such as hatred, jealous, enviousness do not dare to enter and this pious heart becomes so kind that charity and hospitality to men and kindness to animals were enjoyed. Falsehood, treachery, and fraudulence were condemned in Rigvedic age. War was commonly prevalent because to win for virtue is a virtue itself. To remove evil from the society is basic motive of Vedic people. And the same purpose should be of modern educationist, philosophers, and spiritualist. There is a drastic need to remove evils of the society to follow Vedic rules and regulations and rituals, which are quite scientific. Vedic rituals and belief are very useful to maintain purity of inner life. The deities (natural and supernatural deities of Vedic age and gods of puranas).

Strength bends before strength[3]

It is stated that 'Let us stand and straight' that we may walk and live, Jadunath Sinha one of the great philosopher mentioned in his book "Indian Philosophy Vol. II that" The Buddhist ethics of ahimsa was unknown to the Vedic age. I would like to clarify this statement that, Vedic people were also very kind and follow non-violence, charity and hospitality to men and kindness to animals were enjoyed, Lord Buddha was against sacrifice in Yajna and this practice must be followed in present age also, but the point is that Vedic sages had an intuition to follow gods laws and they connected their mind directly with supreme mind super consciousness. During the sacrifice they were permitted by God to perform Yajna like Ashwamegha

Yajna and like that, to follow the reciprocal rule of the universe, to increase the power of the universe that practices had to be done. But aware! Aware! Aware! Not now, because we people of modern Era do not have that much practice of contemplation and due to different set-up of mind can't devote as our sages did. Now the need is to start practice to worship Vedic deities and achieve wisdom to correlate religious-spiritualism with today's technology to lead a happy and prosperous life. The world is said to have been created by austerity (tapas) and self-abnegation of cosmic spirit.

Significance of Om (Aum) sound

Aum (Om) has a paramount importance in Education. Most 0f the Vedic prayers starts with Om (Aum). Aum has a connection with the universe. Vedic seers understood the symbiotic relationship of wave energy. Everything in the universe is pulsating and vibrating – nothing is still.

Science is now proving that what our Ancient Rishis discovered about the facts of natural power and the universe is true. Chanting of Aum when recorded in Tonoscope, it resulted a 3 dimensional representing of the cosmic energy (Sri Chakras Meru). The origination of 'Sri chakra meru' is dated back to 2500–300 BC.

When we chant Aum, it produces a vibration in us, which resonates with the universal vibration of Aum, and we are elevated from our everyday minds to relationship with our true self. We chant Aum to be in tune with the true self. The sound Aum, when chanted, vibrates at the frequency found throughout in everything in the nature. In addition the vibrating and rhythmic pronunciation also have a physical affect on the body by slowing down the nervous system and claming the mind similar to meditation. When the mind gets relaxed, your blood pressure decreases and ultimately the health of your heart improves.

Aum represents many trilogies of meaning. Symbolically the three letters in body the divine energy (shakti) and its' 3 main characteristics.

1. Beginning of the universe
2. The life period of universe
3. Destruction of universe

Aum is the word, which represents the three first forms of God.

1. Brahma (creator of universe)
2. Vishnu (operator of universe)
3. Mahesh (destructor of universe)

As per Mandukya Upnishad:

1. The symbol 'A,' stands for wakefulness, where we experience extremely through our mind and sense organs.
2. The 'U' stands for the dream state, in which inward experiences are available.
3. In the state of deep sleep, represented by the sound 'm,' there is no desire and consciousness is gathered in upon itself.

The sound of Om is omnipresent in the whole universe. Om provides strength to all other words. The sound of Om is a combination of three different sounds. The meaning of this sound has been explained in the Vedas. You can acquire immense knowledge by practicing Om chanting. It is also known as pranav mantra. It is the sound of human-breath. It is believed that Omkar consists of twelve Kalas. Each, notation of this word signifies an important meaning. The first notation is Ghoshini, second vidhyam, third is patangi, fourth is vayuvegani, fifth is Naamdheya, Sixth is Endri, Seventh is Vaishnavi, eighth is shanbari, ninth is Mahati, tenth is Dhriti, eleventh is naari and twelfth is Brahmi.

Om is the solution for all kinds of problems. A person who can concentrate on the sound of Om is able to eliminate all his problems. Aum has always been known as cosmic sound and mystical syllable. Recently scientists of NASA recorded the sound of 'SUN' pronouncing Aum as given at https://youtube/w_toxu2WFSO. It is found in the most ancient scripture of the world "Rigveda" dated to be from the 2nd millennium BCE. The humm 1.1.1 of Rigvedi Samhits

श्ऊँ अग्निमीले पुरोहितं यज्ञस्य देवमृत्तिजम्। हो तारे रत्नधातमम्।।1।।

Rg 1.1.1.

Om (ऊँ) is an agreement with the hymn. Likewise is tatha (so be it) with a song. But Om is divine and tatha is human.

In Jainism, Om is considered a condensed form of reference to the Pancha-parameshthi, by their initials. A+A+A+U+M (o3m) The 'Dravyasmgraha,' quotes a Prikrit time.

ओम एकाक्षर पंथपरमोष्ठिनामादिपम् तत्कथयिति चेत" अरिहंता असरीरा तह उवच्झाया मुणियां

Veneration to the Arhats, veneration to the perfect ones, Veneration to the masters, veneration to the teachers, veneration to all the monks in the world,

AAAUM (Om') is one syllable short form of the five paramesh this 'Arihant, Ashiri, Acharya, Upaji Haya, Muni.'

In Buddhism, Om is often placed at the beginning of mantras and dharnis. Probably the most well known mantra is "Om mani padmi hum."

Scholars interpret the first word of the mantra "Om Mani padmi hum" to be Aum, with a meaning similar to Hinduism – the totality of sound, existence and consciousness.

In Sikkhism Ik Onkar, ironically represented as in the Sir Guru Granth Sabhid, is the statement of singularity in Sikhism that is "there is one God Refers to Absolute monotheistic unity of God."

In Vedic literature syllabi Aum is described with various meanings as, the scared sound, the udgitha (song of the universe, the whole world, the truth, the ultimate reality, the finest essence, the cause of the universe, the Brahma, the Atman.

Various suktas of Rigveda use syllabi Aum in the beginning of the mantras and at the end of the mantras. The Gayatri mantra from the Rigveda O' third mandal sukta 62, mantra 10, begins with...

Om.ऊँ

भूर्भुवः स्वः

तत्सवितुर्वरेण्यं भर्गो देवस्य धीमहि।

धियो यो नः प्रचोदयात्।।90।।90।।

Om' we meditate upon the glorious splendor of the Vivifier divine, May he himself illuminate our mind. There is nothing more exalted them the Gayatri mantra. It is the most renowned mantra of the Vedas. It is addressed to the divine life-giver as supreme God, symbolized in savitra, the Sun*[1], for this reason this prayer is also called Savitra. This mantra derives its name from the meter in which it is written the Gayatri being a Vedic poetic meter of twenty four-syllables by the author "Visvamitra"[1]

The Chand yoga Upanishad is one of the oldest Upanishad of Hinduism. It open with the recommendations that 'let a man meditate on Om (Aum).

In Vase 9 to 12, the Mandukya Upanishad enumerates, four fould etymological roots of the syllable 'Aum.' It states that the first element of 'Aum' is A, which is from Apti (obtaining, reaching) or from Adimatva (being first). The second element is u, which is from utkandra (exalltation) or from Ubhayalva (intermediateness). The third element is M, from Miti (creating, constructing) or from Mi minati, or apti (annihilation). The fourth is without an element, without development, by beyond the expanse of universe. In this way, states the Upanishad, the syllable Om is indeed the "Atman (the self)"[4]

In yoga sutra – Om to Yoga practice.

शतस्य वाचकः प्रणवः ।।27।।

His word is Om

Yogasutra 1;27

Educational value of Aum (Om)

1. The sound of Om encompasses all words, all sounds in human language.
   Om is matrix of all sound, when it is diversified from gives rise to all words used in language. Linguistically, all audible sounds are produced in the space within the mouth beginning at the root of the tongue and ending at the lips. The threat sound is A, and M is the lip sound; and the sound 'U' represents the rolling forward of speech articulation which starts at the root of the tongue, controlling until it ends in the lips.

2. AUM and OM
   In Sanskrit, the sound "O" is a diphthong spelled "au." A diphthong is the blending of two vowel sounds where both are normally heard and make a gliding sound. As a result, the difference between OM and Aum is simply one of transliteration.

3. Aum represents the 3-fold division of time
   A – is the awakning state
   U – is the dream state
   M – is the state of deep sleep.
   At the end of AUM is a pause, a silence. This represents the state known as Turiya, or infinite consciousness.

4. The visual symbol represents the meaning of 'Aum.'
   The symbol OM visually consists of three curves, one semicircle, and a dot.
   ॐ
   The large bottom curve symbolizes the waking state, A.
   The middle curve signifies the dream state V.
   The upper curve denotes the state of deep sleep.
   The dot signifies the fourth state of consciousness Tyriya.

5. Aum is associated with Ganesha – the physical form of Lord Ganesha is said to be that of Om. The upper curve of Aum is identified with the head or the face of Ganesha. The lower curve his belly. The twisted curve on the right side of OM is the trunk.[5]

The Elements: Cornerstone of Reality

Many centuries ago, before the scientific worldview, culminating in the splitting of the atom, led to the predominance of the quantitative, man had a more qualitative conception of the irreducible factors that underlie all manifest realities. For modern man matter and energy (in spite of their different forms and interchangeability) can be said to form the fundamental elements of the universe. Against this dualistic outlook, Vedic man was more pluralistic and believed, as was also true of many other ancient cultures, in the existence of certain basic elements of a qualitatively different nature which underlay the constitution of the universe. These elements should not be understood against the background of a rigid atomic theory; they were to a great extent interrelated and were sometimes even interchangeable, so that the Vedic intuition refers, for example, to fire being born out of waters. The elements are not individualized and separated constituents of a whole but rather, vectors or forces pervading the entire reality. The elements are the real symbols standing for the ultimate constituents of reality; they are the primer dials 'stuff' of the world, but their being the cornerstones of reality is a symbolical and not scientific or merely physical being. They stamp for the underlying unity behind the manifold appearances of all that they symbolize.

Out of five classical elements and others that could perhaps have been chosen. There were three elements concerning, which are, water as the reality before creation, earth as the creation par excellence and wind as the dynamic of the cosmos after creation.[6]

Later classification offer a list of five 'mahabutani' or primordial elements, starting from either or atmosphere (akasha) and including fire (tejas or agni) Agni, who will be introduced later and aksha, which is a particular element pervading everything (Saragata are here omitted. Aakasha though existing in Bandvdoes not appear in RV.

Water

In the satapatha Brahmana it is said that they were produced out of vac, the word'*7, the first element out of "the first principle." The waters are the primeval element, everything else rests on them. 70% of the earth is water and 70% of water present in human-body. Waters are the basic and foundation of the universe.

The life-supporting environment of planet earth is composed of air, water, and soil which are the respective components of what are called atmosphere, hydrosphere and lithosphere. The earth atom is generated from the five subtle essential of smell. The earth atom has solidity. The water atom has viscosity. The light atom has heat. The air atom has mobility. The ether atom has penetrability. The atoms combine with one another and form aggregates (samuha). Ether is modified into space and time with the help of adjacent. So they are included in ether. The elements and substances present in the universe to from cosmic entities are also present in the universe to form cosmic entities are also present in human body to form an individual in entity. Man cannot survive without mutual reciprocation with the nature. You can breathe by receiving the oxygen from the environment. This is the eternal truth. This truth remains fact from the very beginning. From the origin of primordial man. the percentage of oxygen (21%) maintained by the photosynthesis reaction of the trees. The trees get their nutrition from the soil and rain, so purjanya (clouds) dyaus the worshipped as God in the Rigveda because without their presence an (purusha) cannot be survived.

Another important element of the nature (atmosphere) is water. Waters are present in every sphere. In the sky (heaven), in the atmosphere (Antairksha) and on the earth. Without water human life is impossible and due to the presence of water, there is human-life on the planet-earth. Human body's (75%) part is water. So why people forget to destroy water. By destroying water he is gradually destroying himself. In Vedic period Apah (water) has been worshipped as God.

The most eminent and benevolent, grand and sublime beautiful and useful aspects of nature is fire (Agni).

अग्निषोमात्मकं जगत्[8]

Agni pervades in all spaces of the atmosphere. He pervades in all three spheres (adhibhautic) terrestrial, adhidaivic (celestial) and adhyatmic (spiritual) level of the world. Agni is worshipped as fire-god. He is domestic god. He is the lord of the house. "Thy, O Agni, the flaming one, art, born from the heaven, thy art born out of water which is scientifically and spiritually known." Thou art born from the forest and herbs; thou art born bright, O lord of man to men.[9]

Agni is the divine leader of divine tribes, the guardian of the seasons. He knows all rules, where to create and where to destroy. He knows everything that leads astray. He protects us from sin and defiles us.

Agni promotes worshippers prayer. He release men from all sins committed in thoughtlessness. He reigns over immortality.[10]

The sun provides light and heat to the earth living-beings. The planet earth is the abode of many a plant and animal species including men. The life-supporting environment of planet earth is constituted of fire, air, water, and soil. Sunlight is indispensable element in the process of photosynthesis, by which plants prepare food and on the basis of which all living-beings survive. What we have witnessed especially in the last centuries is that, pollution pervades every sphere of life supporting environment. This pollution is destroying the mother plant "Earth." Why has pollution has been occurred. Everyone knows, due to the ignorance of man. The man becomes habitual to live in the world of technology and industrialization. He thinks that by using scientific technologies he is becoming more intelligent and progressive. Of course, he is, but on the other side he is forgetting to save the atmosphere in which he lives, he survives. The man is destroying the elements; water, air, fire, soil without which the life is not possible. And our seers (sages) of Vedic periods worshipped these elements as nature-gods and they lived a healthy and prosperous life of hundred years. So what is here to pay attention is that the modern man should keep progress scientifically, technically by serving and saving our natural, by worshipping, deified, and personified gods. i.e. Apah (water), Agni (Fire) Surya (Sun), Purjanya (clouds) Usha (dawn) etc.

The life-supporting environment of planet earth is composed of these important components, which compose respective components of atmosphere, hydrosphere, and lithosphere. The Human-Mind is so complex and complicated that it can see and understand some elements in different perspectives. When mind sees these elements scientifically and superficially it can see only the one aspect of these elements that these are important for your life, for the survival of human life, but when human mind observe it deeply, with intuitive eyes, it can also see the importance of these components for survival of planet earth also. If you want to be truly prosperous, healthy, and want to lead a successful life. You should try to save the planet earth and to save our mother planet in all the spheres. Atmosphere, troposphere, hydrosphere, and lithosphere must be saved. The living-world or the biosphere and the other three spheres remain in a dynamic equilibrium which is referred to as ecological balance.

The Vedic seers by their intuition obtained the knowledge of the whole universe. Cosmic as well as terrestrial world. They observed the above world, cosmos and got wisdom to study the cosmic world; The Sun, other planets, stars, ether, water, fire, air and earth. The cosmic intelligence provided them the knowledge of the cosmic-mind and made them able to understand the mysteries of the universe. Vedic sages during their contemplation obtained the knowledge of the secrets of the cosmic body, cosmic-laws, laws of the Rita on the basis of which the whole universe works and follow the absolute discipline. It is the physical and moral order of the universe. Human mind possesses capability to obtain the knowledge of the absolute. The necessity is to create will to obtain the knowledge of the things which he is unable to see with his open-eyes but with inner eyes he can understand the knowledge of the God, the absolute, the supreme-being. Thus the Vedic sages did. The cosmic intelligence provided them the secret knowledge of the origin of the universe, working of the universe and the knowledge of Vak (Shabda) from which the whole universe came into existence, that is 'Aum.' The sound of 'Aum' existed in every largest as well as smallest particle of universe. The same sound is present in the Sun, the moon, the stars, in the motion of the earth, in the sound of air, fire, in the murmuring of the leaves of the trees, in the flowing of rivers blowing of wind and ultimately and originally in the breathing of human-being.

In the Vedic-time, the diverse cosmic bodies of the universe had been worshipped. The Vedic-sages by powerful mantras evokes the defied nature to enlighten themselves to maintain the physical order of the universe. The mankind must understand the true purpose of living, the true purpose to born on the earth, which is to live according to the very discipline of the universe (law of Rita) and ultimately human soul should be united in the universal soul to maintain the world.

They contemplate over the question, who hold the earth the sky and the heaven? And got answer in their intuition that "Indra (supreme power) holds the earth, the supreme force which scientifically known the power of gravitation." Vedic sages called this power Indra (the supreme God) who holds the earth, the sky, and the heaven. Indra unites the immeasurable earth and the sky. He originates, wind, storms (Maruts). He maintains the working of the sun, the dawn, and fire God. Indra destroys the enemy power of the universe, the power that tires to destroy the universe. Just think over it "should you tries to destroy the power of water, fire, air and other compositions of the spheres? Indra (the power which hold the earth, sky and heaven) is the terrific destroyer of enemies in the battlefield. He is the killer of the demon Vrilra. He may kill the human also who tries to destroy the universal power. For him all human beings are same. He doesn't' discriminate among humans (who is the saver and who is destroyer) so from time to time he destroy the enemies who unknowingly or unconsciously destroy the important components of the world, that's why calamities happens in the world.

The Vedic sages had written mantras which posses the knowledge of the secretes of the supreme power. The "Purusha Sukta." The most prominent and Supreme Sukta in which they described that "Purush" (Param Purusha) has thousands heads, thousands eyes and thousand feets creates (AVYAY) indifferentiate purush in the form of 'Vak' the Shabda. In the very beginning of the earth, there was only ether. And the substances (elements) which are present in (Vyom) ether, sky is 'Brahma.' There was darkness all over. Darkness was enveloped by darkness. There were no movements. The power of Brahma was in dormant state. The freedom of that power is his supreme peace, supreme bliss, supreme happiness. The substance which blend the whole world is breath' (Pran Vayu) oxygen. That is Rishi (knowledge of Brahma).

Brahma is the seed of (Sristhy) the universe. It is in the form of fire. The whole map of universe hidden in this seed. Just like in a seed of a tree there resides the power of growing the whole tree. The seed possesses the knowledge of the whole tree. And this knowledge is 'Desire' and Desire is knowledge. And there is no 'Karm' (action) without knowledge. The development of action is called knowledge. The whole universe is formed of action of the knowledge of Brahma. It is 'Vivart' manifested, immanent, spreaded all over and possess the knowledge to come back in their original form (the absolute, ultimate power). The (3/4) three forth of the whole power. On the basis of this knowledge Rishi (sage) Narayana wrote Purusha Sukta which describes-

प्रथम मन्त्र

सहस्रशीर्षा पुरूंषः। सहस्राक्षः स्हस्रांपात्।

स भूमिं विष्वतों वृत्वा। अत्येंतिठठदषान्गुलम्।। Rv x 90

Means Purusha, the cosmic person (Param Purusha) whose body is the whole universe. He has thousand heads, thousand eyes, thousand feet. He pervades the whole terrestrial space and transcends it. He envelops the world from all sides and extends beyond in ten directions. Whatever was or will be – all that is Purusha. He is untouched by fruits of action (karma). All creation is his grandeur, but he is superior to the entire creation.[11]

According to the Vedas the origin of the word 'Purush' had been described in various ways. The First one is "पुरूधास्यति इति पुरूषः" Means one who becomes active firstly and acts in different (Bhav) ways of consciousness, is called 'Purush.' The another meaning of पुरूधास्यति (Purudhyasyati) is one who becomes various is 'Purush.' Or पुरा–रूष्यति इति पुरूषः। यहाँ हिंसार्थक रूष धातु से पुरूष बना है।[12]

> "पुरा औषत इति पुरूषः" अर्थात् मन प्राण वाणिमय पुर में मायावरण में घिरे हुए मन–प्राण आदि सम्पूर्ण पाप भाग को सर्वप्रथम जला देता है। वह पुरूष है।
>
> 'पुरे–वसति इति पुरूषः' पुर अर्थात् शरीर में जो वास करता है वह पुरूष है।

The inner nature of Param Purusha is immanent is transcendental, though he is immanent in the whole universe. He is both immanent and transcendent.

> भयथा पिण्डे तथा ब्रह्मण्डें

Like human body, like universe both are same in quality. Both possess same elements which are different in quantity only.

The new generation must understand the; Veda-mantras' and will prove that Adhidevic (cosmic, heavenly) Adhibhut (atmosphere) and spiritual (Adhyatma) all these work on one and single principle only subtle cause of the body, also works like static body and possess the form like: भूः भूवः स्वः (bhuh, Bhuvah, Swah).

"एकं ज्ञानं ज्ञानम्, विविधिं ज्ञानम् विज्ञानम्" and एकोऽहं' बहुस्याम् All these important propositions will be understood and followed by them.

This Purusha Sukta has been composed by Rishi Narayan on Vishnu Narayan so this is not a prayer but description of reality of the universe. It is the process of becoming out of being. Being is (Abhu) and becoming is (Abhava). It is pantheism because is said that

> पुरूष एवेदं सर्वम् यद्भूतं यच्च भव्यम -Means

All the past existence and future existence are forms of purush body. After making so largest and biggest universe it remains apart from it by Ten Fingers above.

स भूमिं विष्वतों वृत्वा। अत्येंतिठठदषान्गुलम्।। 9।।

The mind of Rishi Narayan was able to elaborate the truth of the universe because the mind was totally devoted for the contemplation of the Brahma to discover the reality, the secret of the universe. The new generation should even contemplate on the importance of the components, which are indispensable to create and maintain the universe.

The distribution of gaseous mixture present in air and fire particles of the atmosphere, across the various layers is such that about 95 percent of air is present in the troposphere and the remaining 5 percent in the rest. Most organisms in respiration utilize air. As a mixture, air consists, mainly of two gases, Nitrogen (79%) and Oxygen (21%) besides Argon, carbon dioxide and other miscellaneous gases including ozone, from the composition of air it is clear that quantitatively ozone is an insignificant component. But qualitatively it is its efficacy in absorbing solar radiation that makes it one of the earth's most important life support system and its depletion as one of the most important damages to earth's status as an abode of the living beings.

There is a vital force in your body to keep you alive. This vital force flows through your body, and mind and connect you with the universal force. This is our inner-self, our consciousness and this is our breath. This breath builds a network around us, with the environment. As plants and trees exhale oxygen, human being inhale it. Plants and trees continuously release oxygen during the process of photosynthesis. This oxygen collected in the atmosphere. A molecule of ozone (O_3) is created when UV (ultraviolet) light strikes on oxygen molecule (O_2). A photon splits the oxygen molecule into two highly reactive oxygen molecules to form ozone (O_3). The gas readily absorbs UV light. This is a marvelous process of nature to protect human being from dangerous rays. But human being by his ignorance damages his own protection. Just see the cycle of formation of ozone (O_3) from O_2 is continue which disassociated into its components. Parts (O_2 and O). Given constant conditions, the net result is that ozone settles into a dynamic steady stale, in which the rate of its formation is equal to the rate of its removal. The amount of ozone in the atmosphere is quite small, it constitute less than one part per million of the gases in the atmosphere and if compressed to the earth's surface it would only be three meters thick. It largely resides in the stratosphere and engages the UV radiation in the ozone-cycle.

Clinically, ozone can be obtained by subjecting oxygen to silent electric discharge. The electrodes are covered with insulating materials (glass or mica) so that discharge currents are kept low and high voltage pulses are supplied between the electrodes. This method has to be used so that oxygen acquires the energy it needs to form the ozone but at the same time ozone does not become so hot that the molecules break-up back into oxygen. The gas so obtained is bluish, explosive, and stinky, characterizing its Greek name 'ozein' which means to smell. The atmospheric ozone spares the earth from harmful solar UV radiation; its presence in the troposphere is toxic to human-beings. The toxic effects of ozone are manifested upon its inhalation and absorption in the lungs causing damage in pulmonary and intrapulmonary sites. Besides these effects damage DNA and modify cellar genetic integrity.[12]

In the Vedic times, the ecological balance was not at all disturbed. There was complete harmony, between man and nature. The Vedic seers were conscious of this relationship and so maintain its balance they deified prayers for the gods and put obligations in life to please them. These acts always reminded them the concept of consciousness at all levels in nature. Deity or the god is the name of a natural element or sub-element exiting in various zones of environment. *These* gods provide necessities of life or help to the life cycle-on earth.

The whole biosphere has been divided into three zones in Vedic literature namely terrestrial (Prithivi) midsphere (Antariksha) and celestial sphere (Dyau). The terrestrial sphere is the main also abode of solid and liquid matter such as earth and water etc. and is governed by Agni (fire) as the presiding deity. The midsphere is the abode of such as air and water vapours. It is governed by Indra (or Vayu). The celestial sphere is the main abode of thermal elements and is dominated by the Sun (Surya).

The Vedic word for sphere is 'Rajas' which is sometimes used to denote the above three regions while at other times 'Rajas' denoted atmosphere or the midisphere. The word 'Rajas' for mid-sphere is significant as it means dust particles which are present in the atmosphere. The atmosphere has been divided into various spheres by the modern scientists.[13] Surprisingly Vedic-seers also have made divisions of the atmosphere as-

त्रिरन्तरिक्षं सविता मांहित्वना त्री रजासि परिभूस्त्रीणिं रोचना।

तिस्त्रो दिवः पृथिवीस्तिस्त्र इंन्वति त्रिभिब्रलैर्भि नौ रक्षति त्यानां।।5।।

RV IV 53–5

Means – O' human kind! The Lord who spreaded over all three zones spreads his light around the whole universe and creates the world which possesses all three glams 'Satoguna' (सतोगुण Rajoguna (रजोगुणं) and Tamoguna (तमोगुण), and he himself follow the path of all these three gunas, follow his path.

Not only this, Vedic seers took note of the presence of air, fog, clouds and the water vapours in these regions-[14]

पूर्वे अर्धे रजसो अप्त्यस्य गवां जनित्र्यकृत् प्रकेतुम्।

व्युं प्रथते वितरे वरींय् ओभा पण्शन्ती पित्रोरूपस्यां ।।5।।

Together with the dust particles and water vapours there is heat also in this atmospheric region.[15]

The light of the sun always lit the half-of the sphere of the earth, and there remains darkness in another half-region. In between their present dawn and dusk. During this movement the mankind always resides in present-time. What a wonder to see here that the portion which receives light in day time, the same-portion does not receive light and there remain darkness. And there remains in the sky a wonderful orange and pink colour of light in the conjunctively time (संधिकाल) it is called Usha (deity by praying her you get prosperity. The mocking sees position of movement and stationary at the same-time.

To identity the ozone sphere in atmospheric region in Vedic ecology we may not get a particular word to denote it. But there are Vedic evidences to represent this region. The famous Nasdiya Sukta speaks of it in the following terms.

'Kimavarivah' i.e. 'what covered' we know the ozone layer is the shield which covers the whole of our biosphere. Moreover, the region of lonosphere and ozonesphere. Beyond 'Rajas' there is Vyoma, which can easily be called exosphere. Modern scientists call this sphere as 'air-less.'

The Rigvedic seer also used the word "A-VAT" for the region beyond 'Rajas' in the second mantra of this hymn.

नासदासीन्तो सदासीनदानी नासीदरजो नो व्योमा परायत्

किमावरीवः कुह कस्य शर्मलम्भः कियासीद् गहनं गंभीरम्।।

Another reference we find in the Rigveda (1.141/2). Where three types of Agnis (fires) are mentioned. The Third fire is spoken of as a bull that yields all the rasas some scholars believes this to be the ozonosphere.

वृक्षो वपुः पितुयानित्य आ शेये द्वितीय्मा सदाषिवम् मातृर्षु।

सृतीयेमस्य वृषभस्यं दोहसे दषेपमति जनयन्तं योषेणः।।2।।

The study of Indra's characters as depicted in the Vedic literature also reveals the fact that the Vedic seer were conversant with the characteristics of the atmosphere and its various regions or spheres. Indra is associated with various cosmic activities. Maruts closely connected with Indra act as his helpers in his fight with the Vitra.

RV I. 85

Maruts have been conceived as storm gods[16].

RV I. 85, 7–8

The adjective Marutvan is often used for Indra which relates close proximity between two, Indra's identification with windy (Vayu) is also important to prove our conjecture. The modern scientists describe the stratosphere as the region where strong winds are blowing. So the sphere where Indra and Maruts are conjointly busy in their activities can be surmised as the stratosphere of which ozonosphere is but a part.

In the Vedic 'hymns' Indragni' were also eulogized. This speaks of the relation between wind and heat. Scholars take this principle of heat to refer to lighting of the atmospheric region, which flashes together with its presiding deity Indra. But 'Agni' may not necessarily be taken as lighting. It may be taken as a reference to the solar light, which is beneficial for the earth.

In Vedic Samhitas Indra is sometimes presented as identical with 'Sun' also. This identification is sometimes very precise. Thus at one place Indra says himself-

"I was afore time, Manu, I was Surya." [17]

> अहं मनुरभवं सूर्यष्चाहं कक्षीवां ऋषिरास्मि विप्रः। अहं कुत्संभाजु नेम् न्यृज्जेहं कवि रूषनाः पश्यंता मा।

Once Indra and Surya are called together as if they are one and the same.[18]

The plurality of various forms suggests that Vedic seers are speaking of various forms of solar light. In that sense case atmospheric solar god either Indra or Savitra or Pushan may be taken to represent the ozone sphere, which absorbs the ultra-violet raditatity and allows the beneficial form of light only to let in on the earth. A few characteristics of God Savitra may also prove our conjecture. Savita the essential god may be allotted mid region also. The Rigveda calls Savita as Prajapati, the lord of the beings, the sustainer of the universe.

Catalytic destruction of ozone by atomic halogens. The main source of this halogen atoms in the stratosphere is photo dissociation of man-made halocarbon refrigerants, solvents, propellants and foam blowing agents. These components are transported into the stratosphere by winds after being emitted at the surface.

The Vedic seers had seemed by their intuition all the different layers of the atmosphere, they know stratosphere and ozonosphere. Solar God either Indra or Savitra or Pusham, which absorbs ultra-violet light of sun and allows the beneficial form of light only to let in on the earth, maintains the power of Antariksh. The modern scientists studied much on the stratosphere and proved that "The earth" atmospheric ozone layer plays a critical role in absorbing ultraviolet radiation emitted by the Sun in the last thirty years. It has been discovered that stratosphere ozone is depleting as a result of anthropogenic pollutants. There are a number of chemical reactions that can deplete stratospheric ozone; however, some of the most significant of these involves the catalytic destruction of ozone by halogen radicals such as and bromine.[18]

Humans have introduced gases and chemicals into the atmosphere that how rapidly depleted the ozone layer in the last century. This depletion makes humans more vulnerable to the UVB rays, which are known to cause skin cancer as, well as other genetic deformities.

The absolute consciousness is fully aware of creating, maintaining, and destroying world. As Lord Prajapati is creator, maintainer and destroyer of the universe. The Vedic seers by their wisdom proved that universal consciousness and consciousness of small (particle) tanmatras, are co-related and maintained by the low of discipline; moral and physical order (Law of Rita). They provided the whole knowledge of the universe in the Vedas (Rigveda, Yajurveda, Samveda and Atharvaveda). They anthropomorphized the powers of nature with the glory of supernatural and superhuman spirits akin to mankind. The Vedic gods are supernatural and superhuman spirits governing the phenomenon of nature friendly and beneficial to the worshipper and terrific and deadly to their haters. Means the persons who pay proper attention to save this power by their efforts and prayers because human consciousness has power to know and maintain the universal power, the need is to develop such wisdom to understand it. Modern scientists also study it with their brilliance of thought and prove it by researches and technology but they didn't prove the power by which all the celestial bodies are working. And modern generations mind involve in enjoying the modern industrialists and technological world that they are ignorantly destroying the natural and atmospheric power which are causing diseases to modern man himself. You should be aware of it.

It is said that in Savita energy wise Pushan marches and surveying all existence protects it. Yet another mantra said that Savita becomes mitra (the friend) through his righteous laws. We have already discussed that the ozonosphere protects our earth sending here the filtered light (minus ultraviolet radiation). The Mitra (Friend) form of solar radiation tends to refer to that protective aspect of the atmosphere.

Another god Varuna (who is often associated with Mitra) points out the beneficial aspects of this layer of the ozonosphere Varuna has been depicted as the ultimate god who follow the universal law. Derived from the to encompass, the word Varuna means 'one who covers or encompasses all. According to Mcdonell Varuna represents the element sky, which is, present everywhere. Just as the atmosphere envelops the whole earth and its region known as ozonosphere protects the earth from the ultraviolet rays, in the same way Varuna, the encompass protects the earth. The ozone layer is the part of this natural system, which conserves all types of life on this living planet earth. But when this system is disturbed by some natural or human activities there appears danger to the whole of the creation. The Vedic seer thus prays to Varuna.

O Lord, O Varuna, may this laudation come close to these and lie within Thy Spirit may it be well with us in ksema and yoga.

The Vedic ecology seems to be in agreement with the modern ecology in terms of the description of atmosphere. Vedic consciousness continued man against indulgence in activities that would disturb the ecological balance. The Vedic ritual of sacrifice indeed implied replenishment of supporting system. This consciousness apparently is on the wave now, thanks to reckless consumerism. Self-restraint seems to be paving way for self-appeasement and gratification. The human interference with the ecology must end, developmental requirements not with standing. The human body is quite capable of withstanding natural variations. In weather which in fact are good for human health. Hence limited need for CFC-dominated technologies, air conditioned refrigerators, aroids etc. even if the return to Vedic life style may not be feasible, there is a need to focus our Research and Development (R&D) efforts in evolving eco friendly technologies. Man must learn to live in harmony with nature.

Vedic Deities and Environment

The Vedic sages developed their spiritual forces in the solitude of mountains and confluences of streams. In the roaring of the Parjanya (clouds) and light of lightening. The Vedic sages get cosmic spirit by meditating on the burning and heating sun. They got their wisdom by contemplating on the celestial occurrings. The sages develop "Dhi" which is used to express intellect, action (also sacrificial action), prayer and spiritual force. The ancient seers developed all these faculties in the serene atmosphere of nature and felt obliged towards it. Century's back, the whole of the environment was pure and blissful, just free of pollution. The seers watched the radiant sun god showering upon the earth its choicest boons of light and energy and making all the vegetation and life possible on earth. The shining moon, the twinkling stars guided them in their journey of life. The mid region covered with clouds, poured generously the elixir for both the animate and inanimate. The vast expanse of the earth and far spread Greenland did not merely sooth their vision but also gave them a generous outlook to understand the ecology. The pace of life then was really slow so the people had enough hours of leisure to behold and enjoy the beauty of nature. The nature god bless, present in its bountiful form, inspired them and poetry was the most natural and beautiful thing to happen them. The words of reverence for all these beautiful and beneficial forms of nature were ultered spontaneously. Thus were formed the suktas, the Riks, the mantras in analogy of nature.

Throughout this Vedic poetry, we find deification of natural phenomena. Our ancient seers expressed their reverence in multiple ways like singing song, chanting mantras pouring offerings in the sacrificial fire. The veneration of nature thus become a characteristic of India's culture and tradition. The Vedic word for divinity is Deva *(दानात् दीपनात् द्योतनात् वा)* which means 'one who gives, shines and make other shines. Deva[19] (Sanskrit देव) means heavenly, divine, any thing of excellence, and is also one of the terms for deity in Hinduism. Deva is masculine, and the related feminine equivalent is Devi.

In the earliest Vedic literature, all supernatural being are called Asuras.[18] The concepts and legends evolve in an ancient Indian literature, and by the late Vedic period, benevolent supernatural beings are referred to as Deva-Asuras such as the Puranas and the itihas of Hinduism, the Devas represent the good, and Asuras the bad.[20]

The Sanskrit Deva is derived from the indo Iranian 'dev' which in turn descendant from the proto-Indo-European word,' 'deiwos, originally an adjective meaning 'celestial' or 'shining' which is Vraddhi, derivative from the root 'diw' meaning to shine.'

The Samhitas, which are oldest layer of text in Vedas enumerable 33 devas; II for each three worlds or as 12 Adityas, 11 Rudras, 8 Vasus, and 2 Aswins. Rigveda states in hymm 1.139.11,

भये देवासो दिव्येकादष स्थ पृथिव्यामध्ये कादष स्थ।

अखुक्षितो महिने कादषस्य ते देवासो यनापियं जुष्ध्वप्।।

O'Ye eleven gods whose home is heaven, o'ye eleven who make earth your dwelling.

O'Ye who with might, eleven, live in waters, accept the sacrifice, O gods, with pleasure.[21]

MaxMuller states that the Vedic hymns are remarkable in calling every single of different devas as the only one, the supreme, and the greatest. Muller concluded that the Vedic ideas about devas are best understood neither as polytheism nor as monotheism, but as henotheism where gods are equivalent, different, perspective, different aspects of reverence and spiritually unified by principles of Rita and Dharma.

The oldest Upnishads mention Devas, and their struggle with Asuras. The Kaushitaki Upnishad, for example, in Book and states that "Indra was weaker than the Asuras when he did not know his own Atamn (Soul, self)[21] once Indra had self knowledge, he become independent, Sovereign and Victories over the Asuras. Similarly, states Kaushitki Upnishads" the man who knows his inner religious independence, sovereignty and is unaffected by all evil.

Conception of Brahma as cosmic principle: The origin of the meaning of the word "Brahman" is uncertain. the view of MaxMuller[21] is that, "it denotes what grows from urn in the sense of 'grow,' that which expresses itself in speech or in nature as force. The view of Deussen is that it is human will in its striving to the divine, when the individual in prayer returns to the timeless, space less, individualizes self of his, which is God. Neither for the views of Max Muller nor for that of Deussen[22] is there any support in the actual use of the word in the Rigveda. These at any rate the word naturally and normally means prayer, but there is further development. It can mean spell, for the prayer may be spell, and not real prayer, and often means holy speech and the holy writ, the three fold Veda. The Brahma is that which fills all beings, stimulates the sense organs, penetrates the whole world, and encircles the universe. Its true nature is revealed in those passages of the Upanishads, which described the Brahma as qualified, the unqualified Brahma being manifestly the prudent of further refinement of speculative thought. It is also found that the Brahma is the bodily warmth in man, which identified with his self, Atman, and also with the cosmic light or fire (tejas or jyotis). The fire, which composes the self of individual, is essentially bound up with the power of thought. The cosmic Brahma on the other-hand is fire (jyotis) in no metaphorical sense, the 'brahmanah Parimarah' of the Aitareya Brahmana really means that all comes from fire and resolved into it again. Now the connection of the individual and the cosmic fire is simple; the rays of the sun bring fire into the heart of the individual and at death the fire departs from him back to the sun when it come, or rather to the heaven of fire, which lies above the earth and of which the sun and the moon are doors pierced in it. The idea of this path of light is older than the Upanishads, for it occurs in verses cited in the Brahdaranyaka Upanishad and the Atharvaveda knows the threads of which life is woven and calls this knowledge the great Brahmana, that is the great secret of the Brahma, prior to the Upanishad we find the conception in a personal shape, Brhaspati, the lord of heaven of light, the peer of Zeus, Pater, of Jupiter, German war god, a form of Dyaus himself. It is for this that he appears in the Rigveda as the highest of gods, their father and ruler, guardian of the Rita, leader of men, enemy of all that is false, an Indian parallel to Ahura-Mazdiah."

'Brahma,' the frequently used term is usually questioned but it is because of "cause is used for the effect" and similarly the use of ric and Dhi, dhits, and didhitt is explained.

The idea that fire pervades and constitutes the essence of the universe is based on the interpretation given to the Brahma. It is stated that fire existed in the earth, the plants, the waters, stones, men, cattle, and horses fire is the essential principle of the universe. The Brahma is manifested in the breath of men and in the wind, and it is to exaggerate one element out of all proportion to find the fundamental reality in fire, even when fire is deemed to be endowed with intelligence and therefore to be much more than merely material.[23]

पृथिवी–अन्तरिक्ष–द्यौ[24]

The earth, the atmosphere, and the sky having Agni, Indra, Aditya, Mitra-Varuna, Vayu as presiding deities. All the natural forces in between were also termed as divinities. The Indra, armed with lightening and thunder stood for rain, the storm deities who were raging the sky, called Maruts.

For our daily requirement we get things for nature. But nature is not just a conglomeration objects. It is a complete system. Man is a part of this system. He is neither different nor over and above nature. That is only in Indian tradition we don't have the concept of conquering nature. Nature here in all its infinite forms and countless modes is nothing but a manifestation of god himself. That is why all beings in the universe are interrelated. In our external experience. We see the world in its plurality but in our mind, in our internal experience, we can see the world as one. The need is to intuite on it, to contemplate on it. Inspite of the plurality of gods and the Rigvedic seers are able to establish the principle of one ultimate reality. ;एकं सत् विप्रा बहुधा वदन्ति RV 1.164.46)

यो देवोषु अन्नौ यो अप्सु या विष्वं भुवमाविवेष।

य ओपधीसु यो वनस्याषियु तस्मै देवाय नमोनमः।।

उपनिषद्

It means "That is the god who is the fire who is the water, who pervades the whole universe who is in medians, who is the vegetation, we solute that god."

Whatever exists in this world emanates from God. As Purusha Sukta is mentioned various times here.

स भूमिं विष्वतो वृत्वात्यतिष्ठदषांगुलम्

त्रिपादूहर्य उदैत्पुरूषः पादोमेहाभवत्पुनः

RV X 90 [24]

When you perceive and understand this truth you automatically form a relationship with everything in this world. And this relationship is the thing that does wonder in preserving the environment and protecting the nature. Recognizing this relationship our questions never allowed their material development to move in wrong direction. They never allowed their material development and progress. They were always conscious that whatever means they adopt to achieve happiness and progress. They were always conscious that whatever means they adopt to achieve happiness and property, nature should always be given precedence over their individual and immediate ends. Thus developed the Vedic culture which was not egoistic but which worked for the benefit for all. That is why they pray not for their own well-being but for the general welfare. The स्वस्तिवचन, the शं – prayers and famous शांतिपाठ of yv speak of the generous outlook of the Vedic seers.

Another remarkable trend to be noted in this connection is that the Vedic seers have lent humane touch to this relationship of man and nature. This has made relationship[25] between two, more strong and everlasting. In their most exalted moments of their realization, they call द्यौ[26] (sky) as their father who sustains them, and earth (पृथिवी)[27] as their mother who nourishes. Them, Aditi the indivisible nature gets the epithets father, mother, and progeny.[28] The sky and the earth have been called as sisters.[29]

संगच्छेमाने युवती समेन्ते स्वसारा जामी पित्रोरूपस्ये।

अभिजिधेन्ती भुवेनस्य नाभिं द्यावा रक्षेतं पृथीवीनो अभ्वात्।।5।।

V I 185.5

Of all the relations the most exalted and selfless relation is that of mother and progeny. Naturally the Vedic seers express it then and often with reference to see many deities. The herbs are thus being presented as loving mothers. An affectionate mother cannot see her issue die. That is why the Rishi invoking the herbal plant submits.

शतं वो अम्ब धामानि सहस्त्रयुत को रूहः।

अधा शतक्रत्वो यूथमिमं में अगदं कृतः।

Ye mother, have a hundred homes, you and a thousand are your growths.

Do ye who have a thousand powers free

This patient from disease.

In the same spirit, the seers go on describing the goddess of forests as the carrying mother.

समुद्रज्याष्ठाः सतिलस्य मद्ययात् पुनाना यन्त्यनिविषमानाः।

इन्द्रो या वज्री वृषभों रसद् आपो देवीरिह मामवन्तु।[29]

Forth form the middle of the flood the waters their chief the sea – flow cleansing never sleeping.

Indra, the Bull, the Thunderer, dug their channels: here let those waters, Goddesses, protect me.

The chief, the eldest one of water is the sea, who flows continuously, fluently without rest or sleep. Although, Indra, the Bull, the Thunder dug deep channels, the flow of water never stop and Apah – The goddess always protects us.

From the above mantra it is obvious that waters the Goddess protect mankind and make body and spirit. But the present age is destroying it. The people of present time don't have the knowledge of divinity of the apah, the water and due to ignorance they don't save water but destroying it and in true sense people destroying themselves.

या आपो दिव्या उत वा स्रवन्ति खनित्रिमा उत वायाः स्वयंजनाः

समुद्रार्था याः शुचयः पावकास्ता आपो देवीरिह सामवन्तु[30]

Those amid whom goes Varuna the Sovran, he who discriminates, Goddess self protect me.

Earth, the Prithvi, is the mighty god and sage Atri stated-

बलित्या पर्वतानां खिद्र विभार्वि पृथिवि।

प्र या भूमि प्रवत्वति महा त्रिनोषि महिति।।[31]

Thou, of truth, O Prithvi, bearest the tool that rends the hills:

Thou rich in torrents, who with might quickens earth, O Mighty one.

स्तोमासस्त्वा विचारिणि प्रति सहो भन्त्यवतुभिः।

प्र या वाजं न हेषन्त पेरूमस्यस्यजुनिं[32]।।

To thee, O wonderer at will, ring out the lauds with beams of day.

Who drivert, like a neighing steed, the swelling cloud, O bright of hue.

In the above mantra "UpmavachakIuptomalankar is over there. And it denotes that The earth wonders at her own will and, it divert like a steed; neighing steed like person appreciate laureates, just laureate like it knowledgeable women at her own will, appreciates another knowledgeable woman."

बलित्या पर्वतानां खिद्रं बिभार्षि पृथिवि।[33]

The mankind must possess religious values in their heart just like earth possess salable mountains in her heart. The mankind must perform his duties towards nature to protect it. The environment can be saved in this condition only.

Vayu: God of wind, which purifies the atmosphere and provide essential substances to each and every living beings of the earth as a great nutrition and possess oxygen (Pran Vayu) which connects human beings to the power of the universe, power of the ultimate and supreme being the God. Vamadeva said in the Rigveda about Vays, the wind God-

विहि होत्रा अवीता विनो न रायो अर्थः।

वायवा चन्द्रेण रथेन याहि सुतस्य पीतये।।

Taste offerings never tasted yet, as bards enjoy the foeman's health.

O' Vayu on refulgent (shining bright) chariot come to the different spheres of the earth and drink juice.

Again Vamdeva the seer described that-

वहन्तु त्वा मनोयुजो युक्तासो नवतिर्नव।

वायवा चन्द्रेण रथेन याहि सुतस्य पीतये।।[34]

May nine and ninety harnessed steeds who yoke then at they will bring thee,

O' Vayu, on refulgent chariot come to the drinking of the juice.

वायो शतं हरीणां युवस्व पाठेयाणाम्।

उतवा ते सहस्रिणो रथ आ यातु पाजसा।।

Harness, O' Vayu, to the chariot a hundred well-fed tawny steeds, yea, or a thousand steeds, and yet thy chariot come to us with might.

Air originated about 2.7 billion years ago, prior to this, the level of oxygen was too low to breath as it is present in the mars. App 2.7 billion years ago there was a great process of oxidation happened.

The atmosphere of early earth was primarily Co_2 carbon dio-oxide. With the advent of oxyphotosynthesis in microorganisms, this carbon dioxide was progressively consumed. Creating the waste produce of element oxygen. The oxygen catastrophy is clearly demarcated in the geological record by the introduction of large amounts of oxygenated iron (rust). These relies are called banded iron formation. The event is called 'catastrophy' because oxygen is toxic to anaerobic organisms, which the event wiped out in large number.

There was a time log of about 300 million years before the evolution of the first oxygen-producing organism and the fault fledged oxygen.[35] In the subsequent billions of years, oxyphotosynthezing organisms flourished, producing more and more elemental oxygen. The history of air, from practically zero oxygen to 20% oxygen, stretches over more than two billion years. During the carboniferous period, approximately 250 years ago, when plants, oxygen levels were even higher dragonfly, Meganeura with a two-foot wingspan. Today air would be not breathable to meganeura, due to its relative lack of oxygen.

The principal deity of Antariksha is vayu. Jaiminiya Brahmana quotes; Vayu brightens in Antariksha field is another form of energy and, therefore, yajervada says; Vayu has penetrating brightness. The meaning of Vayu is made clear in Shatpatha Brahmana in the following mantra "Sun and rest of universe is woven in string. What is that string, that is Vayu! The apparent meaning of Vayu air. The Vedic seers knew the importance of air for life. They understood all about air in the atmosphere and also about the air inside the body."

Prana, Vrana, Apana, Udana and Samano. Air resides in the body as life concept and significance of air is highlighted in Vedic verses Rigveda mentions – O' Air! You are our Father, the protector.[36] Air has medicinal Values.[36]"Let wind blow in the form of medicine and bring me welfare and happiness."[37] Medicated air is the international physician that annihilates pollution and imparts health and hilarity life and liveliness to people of the world. Hilly areas are full of medicated air consisted of herbal elements. Another verse describes characteristics of air – 'The air is the soul of all deities.' It exists in all as life breath. It can move everywhere. We cannot see it. One can hear its sound only. The Vedic sages prayed Vayu God for blowing continuously to keep the atmosphere and people healthy and happy.

Akasha: The first sound "Aum," is originated from ether, the Akasha. The waves of sound moves move everywhere at various frequencies and from various sounds. The mankind resides on the earth can see akasha which exists only in the vicinity of earth, but taitiriya upnishad throws light on two types of ether i.e. one inside the body and other outside the body.[38]

स य ऐसो अन्तर्हृदय अकाषः सुवरित्यसौ

The ether inside the body is regarded as the seat of mind an interesting advice to the mankind is found in the Yajurveda. Do not destroy anything of antariksha.[39]

द्यां मा लेखनन्तरिक्षें या हींसी

The sun shines in Dyuloka and we get light from sky. The sunrays strengthen our inner power and are essential for our life. Thus importance and care for ether is openly mentioned in the Vedic verses.

The Manas: Many prayers are found in Vedas requesting the God to keep the mind free from bad thoughts, and controlling of senses from wandering over here and there learn to make the mind stable. In this regard Shiv Sankalpa Sukta of Yajurveda is worth mentioning-[40]

Yajjagra to duramudaiati
Daivam tadu suptasya tathal vaiti
Duramgamarn jyotsam jyotirekam,
Tanme manah 'sivasamkalpamastu......

The mind which in the waking state through the means of the senses roams through this world, and which in the dream state roams through many worlds, and in the state of deep sleep return to its original state, that light of knowledge, my mind, may you have good intention. Considering the havoc that the polluted minds may create, our ancient sages prayed for a noble mind free from bad ideas. The logician recognizes Manas as one of the nine basic substances in the universe.[41] The mind is most powerful and unsteady. Although the study of mind does not appear directly under the contents of modern environmental science but in reference to cultural environmental consciousness of Vedic seers, the environmental Vedas must be studies.[42]

It is also said in Rigveda X.58 about Manas the spirit (Bemdhy)

यत् ते भूमि चतुर्थृष्ह्रिं मनो जगाय दूरकम्।

तत् त आ वर्तयामसीह क्षयाय जीवसे।।

The above hymn is an address to recall the fleeting spirit of a man at the point of death.

The spirit of man went away from different corners (here four corners) of the earth. We cause to come to the again that thou mayest live and sojousm here.

This hymn can be used to the Manas, (the spirit) of man which wonder everywhere, so we pray to God to let the spirit cause to come back at their seat (mind) and sojourn in the right place.

Animals and Birds: Animals and birds are part of nature and environment. It is natural, therefore, that Vedic seers have mentioned about their characteristics and activities and have desired their welfare. Rigveda groups – sky animals like birds, forests animals and animals in human habitation.[43]

All the three types of living creatures found in the universe have distance environment and every living creature has an environment of its own. But when we leave from man's perspective all of them constitute his environment. There is a general feeling in the Vedic text that animals should be safe, protected, and healthy. Domestic animals, as well as wild animals along with human beings should live in peace under the control of certain deities like Rudra, Pushan etc. Vedic people have shown anxious solicitude for welfare of all the creatures of the earth.

Plants and Herbs "Oshadhis": The knowledge about the origin and significance of plants can be traced out from Vedic literature in detail. In Rigveda Aranyani Sukta is addressed to the deity of forest.[44] Aranyani queen of forest, received high praise from the sage, not only for her gifts to men but also for her charm. Forest should be green with trees and plants. Osadhi sukta of Rigveda addresses to plants and vegetables as mother. O' Mother! Hundred are your birth places and thousands are your shoots.[45]

शतं वो अम्ब धामानि सहस्रयुत वां रूहः

The plants came to their existence on their earth before of the creation of animals.[46]

या ओषधीः पूर्वा जाता देवेभ्यात्रियुगं पुरा

Chandogya Upnishad elaborates "Water have generated plants which in turn generated food."

त अन्नम सृजन्त तस्यायत्र क्वचन वर्षति भूमिष्ठमन्नं भवति

The Rigveda instruct that forest should not be destroyed.

वनानि नः प्रजहितानि।

The Aharaveda talks about the relation of plants with earth. The earth is keeper of creation, container of forests, trees and herbs.[47]

मन्द्रागेत्वरी भुवनस्य गोपा वनस्पतीनां मृभिरोष धी नाम्

There is an important quotation in Purana which says one tree is equal to 10 sons.[48]

दशपुत्र शमो द्रुमः

The Athraveda prays for continuous growth of herbs – 'O Earth' what on you, I dig out, let that quickly grow over.

यत् ते भूमे विरवनामि क्षिप्तं तदपि रोल्यु

Another prays says, 'O Earth let me not hit your vitals.

The 'Avi' element referred in the Atharvaveda, as the cause of greenness in trees.[45]

अविव नाम देवता.........

तस्य रूपेणेने वृक्षाः हरिताः हरितस्रजः

Is considered generally by Vedic scholars as 'Chlorophyll' the term 'Avi' is derived from the root Av and thus gives the direct meaning of protector. Hence, plants were studied as the Vedic seers prescribed a part of environment and their protection.

Importance of Yajna in purifying environment: The sacrifice 'yajna' is regarded as an important concept of Vedic philosophy and religion but when we study it in its broader sense, it seems to be a part of Vedic environmental science. Yjaurveda and Rigveda describe it as the 'neval' (nucleus) of the whole world.

अयं यज्ञो विष्वस्य भुवनस्य नाभिः

It states that Yajna is regarded as a source of nourishment and life for the world, just as neval is for the child.

Yajnas were the true source through which the Vedic seers become able to understand the true meaning of mantras to be manifested to the world.

Yajna. created all sort of knowledge[49]

तस्माद् यज्ञात् सर्वहुत ऋचः सामानि जज्ञिरे[50]

Sacrifice (Ritual) Yajna is considered as noblest action.

यज्ञो वे श्रेष्ठतम् कर्म [51]

In simple words Yajna signify the theory of give and take. The sacrifice simply has three aspects: Dravya (material), Devata (deity) and Dana (giving) when some material is offered to a deity with adoration, then it becomes Yjana. Pleasing deity returns desired material in some different forms of devotees. This Yajna is going on in the universe since beginning of the creation and almost everywhere for production and, also for keeping maintenance in the world. Even the creation of universe is explained as Yajna in the Purusha Sukta. Thus, the concept of Yajna seems to be a major principle of ancient environment as science.

In environment all elements are inter-related and affect each other. Sun is drawing water from ocean through rays. Earth gets rain from sky and grows plants. Plants produce food for living beings. The earth pours oceans water drops in the fire of sun rays (water drops are oblation), the clouds pour water on the earth by raining. The sunrays and water produce food mixing with chlorophyll and produce food. Mankind gives oblation of food to the stomach to grow. This is essential for maintenance of environmental constituents. The Yajna cleans atmosphere through its medicinal smoke, and pervades longevity, breath, vision etc. According to Vedi thought Yajna is benefited to both individual and community. Yajna helps in minimizing air pollution, in increasing crop yields, in protecting plants from disease, as well as in providing disease free, pure and energized environment for all, offering peace and happiness of mind. Moreover Yajna serves as a bridge between desired fulfillment.[52]

It is the matter of proud for humanity to feel that our ancestors (ancient seers) obtained such a true and deep knowledge about the truth of the universe, interrelation among all the planetary and earthly bodies, unbroken bond between the human mind and cosmic mind. Unbelievable relation of environmental elements. Law of rit through which the whole universe working in a proper discipline Ancient seers through their wisdom got mysterious knowledge about the environment and cosmic and physical order of the world. They were quite aware of purpose of universal working and purpose of human being to know about the orders of the universe to keep ourselves, healthy, prosperous, successive moral and aware of achieving goal of the life of mankind. They also know about the importance of co-ordination between all natural powers for universal peace and harmony. When they pray for peace at al levels in the 'Shanti Mantra' they side by side, express their belief about the importance of co-ordination and interrelationship among all natural powers and regions-

ऊँ असतो मा सद्गमय।

तमसो मा ज्योतिर्गमय।

मृत्योर्मा अमृतं गमय।

ऊँ शांतिः शांतिः शांतिः।।

Om (O Lord) keep me not in the unreality of bondage of the phenomenal world, but lead me towards the reality (of Eternal self). Let me know the truth of the universe without which I can't live my life successfully.

O Lord keep me not in fear (of death) or ignorance, but lead me towards light (of spiritual knowledge).

Lead me towards immortality (gained by the knowledge of the immortal self beyond death).

Om peace, peace, peace (at the three levels – Adhidaivikas Adhibhautika and athyatmika).

The above mantra clarifies that there is unbroken relation between human-life and of environment. Without the knowledge of environment, how does mankind obtain prosperity, good health and peace.

ऊँ भद्रं कर्णेभिः श्रृणुयाम देवाः।

भद्रं पश्येमाक्षमिर्यजत्राः।

स्थिरेर॰गैस्तुष्टुवाँसस्तनूभिः

व्यषेम देवहितं यदायूः

- Om, O' Devas, may we hear with our Ears what is Auspicious,
- May we see with our Eyes what is Auspicious and adorable
- May we be prayful with steadiness in our bodies and minds.
- May we offer our lifespan allotted by the Devas for the service of God.

To obtain the true knowledge our mind should be free of all types of negative thoughts and thoughts enter through words which enters through ear, so it is prayed that keep our mind pious and auspicious.

Keep our eyes auspicious so that we can see whatever is right. All the senses are means to gain knowledge, the food of mind and spirit so we should maintain to gain positive thoughts only.

स्वस्ति नः इन्द्रो वृद्धश्रवाः।

स्वस्ति नः पूषा विष्ववेदाः।

स्वस्ति नस्ताक्ष्र्यो अरिष्टनेमिः।

स्वस्तिनो वृहस्पतिर्दधातु।

ऊँ शांतिः शांतिः शांतिः

- May Indra of great wisdom and glory grant us well being.
- May Pushan (The Sun God, the nourishes) of great knowledge grant us well-beings (by nourishing us and granting knowledge).
- May Nastaarkssyo (Tarksya – A mythical bird) of great protection power (a thunderbolt to misfortune) grant us well-being.
- May Brihaspati grant us well-being.

Om peace, peace, peace.

The mantras take about the concord with the universe –

"Peace of sky, peace of trees, peace of all gods, peace of Brahma, peace of universe, peace, peace may that peace come to me."

The concept of the form of the earth is the Rig-Veda is most fascinating. It is mostly addressed along with the heaven into a dual conception (Rodasi, Dyavaprithvi) one of the most beautiful mantra of Rigveda says 'Heaven is my father, brother atmosphere is my navel and great earth is my mother.[53]

द्योर्मे पिता जनिता नाभिरत्र बन्धुर्मे माता पृथिवी महीयम्[54]

May Peace Bring Peace!

Santi

Man may possess everything: health, wealth, wife and chilren, knowledge and skill, power and glory; but still he can be the most miserable creature if he is lacking that gift of the Gods which does not depend on any other gift, and on which all other gifts depend if they are to be real blessings for Man: peace. Human fullness is incomplete without peace, whereas even the one who lacks everything else can still have peace withing himself and peace with all beings, which in fact constitutes happiness. The Vedas were deeply aware of this and thus of the constant necessity to invoke peace with all the power of the mantra.

The *santi* mantra[55] or invocation of peace is an essential utterance at any beginning, and especially at the end of a sacred action or of the recitation of a sarced text. How can a holy word be uttered or heard unless there is peace in heaven, on earth, and in the human heart? The discord and dissonances in the universe and among Men have first to be pacified before any real, that is, sacred, pocosmic interaction. There can be no peace in the human heart if there is no peace on earth, but, conversely there can be no earthly peace if there is discord in Man's inner being. The one affects the other and, at the same time, both interact with the world of the Gods in the same kind of double relationship.

Man is the powerful mediator, becauses he alone is capable of uttering this prayer for peace. He even dares (in our second short text) to wich peace to Brahman! God is not only in and throught prayer-he *is* Prayer.

Peace-and the *sānti* mantra-must be at the beginnign and end of everything. Nothing is achieved by external discord or internal unrest, and nothing is accompleshed in the world or in human life unless it is grounded in peace. For this Man needs the collaboration of all the Gods: to establish peace in heaven, in the atmosphere and on earth. This is the meaning of the threefold wish: *sāntih sāntih sāntih!*

Sānti

AV XIX, 9

i). 1. Peaceful be heaven, peaceful the earth,
peaceful the broad space between.
Peaceful the plants and herbs!
2. Peaceful to us be the signs of the future,
peaceful what is done and undone,
peaceful to us be what is and what will be.
May all to us be gracious!
3. This supreme Goddess, Word, inspired by Brahman,
by which the awe-inspiring is created,
through her to us be peace!

4. This supreme Spirit, inspired by Brahman,
by which the awe-inspiring is created,
through her to us be peace!
5. These five sense organs, with the mind as the sixth,
within my heart, inspired by Brahman,
by which the awe-inspiring is created,
through them to us be peace!
6. Gracious be Mitra, gracious Varuna,
gracious Visnu and Prajāpati,
gracious to us be Indra and Brahspati,
gracious to us Aryaman.
7. Gracious be Mitra, gracious Varuna,
gracious be Vivasvant and Death,
gracious the wandering planets.
8. Gracious to us be the trembling earth,
when struck by the fiery meteor.
Gracious be the cows yielding red milk,
gracious be the earth receding.
9. Gracious be the constellations struck by the meteor,
gracious incantations and all magic!
Gracious to us be buried charms,
the meteors and plagues that afflict us.
10. Gracious to us be the stars and the moon,
gracious the sun and Rahu,
gracious be Death with his banner of smoke,
gracious the powerful Rudras.
11. Gracious be the Rudras, gracious the Vasus,
gracious the Adityas and Agnis,
gracious to us be the god like sager,
gracious all the Gods and Brhaspati.
12. Brahman, Prajāpati, Dhāti, the worlds,
teh Vedas, the Seven Sages, and the fires,
prepare for m a blessed path!
May Inda be my refuge,

may Brahman be my refuge,
may all the Gods be my refuge!
May the Gods united be my refuge!

13. May whatever appeasements there are in the world,
known by the Seven Sagar,
may they all be gracious to me!
May peace be with me!
May fearlessness be with me!

14. Peace be to earth and to airy spaces!
Peace be to heaven, peace to the waters,
peace to the plants and peace to the trees!
May all the gods grant to me peace!
By this invocation of peace may peace be diffused!
By this invocation of peace may peace bring peace!
With this peace the dreadful I now appease,
with this peace the cruel I now appease.
with this peace all evil I now appease,
so that peace may prevail, happiness prevail!
May everything for us be peaceful! YV XXXVI, 17

Shabda Brahma: Shabda Brahma (शब्द ब्रह्म) means transcendental sound (Shatpatha Brahmana 111.12.48) or sound vibration (Shatpatha Brahma VI.15.15) or the transcendental sound of the Vedas (Shatpatha Brahman IX.21.36) or of Vedic Scriptures (Shatpatha Brahma X.20.43).

Shabda stands for word manifest by sound (verbal) and such a word has innate power to convey a particular sense or meaning (Artha). According to the Nyaya and Vaisheshika schools, shabda means verbal testimony; to the Sanskrit grammarians, Yaska, Panini and Katyayana it meant a unit of language or speech or Vac. In the philosophical terms this word appears for the first time in Maitri Upnishad (sloka VI22) that speaks of two kinds of Brahma – Shabda Brahma (Brahman with sound) and Ashabda Brahma (Soundless Brahma). Bhartrhari speaks of creative power of shabda, the manifold universe is a creation of Shabda Brahman[56] (Brihadaranyaka unnishad IX.1.2). Speech is equated with Brahma (Shatpatra Brahma

2.1.4.10). The Rig Veda states that Brahma states as far as Vac (R.V.X.114.B) and has hymns in praise of speech as the creator (R.V.X.71.7) and as the final abode of Brahma (R.V.I. 164.37).

Time is creative power of Shabda Brahma purva minansa deals with Shabda Brahma (Cosmic sound or word) which is endowed with names and forms and is projected in Vedic revelations (the mantras hymens, prayers etc.)

Savara defines testimony (Shabda) as the knowledge of an object which is not present to a sense-organs, produced by the knowledge of words[57] Kamarila defines it as the knowledge of objects, which are supersensible, derived from sentences by comprehending the meanings of the constituent words. Shabda is verbal authority. Kumarila divides testimony into human and superhuman. The former is the testimony of trustworthy persons, while latter is the testimony of the Vedas. The former is valid, if it is altered by persons of trustworthy character, while the later is valid in itself. Both are valid, since they are free from the defects of being composed by untrustworthy person, and words are valid in themselves.

Mimansa is called purva mimansa, while the Vedanta is called the uttara mimansa. The former is earlier than the later in the sense that it deals with rituals (karma), while the latter is concerned with knowledge (jnana). Vedanta deals with Parama Brahma (the ultimate reality) which is transcendent. One has to become well established in Shabda Brahma before realizing Param Brahma. Vedas are not the product of conventional language but the emanation of reality in form of Shabda (sound word) which is the sole cause of creation and is eternal. Purva Mimansa, an esoteric discipline from the point of view of spiritual growth aims at attaining the heavenly happiness by realizing Shabda Brahman (cosmic sound) by conducting Yajans that help control the senses and the mind; when the mind and the senses are subdued the inner subtle sound is realized as Shabda Brahma.

The fundamental theory of Indian classical music, art and poetry is grounded in the theory of Nada Brahma or Shabda Brahma, and is linked with Vedic religion.[57]The Apara Brahma mentioned by mandukya

Upanishad is Nada Brahma or Shabda Brahma. Shiva Samhita statement whenever and whatever is the causal stress or Divine action, there is vibration (spandan or Kalmpan) and whenever there is vibration or movement there sound is inevitable. 'M' of Aum, the primordial Vac represents Shabda, which is the root and essence of everything; it is Pranava and Pranav is Vedas, Vedas are Shabda Brahma. Consciousness is all beings is Shabda Brahma.

When the necessity of directing the mantra internally and to objects externally is transcended then one gains mantra chaitany, which then awakens Atma Chaitanya, the Divine consciousness, and unites with it.

In the Bhagwat Gita (Sloka VI.44) the term Shabda Brahma has been used to mean Vedic injunctions. Adi Shankra explains that the Yogic impressions do not perish even when held up for a long period, even he who seeks to comprehend the essence of Yoga and beings to tread the path of Yoga goes beyond the spheres of the fruits of Vedic works, he sets them aside[58] Gaudpada clarifies that the letter 'o' of Aum leads to Vishva, the letter 'u' leads to Taijasa and the letter 'm' is leads to prajna. With regards to one freed from letters, there remains no attainment. Aum is Shabda Brahma, Aum is the Root sound of which creating is a series of permutations.[59]

According to the Tantric concept, sound is the first manifestation of Param Shiva; in its primary stage it is a psychic wave. Its very existence entails the presence of spandan or movements of waves (vibration) without which there cannot be sound; spandan is the quality of saguna Brahma and the world is the thought-projection of Saguna Shiva.

The Brahma (the universal soul) spreaded in the form of Vac (Shabda) word, the first thing is Shabda Vac, means power of Brahma, another thing is Arth Vac means power of Vishnu (that is Lakshmi)-

शब्द वाक परा–पश्यन्ति – मध्यमा और बैखरी रूप में आगे बढ़ती है।[60]

Prikriti (Nature) follows eternal principle – Every individual, consciousness and unconscious (जड़–चेतन). Either static or dynamic, all follow a single principle and law. This is "Law of Rit," physical and moral order.

According to the science in this world only two substances are existed – matter (पदार्थ), energy (उर्जा) these substances never destroy, instead changes in another form (परिवर्तित). Vedas are the origin of Indian wisdom and very ancient. Vedas depicts the same thoughts. From the linguistic point of view, these can be described as Ras (रस), power (बल), Brahma and Maya (माया) Water converted into ice, this is not called change (परिवर्तन) but this is inversible change (विवर्त) because in turn, ice again can be converted into water, curd can't convert into milk again so this is a change only. In nature, time is very indispensable element, and basis of law of Rit, but we cant see the time; in the point of view of (काल भेद) time-discrimination. It is decided in the Nature (प्रकृति) that, one who born, must die and one who dies, born again (पुनर्जन्म). The souls perform their tasks between birth and death and virtue is awarded and vice is punished. Every soul is affected by the fruits of action. The Reincarnation of the soul takes place on the basis of the fruits of action. In the Prikriti (environment) there are both types of substances existed; gross and subtle. Gross is visible and subtle exists in the root of gross. Subtle substance also possess, cause element because without cause there is no effect. The world moves on the basis of cause. The cause based on the conception of Rita. Rita further harmonizes the goods with one another, and paves the way for monotheism. Rita governs the uniformities of nature. Rita reigns everywhere in the sky, in the sun, in the mountain, is the sacrifice and in truth.61

RV ii.1.3–5-

The principles and law of Rit on which the whole universe works in a determined order are called Vedas. The elements and substances present in the universe are called. Tatva Veda, and these elements are depicted by words name; these words are called Shabda-Veda, or Shabda of Brahma because these Shabda described the knowledge of the universe and that of law of Rit.

Shabda Brahma depicts that Lakshmi and Saraswati are two sisters. Both exist together occasionally. Both are identified by Vac. Lakshmi 'Artha Vac' and Saraswati 'Shabda Vac.' Lakshmi and Saraswati possess two forms;

first one has 'Lakshmi' and 'Shri.' Lakshmi means 'sign (चिन्ह);[62] silver, gold, note, rupees, grain, vehicle etc. are form of Lakshm. Shri means 'Shobha,' beauty. Lakshami and Shri both rarely reside together. Some person posses too much Lakshmi but no beauty is there and some person possess too much beauty but no Lakshmi is there. God provides both the things to those who are able to get showering of special blessings of Him.

Saraswati also has two forms; Shabda and Naad. The field of Naad is Manas. It is Madhyama Vac, the Shabda originated by this gross form of Vac. The movements of Shabda, word is not continuous but the movements of Naad is always keep continuity. Where there is person, mind, word and goal becomes one, both the goddesses, Lakshmi and Saraswati resides together. Our scriptures exemplified that 'Shabda' originated the universe. Chanting of mantras, Yajnas, appears all the cosmic bodies. Moreover human beings are come into existence by chanting mantras. Scientifically words have waves and vibrations. We can listen voice on Radio on the basis of these waves. We are using mobile phones and T.V. on the basis of the same science of waves of words. Each wave has a definite wavelength. Each wave has a definite colour, and an effect. We can produce and gain our desire by chanting mantras.

Waves of same colour, when produce again and again become dense which crosses or Aura and affects our body. When the consciousness is fully involved with words and goal and all three become one, this oneness of contemplation is called meditation. In this condition of mind, the mind becomes silent and the consciousness possesses 'vid' of God. This is Veda, and this is Rik – The mind of the person is fully involved in knowledge and performs works with this knowledge, here in this state of mind both Lakshmi and Saraswati are present.

Words possess life and movement. The task of life force is to provide movement, activeness, and alertness. We do jap (recitation of mantra) for the purpose to produce life-force. We can go on this path by complete determination of will, but most important thing of this purpose is to set a goal without willingness of fruit. The God become clear by developing concentration. The word enter in sub consciousness of mind becomes subtle and converted in complete silence.

The control of speech is called silent. This silent is of many kinds. In the house, any person keeps silent due to bad behaviour but this type of silent is not meditation but an obstacle (साधक ना होकर बाधक होता है). The silent, which arises by contemplation, is called true silent, here divine feelings and power is prominent. Mahakavi Kalidas wrote 'Satyaymit Bhashinam' Raghuwanshi spoke few words to follow truth, "This is the truth that one who is truthful and dosen't need to speak much."

Silent state of mind is important during contemplation or it is described in this way that contemplation can only be done in silence. In silence, there is word exists, communication also present but pronunciation is absent. Practice of silence is helpful in control of sense organs. Speaking his capacity of meditation and contemplation decreases reduces the power of mind. Mind becomes unable to concentrate on subject while speaking much. Speech closed the path of contemplation, and goal disappeared from the horizon of mind.

In silence, ego last its existence. There is no need to say about oneself by which ego can be nourished. The experiences of sense organs become subject of contemplation. Mind becomes silent and concentrated this Dharma, knowledge, penance, obstination brings prosperity in the life of human-being.

Shabda Brahma is word which is produced after a long period of silence, while Shabda (word) provides scientific level to the life of human being. Language decides the path of life. It prepares the filed and atmosphere of feelings-expression of mind becomes possible by means of communication that is language. The union of letters prepares words. Letters are came in forms with the union of vowels and consonants. No act is performed without the union of soul-mind and body. Meaning is connected with words. Words are alive, they have life, breath and soul. Knowledge is born by words, knowledge is converted into action. The balance between knowledge and action is peace of life. Knowledge is gross state of Brahma and action is gross state of intention. Sound and pronunciation is connected with every word. Vibration originated by producing words. It gets life by breath, soul, letters are formed by the formation of consonants and vowels. It takes a definite forms. 'अकारो वसुदेव:'[63]

Whenever a consonant come towards the vocal cards from Nabhi Chakra, then 'v' sound produces and 'विसर्ग' goes back to 'नाभि.' Because of this scientific reason of sound waves, mantras are produced. Mantra Shastras are come into existent. The subtle vibrations of our body are identified and analyzed.

The whole reality of our life is based on vibration (स्पंदन). Every word has a special and particular vibration. Gross and subtle also. Gross is converted into subtle. The mind of human being is subtle, the wisdom is also subtle. Soul is subttest. All the above things have their won space, sky (आकाष). The soul of subtle body takes place because of subtle movements. Where there is only space, the breath, soul and Shabda cannot be differentiated. An another element also affects all these procedures and this is 'Prikriti,' which is; Satva, Rajas and Tamas.

With the words, Shabda, Pran Vayu, breath unites on the basis of Prikriti. When an individual do Jap (reciting Mantras), vibrations produces. He recites in three ways. Vachik (by speaking), Upanshu (by wispring) or Manas (mentally). He goes from gross to subtle. The form and body of words, in this condition space between them reduced. The waves go towards space (आकाष) Space is Brahma. There is vibration in the space. These vibration of sky reach to the mind of the person. Mind brings these vibrations to the intelligence of person. Intelligence takes decision, and returns to the mind. These vibrations pervades throughout the space. The entire environment becomes 'Brahma.' The knowledge of 'Brahma' come into existent. Wisdom awakens and the person becomes enlightened. Shabda assimilated into Brahma means word (Shabda) becomes Brahma. Pleasure spreaded all-over, in the form of light. The colour of which light depends on nature (Prikriti) of the person. With the help of Vedic mantras, by performing Yajna we can receive our desired things and goals this truth is written in Vedas and Puranas. In the present age, this Yajna ritual is also performed for achieving desired goals.

* * * * *

References

1. Manu II 83.
2. the vedic experience by Pannikar pg 38–39.
3. Jadunath sinha "The indian philosophy" pg 422
4. Later classification after a list of five Mahabhutani or Primordial elements stsrting from etheror atmosphere (akasha)
5. Rv i.1
6. Rvi 59,2; 1.
7. Purusha sukta Rigveda karpur bhashya.
8. ibid
9. ibid
10. vedo me paryavaran sanrakshan.
11. RV124.5
12. Rv x 45.3
13. chem vikki.vcdavis.edu –division of atmosphere.
14. En.m.wikkipidia.org
15. Wash Adward Hale.(1999) Asura in early vedic religion
16. nichobar gier(2000) spiritual titanism
17. RTH Griffith the oldest divine book.
18. Paul Deussen sixty upnishads of veda.
19. six systems of Indian philosophy pg 68
20. Aurther keith 461 pg
21. Unfortunately man has forgotten this relationship
22. dhaurstunh pita Rv I 90.7
23. mata bhumi putro aham prithivya athrvaveda 12.1.12
24. Rv I 29.10
25. Rv I 185.5 Rv viii.49
26. Rv v 84.1

27. RV v 84.2
28. Rigveda the oldest divine book RTH Griffith pg 26
29. Rigvedbhashyam 'Maharshi Dayanand Sraswati'
30. Rv iv 48
31. Rv iv 48
32. wisw greek.com
33. Vayurva va prano bhutva sharirmavishat 'taitiriya upnishad 2.4
34. utavath pitasi nah rig veda 10.186.2
35. aa vahi bheshjam rv 1.37.2
36. vat aa vatu bheshtam shambhu mayambhu no hude rv 10.186.1
37. Taitiria upnishad
38. yajurveda 5.43

    The shiva sankalpa sukta is a divine song, has six versesIt is regarded as upnishad. some people call it shivsankalpaopnishadas.
39. Tarkasangrah.
40. Nandita sanghvi vedo me paryavaran sonali publication jaypur pg 313–356
41. Rigveda 10.90.8
42. Rigveda 10.90.8
43. Rigveda 10.97.2
44. IBID
45. chandogyaupnishad 6.2.4
46. Atharva veda 12.1.57
47. padma purana 1.44.455
48. Atharvaveda 12.1.35
49. Avirve anmh devta… Atharvaveda 12.1.57
50. Yajurveda 13.62
51. Yagnen vachah vadviyamam rigveda 10.71.3
52. Rigveda 10.90.9
53. RIGVEDA 10.71.3
54. origin of environment science from vedas
55. Rigveda 1.164.33

    shashtram shabdavijnanat asannikrs for the vijnonam

56. Rajshri yoga; The ultimate spiritual path Llewellyn world wide pg 32–33
57. Vinayak purohit Arts of transitional India Popular prakashan pg 856
58. Bhagvat gita
59. swami prabhupada bhagvat gita
60. Devi sukta –pt. Devidatta chaturvedi
61. RV ii 1.3–5
62. shabdavadah by Karpurchand kulish pg 23–28
63. shabda vedah Karpurchand kulish pg 30
Rigveda

Chapter - VII

Conclusion

The Vedic religious belief and ethical values are embedded in; chanting of hymns, adoration, prayer, Yajna, sacrifice, penance, contemplation on cosmic and supreme power, optimistic outlook in life following the law of Rta (Natural order). Sacrifices were made, in which milk, butter, honey, the soma juice and food were offered to the gods. The fire god, Agni is the mediator between men and gods which transmit the emotions, will in the form of prayer and adoration to the Lord Agni (cosmic fire) the Sun (Surya) the dawn (Ushas), the earth (Prithivi) the rain-cloud (Parjanya), the storms (Maruts), the winds (Vayu, Vata), the sky (Dyaus), the bright sky and day (Mitra), the dark sky and evening (Varuna), the morning Sun (Savita) and the like. The sacrifices were made for the purpose of purifying the environment, to maintain the ecological balance.

At the present age even a civilized person is not aware of fact that he is causing ecological imbalance for a merge selfish reason. It is the duty of every person to purify the environment and improve the ecological instance. Through Yajna the whole atmosphere and nature can be healed. Agnihotra is a healing process, it is not only a form of worship for praying the Almighty for just fulfilling our needs but it is very scientific process which must be known by each and every person and even each and every child.

During the Agnihotra (Yajna) various substances, herbs, vegetation, and even animals used as obligations are offered into the fire. Among the oblations offered as oblations in the Yajna are ghee (purified butter), milk, grains, cakes and soma. All the activities of the entire cosmos revolve around the axis of Yajna. The deep import of Yajna connotes spirituality and also an act of generosity.

According to the Rigveda Yajna is a Purohit (priest) appointed by Almighty God and despite the speech remaining mute it inspires world denizens to aspire for all round progress and peace via its activities Yajna purifies foul air, kills bacteria and rendering it very fragrant. Thus man's very life support viz. air (oxygen is rendered clean and pollution free. Today air pollution has become a very big world problem and hence if the concept of Yajna is given due importance air pollution can be demolished from its very roots. Yajna energy abounds with power to destroy bacteria and other germs that cause various diseases. It is healing method both as far as the mind and physical body concerned.

During the Yajna, butter, milk, sugar, and different kinds of vegetation and herbs burn with slow consumption, which create CO2, but in very little amount, which stimulates the mind to be relaxed and think better. The pure air entered through the breath, which destroys the bacteria, and germs present in the body and cause various diseases. If today's world situation is analyzed very deeply what stands out that more than physical diseases, it is vile mental taints like bad habits, addition to drugs etc. criminal tendencies, unruliness, anger, erroneous thinking, hatred and stressful life which gives more hardships to world humanity. Thus when Yajna Therapy will be presented in a very compact form to the entire world it will surely help to overcome mental stress and bodily diseases in a big way. Special Yajna can be conducted pertaining to rain bearing cloud formation more than purification of air it is more prudent to sanctify the world's atmosphere.

The atmosphere influences every nook of our life and personality. It means that one must imbibe idealistic inspirations embedded in the subtle aspect of fire. Fire is always manifesting heat and lift. Thus fire inspires to heat up our perseverance and hard work and its light inspires to become brilliant and well known in a wholesome way. The flame of fire always points in the upward direction. One may try to pint it down and yet it will elude you and continue its upward march. This inspired to ignore that pressure which tries to induce us to lend a demand life of eat drink and be merry whatever be the enticement and allurement we must pay no heed to it and instead march in the upward direction of glory and greatness. Any objects thrown into the fire merge into the fire our greatness should be such that whoever contacts us becomes great too. Thus a cascading effect of greatness can take place in the entire world whenever anything is given to fire. It will not hoard but instead after making it gaseous spreads it in all directions of the atmosphere. The remnants of fire are in the form of ash, which is applied on the forehead to uplift our life. This is Puchanagni Vidhya.

In Hinduism the dead body of human being is given to fire god to demolish the bacteria of the body and all the oils and good elements of the body is oblated to the universe which receives all the five-substances (पंच तत्व) and become one with the nature.

अथ यद्यश्र इत्याचक्षते ब्रह्मचर्यमये

तद्धह्मचर्येण द्येव यो ज्ञाता तं.

बिल्दतेय यविष्टमित्याचक्षते बह्मर्वमेव

तद्धह्मचर्येण द्येवेष्टद्वत्मामासनुविन्दसे

ChandyogaUnanishad 8.5.1

Prayers and sacrifices were intended for obtaining cattle, wealth, sons and grand sons, a life of hundred years, victory in battles, and happiness and bliss.

The process of becoming one out of diversity is called "science" 'विज्ञानंयज्ञं तनुते कर्मापिच' (Taitirya Arenyak 8.5.1)

Just contradictory to this out of diversity, becoming one is called knowledge. Lord Shri Krishna described (ज्ञान–विज्ञान) knowledge and science as ज्ञानं तेऽहं सविज्ञान मिदं वक्ष्याम्यशेषतः (Gita 7.2). It is obvious that-

यतोभ्युदयानिः श्रेयससिद्धिः स धर्मः

The scholiast Sayana opens his commentary on the Rigveda with the declaration that-

Vedavatara adyaya redrthah Prapcintah

Vijnatam Vedagambhiryans atha samksipya varnyate

(SRB I.II)

Vedas were revealed for the purpose of sacrificial rituals.

Sarve Veda Yajnirtham Pravytatah). According to the Indian tradition, the Vedas were revealed in the beginning of the human creation and that the sacrificial ritual accompanied with material offerings to the gods began in the beginning of Treta age or at Juncture of the Krita age and Treta age. Later on, they developed into an elaborate and complicated system of rites and ceremonies which degenerated in the Dvapara age.

Treat-youa-vidhis tu esa yajnanani nakrta yuge.

In the beginning, to be sure, nothing existed, neither the heaven nor the earth nor space in so nonbeing, having decided to be, become spirit between and said: "Let me be! He warned himself further and from this heating was born fire. He warned himself still further and from this heating was born light. In the beginning, things undoubtedly began. But what about the beginning itself 'before' the actual 'beginning'? We cannot say "before" the beginning is precisely the beginning, because it has no before, because it is itself beginning led. Thus, if we want to speak about the beginning in itself, we shall have to use a language of opposites and make ample use of paradoxes: in the beginning there was neither space nor the sky beyond neither death nor non-death, no distinction between day and night. In the absolute void the one breathed by its own propulsion without breath."

The one unwrapped in the void took birth. Nonbeing made himself 'atman' and cried. I will be! let me be! This was the self in the form of a person. But the primal being is not yet fully born, he is not yet fully 'out' for whom has looking around. So he forced to took upon himself and take cognizance of himself only then he is born.

Breath is soul 'Atma' in Vedas. The sovereign field of 'sun' (Surya) is called 'Devlok' or 'Premlok.' Another name of Sury (the Sun is Devraj Indra next of which is Pitraprem Sansthan and then Rishi Pransansthan. Veda has threefold interpretation on the basis of Devpran (Cosmi breath) Pitrapran and Rishipran that is (Adhyatmika) spiritual, (Adhidaivika) relating to gods) and (Aadhiyajnika) ritual. The subtle body is the body of breath (Pran, Atman). This is the only reason of the whole cosmic region. This is the science of Veda and called "Vid" (विद). In Sanskrit which is not a simple term but knowledge of the whole cosmos, the law and order of Rt' (Rita).

The whole universe is pervaded through Rik, Yaju and Sam. Rik is centre, Sam is idol (symbol) and Yaju is mobile part of the universe. This is 'Vid' from which the word Veda is derived. Rik, Yaju-Sam are called manas, breath and word. Manas is centre word is in image form and breathe is like Yaju pervaded thoroughly in motion form. Pt. Madhusudan Oza wrote in "Brahmavigyan that all these three Rik, Yaju and Sam" are called 'Ras,' 'Bal' (force) is "Abhva." The most ancient form is 'Ras,' force is cause and word is "Abhva." Three forms of 'Ras' are 'Mahokth,' 'Mahavrat' and Agni, these are called Rik, Yaju and Sam (ऋक, यजु, साम). The breath, soul, pran, which is part of supreme Brahma, is called 'Mahokth.' The part, which fills the space by entering into the body, is called 'Mahavrit.' The substances and elements, which make the body, is called Agni, the Yaju. Mahokth is the sea of Richas (Suktas) of the Rigveda; Mahavrit is the ocean of Sam and Agni is ocean of Yaju.

Veda are science of producing universe and the whole cosmos. Vedas are principle and order of process happens in the cosmos. The explicable and able to menifest form of these cosmic processes in words is called "Shabda Veda." Originally Vedas are "Mantra Sukatatmak"; can be expressed in the form of hymns (Suktas) only because these are prayer for adoration of God. It must have Alliteration and rhythm. The hymns consist of sounds composed by letter, which have the nature of Shiva. All the vowels are seeds and the consonants are womb, they are of the nature of Shiva and Shakti. All the hymns of Rigveda are written in different meters.

Thus the whole knowledge; the knowledge of the working process of the cosmos, law, and order, and principles on these processes are working. Following with adherence the law of Rit. The knowledge of Rishis (sages), the meters by which all the hymns are written is called vid which forms the name Vedas.

Vedas are called "shruti," as Vedas follow the tradition of listening hymns and handed down to the next generation. These are four Vedas – Rig Veda, Sama Veda, Yajur Veda; and Atharva Veda. Each of them has three divisions viz., the Samhitas, The Brahmanas, and the Aranyakas. The samhitas are collection of sacred texts mostly inverse. The brahmanas are commentaries in prose. The Aranyakas are forest treatises. The Upnishads are mostly parts of the Arnyakas. The Samhitas and the Brahmenas are called karmakand, the portion pertaining to rituals. The Armyakas are called "Upasonakanda," the portion relating to meditation. The Upanishads are called Jnanakanda, the portion dealing with supreme knowledge. The Rig Veda; Sama Veda, and Yajur Veda are said to be the triad (trayi), and considered to be the original Vedas. The Atharva Veda is later addition.[1]

Rig Veda is the oldest one and there are signs of considerable elaboration of ritual and of the employment of a number of priests at the sacrifice, and the later samhitas and the Brahmana revealed to us a time when the functions of the priesthood have been definitely divided up and apportioned among sets of priests. The manual acts of the sacrifice are ascribed to Adhvarya priest and his assistants and accompanied by muttered formulae, in prose or verse, styled yajus.[2]

At the greatest sacrifices, such as the Soma sacrifice, sages chants samana, and recited castras (Shastras) while the Brahmana priest supervises the whole performance, usually in silence. On this division of functions is based the division of the later Samhitas: the Samans are preserved in the song book of the Sam Veda, the Yajuses in the Yajur Veda.

Thus the Rigveda belongs to the hotr priests and was recited by them at the sacrifices. The Sama Veda contains chants and melodies (saman), chanted by the priests of that name. the Yajurveda consist of sacrificial formulas of the Adhverya priests, and many of these also are taken from the Rig Veda. It has come down to us in several recensions, the Krishna or Black Yajurveda whose samhitas are the Taittriya, the Maitrayagni, and the Kathaka, and the 'white' or 'shukla' Yajurveda whose Samhita is the Vajasaneyi. The Upanishads are the fourth or final stage of the process, and are known therefore as the Vedanta or end of the Veda. They represent the mystical and philosophical culmination of the Vedas. They contain the teachings of the great masters which point toward the path of moksha or liberation.

With the passing of time a further literature grew up whose main concern was the exegetic study of the Vedas. It is grouped under the six headings as Vedangas or "limbs of the Vedas." The Vedangas include the study of phonetics, and correct pronunciation of the Vedas, of metrics, etymology, grammar and astronomy, needed to ensure the correct timing of the sacred rites. The sixth Vedanga is concerned with Kalpa, or the correct ways of performing the rituals.

The Rig Veda samhita has come down to us in the sakala school recension. It consists of ten mandalas, which are divided into 1028 suktas and suktas, in turn are divided into 10552 rics or 39831 pada.[4] The satpatha Brahmana gives the number of syllable to be 43200014. Each Mandala belongs to a particular family or school and the hymns are arranged according to a hierarchy of the goals addressed; thus the order of the first eight Mandalas is arranged in the following order. The first hymn is usually addressed to Agni; next comes Indra; and then come hymn addressed to the Visva-devates and special deities. These mandalas are known as "family books." The eight mandala is dedicated to Indra and then soma. The first and the tenth mandala are the latest additions.

As far as authorship of the hymns is concerned, there is no certainty about it. We entirely depend on the Veda itself and on tradition. It is assumed that the second mandala composed by Gristmad; the third by Vishvamitra; the fourth by Vamadeva; the firth by Atri and his family, and seventh by Vashistha, and the first, eighth and tenth by various other poets.

The composition of the Rigveda Samhita does not seem to have been liturgical. Not all the hymns of this Veda, like the other two liturgical ones, are used in sacrifices. These hymns, which have no liturgical function, have a purely poetical or mystical character. The non-litergical nautre of these hymns can be inferred from the structure of the poems. We may here quote a hymn in which the Brahmana are composed to frogs who, during the rainy season make too much noise., viz.,

As priests that have their vows fulfilled. Reposing for a year complete, the Frogs have now begun to talk, Parjanya has their voice aroused.

When on the longing thirsty ones it rainath, then akkala! They cry: and one the other

Greets with his speech as sons address his father.

The priests about the intoxicating soma

Talk as they stand before the well filled vessel,

So stand ye round about this day once yearly.

On which, O frogs, the time of rain approaches. The vision of the knowledge of Rigveda comes out of a profound insight into the mystery of reality. It is the product of mystical experiences that for transcends the limits of logical thinking. The message of the ultimate reality can be conveyed only in musk or poetry, which is able to invoke in splendid verses the primal mystery that transcends all categories, both human and divine. These hymns, while trying to plumb the depths of the mystery, formulates no doctrinal system but expresses itself by means of a rich variety of different symbols related to the one single insight. The hymn, in fact, presents on extraordinary consistency, which is patent only to the contemplative mind, in the absence of this latter, however, it is bound to appear either as syncretistion as agnostic, as has in fact been sometimes asserted.

In the beginning there was neither existence nor non-existence, there was no sky, nor heaven beyond, only space was there (Void Space). The Temmatra essences of the space is Nad (the sound with vibration), the essence of sound which generates ether. The essence of touch generates air, the essence of colour generates light, the essence of taste generates water. The essence of smell generates earth. The essence of sound, touch, colour, taste, and smell are the chief constituents of ether, air, light, water and earth respectively.

The air breath, pran, Rishi Pran Agni (Agney) water (Soma) was forceful, Agni was weak before soma so there was no nothing in perfact form, but vibration (spandan) was all over. There is expansion and contraction in vibration. This expansion is called 'Bramah' and contraction is called 'Maya.' The form of prikriti and purusha embaded in it. The coordination of prikriti and purusha is because of the process of vibration (spandan). All the creation and destruction of the universe happen because of this 'spandan' vibration. To know the vibration of our own heartbeat, body, mind and spirits, vibration of the environment; air, water, fire etc. and vibration of cosmic bodies are means to know the life. To know the reality from diverse (various) bodies and elements of the world to the one and supreme power is development of human being.

The 'Brahma,' ultimate power, which expands at every moment in the form of substance has power, manifested in the form f vibration. The very subtle part of the Brahma comes into existence as an atom. The centre of which is Rik, periphery is Sama and the mobile part in between is called Yaju.

This is 'vid,' the Vedas. The soul, the centre point of the atom, goes downward from "Swayambhuloka" falls in Permesthi loka. Here the soma form is pitra pran. Seven lokas are here Bhu: Bhuwah, Swah, Mah, Jamah, Taph, Satyam, भूः, भूवः, स्वः, मह, जनः, तपः, सत्यम्) Satyam is known as "Swaymabh" Janah (जनः) is known as (Permesthi). In between Satyam the Swaymabhu and janah permesthi Taphlok existed, this is Antariksha, Surya (the sun) is satellite of permesthi which revolves in Tapahlok.

From Swayambhu, the unmanifested prakriti generated.

From permesthi, chetana, the consciousness originated.

From Surya (the sun) wisdom born.

From moon, manam (man) forms.

From eternal Agni, Prem, breath & senses come into existence.

From mrutya Agni body takes its form.

And this is 'vid,' the knowledge.

The Vedic religion traverses the whole gamut of polytheism, organized polytheism, henotheism, monotheism and monism. The Vedic poets were simple children of nature. They wondered at the grand and sublime, beautiful and useful aspect of nature, and were thrilled into ecstasy. The different gods are the personification of different powers of nature. They are sometimes worshipped individually. This is not naturalism, but anthropomorphic polytheism. The Vedic poets were not worshipper of nature. They worshipped supernatural and superhuman deities pervading the whole of considerable part of nature and beyond and endowed with some qualities in groups.

The gods were gradually related to one another. Gods are divided into four groups;

1. The Great Gods – Celestial
2. The Great Gods – Aerial
3. The Great Gods – Terrestrial
4. The Minor Gods of Nature

The different Gods are personification of different powers of nature. All the major and minor Gods are gradually related to one another, as dependent on each other. The conception of Rta harmonizes the gods with one-another, and paves the way for monotheism. Rta is the physical order, it governs the uniformity of nature. Rta reigns everywhere, in the sky, in the sun, in the mountain, in the sacrifices, and in truth.

हंसः शुंचिषद्वसुरन्तरिक्षसद्धोता वेदि्पदतिथिर्दुरोव्सत्ः

नृपद्वेर्स दृत सद्वयो मुसद्ब्जा ग्रोजा ऋत्जा अद्विजा।।

Meaning-

It is the course of nature. It is the natural order. The sacrifices should corform to Rta. It is the law of rites. It is the social law. It is the law of truth, right, and justice. It is the moral law.

The first category of Gods is celestal goal. These are;

1. Dyaus the father
2. Varuna, Mitra, and the Adityas
3. Surya, Savita and Pusan
4. Vishnu
5. Vivasvant
6. The Acvin (Ashwin)
7. The Goddess dawn
8. The Moon

The second category of Gods are Arial. These are;

1. Indra
2. Trita, Aptya
3. Apam Napat
4. Ahi Budhnya
5. Aja Ekapad
6. Matarisvan
7. Vayu and Vata
8. Parjanya
9. The Waters
10. Rudra
11. The Maruta are Rudras

Third kind of Gods are Terrestrial which are-

1. Agni
2. Brahaspati and other forms of Agni
3. The God Soma
4. The Rivers
5. The Earth
6. The Sea

Fourth one is – Minor Gods of Nature-

1. The Rbhus and the Rtus
2. The Gandhavras and Apsaras
3. Spirits of the forest, the trees, and the plants.
4. Spirits of Agriculture, pasture and the mountains
5. Deities of house
6. Divine implements
7. Divine Animals
8. Totemism
9. The lesser nature goddesses
10. Constellaticms and time periods

Varuna is the custodians of moral law or Rta. He adheras to the right, and punishes sins. All the four types of gods follow the law of Rta. It points to be existence of one supreme God whose law is unalterable and inviolable. The conception of Rta prepares the way for monotheism, though it is an impersonal order which upholds the gods and the world.

Hiranyagarbh or Prajapati, Vishnukarma and Param Purusha gradually take the place of one supreme God. Hirnyagarbh is prajapati, the lord of all creatures. He arose in the beginning. He establishes the earth and the heaven. He is the sole king of entire universe.

The celestial God Dyaus has the honour of being the only Indo-European god who is certainly to be recognized as having existed in the earliest period, and he has been claimed for that time as a real sovereign of the gods, much as zeus among the Greeks. In the Rigveda he has not a single hymn of his own and his appearance is nearly always in one or other of two capacities either he is the parent, who has as children. Usas, the Acvins, Agni, Parjanya, Surya, the Adityas, the Maruts, and the Angriases or he is couple with the earth, prithvi.

The slight prominence of Dyaus in the Indian period is doubtless in part at least due to the prominence of Mitra and Varuna, of which pair the greeted by far is Varuna. Mitra, indeed by his close association with Varuna has lost any real independence of character. Though Varuna is anthropomorphic and has arms, hands, feet, walks, drives sits, eats, and drinks. The eye of mitra and Varuna is repeatedly declared to be the sun, and it figures conspicuously in all the hyams regarding Varuna. Mitra is said to have produced the day, Varuna the night.

Surya the Sun God is major god of Rigveda and the bymns are devoted to him. In the purushasukta he is made to be born from the eye of purusha. Many gods stand in close connexion with Surya. From the lap of the dawns he shines forth, and he is also the husband of Dawn: Pushan is his messenger, Varuna, Mitra, Aryaman make hispath; Indra, Vishnu, some Dhatr, and the Angirases all are said to create him or produce him.

In Rigveda lord Vishnu is worshipped as prominent God but his name occurs not more than hundred times at all. Vishnu is closely associated with Indra: Ashwins are next to Indra, Agni, and Soma, the gods most frequently mentioned in the Rigveda, more than fifty hymns are written about him.

Indra is the greatest God of the Rigveda with the solitary, exception of Varuna, who is equal to him in might. The birth of Indra is mysterious, like that of other heroes; he declines to be born save through his another side. The deeds of Trita have often the closest resemblance to those of Indra. The real wind Gods of Rigveda are Vayu and Vata, who differ however quite distinctly in character and in importance. Vayu is beautiful, touching the sky, thousand-eyed; he travels on his implements course, in a chariot at his own will in indefinite speed. Indra rides with Vayu. He generates Maruts. In the purushsuketa he is born of the giants breath. Like is friend Indra he is fond of Soma.

Vata is merely the wind in its power, sweeping along great clouds of dust, shattering and thundering. He is the breath of god and recipient of oblation Parjanya like Vata, is a god whose natural character is obvious and undeniable. Three hymns are allotted to him. The rain cloud is made into a real person, often in theomorphic shape; thus he is bull who roars and impregnates the plants, and its roaring waters delight the earth. The nature of Parjanya as the thunder cloud is preserved threrghant the Vedic literature and is recognized in the later period, where his name is also applied to Indra.

Four hymns of the Rigveda and many verses praise the waters as goddesses. Their anthropomorphic from is the Apsara, who will be treated below. They are also celestial. They abide in the seat of gods and of mitra and Varuna. In them Agni dwells and they are his mothers. Maruts share the greatness of Indra, and therefore, they have a prompt place in Regveda. Thirty-three hymns being exclusive theirs, while they share seven with Indra, and one each with Pusan and Agni, maruts are great, young, imaging, terrible like wild beats, but play-full like children or calves. The main deed of the maruts is the rendering of aid to Indra in the staying of Vritra.

The great of terrestrial God is Agni, priest, hotra. In Rigveda 200 hymms are devoted to him. He is like the Sun, dispels darkness, and bears the epithet 'waking at dawn.' It has the place in the naval (nabhi) of earth, hence it is nevel of immortality Agni is born from the wood so it dwells in plants. It is also born from the waters. He is embryo of waters, kindled in the waters, a bull who has waxed great in waters, and descendents from clouds.

Agni has the birth in the heaven; he is born there and was brought down by matarisvan. The domestic side of the fire worship is revealed namely by the constant reference to Agni as a friend in the homes of men. He is the fire god, domestic god, Lord of house. He is the youngest, resplendent, and beautiful god, righteous, omniscient, and benevolent. He is mediator between men and gods. He is the messenger of gods. He carries the oblation to the gods. He brings them to the sacrifices. He is the steward of both worlds. He is in fallible. His blessings are flawless. He is intent upon right (Rta) and true. He adheres to his own power of mind. He knows all rules. He has proclaimed his rules to the mortals. He protects us from sin that defiles us. He is self dependent gods. He releases men from all sins committee in thoughtlessness. He reigns over immortality.

Soma is Amrta, "ambrosia" the drink of immortality and the whole ninth mandla is devoted to Lord Soma and six hymns from other mandals also. A common name of plant and the drink is Indu, the bright drop. The plant is brown, ruddy, or most often tawny. In the purified form the juice of Soma is called Cukra or Cuci, 'the bright; and offered to Indra meet and Vayu. The various names of juice is andhas, pitu, mada, the intoxicating beverage.

Goddess Prithvi plays a singularly restricted part in the Rigveda except in so far as she is invoked along Dyaus she has but one short hymn of her corn.

She is rich in height, bears the burden of the mountain, and supports in the grounds of forest trees. She is great shaking firm, and quickens the earthy by scattering rain from the cloud, fact which shows that she is not rigidly confined to her element, doubtless because she has borrowed an attribute of Dyaus himself. The Brahmas follows the Rigveda in referring her name as broad to the fact of her having been extended.

All the goals are gradually relatd to one-another as the major and minor (angapartyangabhava), as dependent on one another (anyanyasraspa, and as generating one another (anyanyasraya), and as generating one another (anyonyotpatti). The relationships among the gods organizes plurality of nature gods.[6]

Among the multitude of nature gods any one is treated as supreme god for the time being when he is worshipped. MaxiMuller calls this religion henotheism.[7] "O' Agni, thou than art mighty Indra, the wide ruling Vishnu, the king Varuna, whose laws are firm, the wondrous mitra, Aryaman, the lord of beings. Thou art Rudra, the maruts, the winds, the pushan, thou art Savitra, a bestower of treasures, Bhaga, the lord of wealth, Rbhu, Aditi, Bharti, Ida and Sarasvati. Thou art united with all gods and equal to them in strength, and, than surpassest them, when their power has expanded over heaven and earth."[8]

From book RV 113.5.

Agni is identified here with many gods and treated as superior to them. This is henotheism. It is a step from polytheism to monotheism.

This is one of the most prominent religious belief of Rigveda, that sometimes the gods were invoked in groups. A number of dual gods such as Mitra and Varuna, Indra and Agni, Agni and Soma were invoked. Sometimes three gods working together such as Aryaman, Mitra and Varuna, or Agni, Soma and Gandhavra were praised. Sometimes four deities such as Bharati, Ida Saraswati and Mahi were worshipped. Sometimes many gods together were praised. May Mitra and Varuna, Aditi, the Sindhu, the Earth and the sky grant as happiness and long life. Some times all the gods together, Visve Devas, were praised and invoked. "Sit down on the sacrificial altar, O Vasus, O Vishve Devas, O Aditiyas worthy of worship. 'May all gods protect us for our welfare.'"

RV 11, 3, 4; IV 46.3, V 51.13

Thus gods were interrelated to one another. When all gods were worshipped together, they were implicitly conceived as partial aspects of one supreme God. A collection of gods working in harmony paved the way for one God. This stage may be called organized polytheism.

Polytheism, Henothesism, Monotheism and monism philosophical and spiritual outlook of Rigveda is religious belief of Rigveda. These religions belief is maintained by law of Rta. To be united with the Gods (devayana were mentioned). To be united with the gods and to attain immortality were also regarded as the goal of religion. Religion aimed at earthly happiness and heavenly bliss.

Law of Rta is the most prominent ethical value of Rigveda. It is the moral law. It is truth and righteousness. The gods are the custodians and followers of the moral law.

Varuna is of fixed, unswering right conduct (dedhavrat). Sin is untruth and unrighteousness. It is falsehood (amita) and delinquency. Virtue is rewarded. Vice is punished. Virtue is purity of inner life. The gods descry the impure motives and intentions, and punish them.

वि घ् त्ववाँ ऋतत्रात यंसद्गण्शानो अंग्ने तन्वेइबरूयम्।

विश्रोद्रिरिक्षरूत् वा निनित्सोरेभिः द्वतामसि दैव, विठ्पट्।।6।।

The persons who is able to discriminate right and unright, truth and untruth by his own conscience follow righteousness and keep away violent, evil and corrupt persons from them can obtain prosperity peace and happiness of the world.

प्र साँ अग्निर्व भसन्तिग्मजेम्भ्स्तपिठठेत शोचि्षाचः सुराधांः।

प्र यं मि्नन्ति वरूेणस्य धामे प्रिया मित्रस्यु चेतेतो ध्रूवाषि।।4।।

Vachakluptopmalankar As Agni, the fire destroy wet and dry substances, the right person destroy the selfishness and sorrow creating persons from the world and the person is able gain precise.

These are the ethical values of Rigveda.

In Rigveda this tendency to dissimilation which may be called in some degree monotheistic, but with a pronounced tendency to pantheism, practically excludes the grown of any real hierarchy among the gods. The Rigveda indeed, expressly says of the gods that some are great, some small, some young, some old, and there is no-reason to doubt that this was a view widely held: the mere fact that another poet assures the gods that they are none of them small or young but all great, is rather proof of the prevalence of the contrary view than an indication that the assurance which he gives was generally accepted as correct. Moreover, there is the patent fact, when all allowances are made for the nature of the subject matter, two vedic deities do appear as being much greater importance than the others. Indra as the great ruler, and Varuna as the lord of physical and moral order. It is therefore natural enough to imagine that the original great god of the Aryans was Varuna and that it was in India that Indra was made up to the stature of Varuna, and even overthrew his performance.

Indra holds the earth, the sky, and the heaven. He unites the immeasurable earth and sky. He is father of the Maruts, the Sun, the dawn, and the fire god. He is the terrific destroyer of enemies in the battlefield. He is the killer of the demon Vrtra. He is the lord of the word. He is resplendent, ever young, and infinitely great. He is a voracious drinker of soma juice. He is the possessor of infinite wealth. He is the giver of food, wealth, prosperity, victory, and long life. he entered into the earth and the sky, and created the world. He is the creator of waters. He is bountiful, generous, self controlled and immoral. He is the protector of worshipper.

All gods are inspired by the same divine power. Their great divinity is one. There is unity and order in the phenomena of nature. They acquired divinity and immortality by serving Rta rightly. Varuna walks and round the earth on the straight path of Rta. Rta is the course of nature. Gods know the pure thoughts of the worshippers, and promote their prayer.

Duties of men and duties of gods were recognized. Charity and hospitality to men and kindness to animals were enjoyed. These are ethical values of Rigveda. Falsehood, treachery and fraudulence were condemned. Gambling was denounced, though it was prevalent. War was not condemned. Ethics of non-violence (ahimsa) was absent. Violence is to be met by violence. Strength bends before strength is vital belief of Rigveda.

Let us stand straight that we may walk and live. The Buddhist ethics of ahinsa was unknown to the Vedic age. Asceticism was foreign to the spirit of the Vedic people, thought it might be practiced by a few people. The world is said to have been created by austerity (tapas) as the Nasadiya Sukta of Rigveda is stated that-

"Then there was neither existence nor non-existence, there was no sky, nor heaven beyond. Then there was neither death nor immortality. There was neither day or night nor distinction between them. There was sole one (Tad-ekom) that breathed by itself without breath; there was nothing other than the one. Then there was darkness without light. All was engulfed in the primal cause. That one was born by the power of austerity (tapas). There first arose desire or will in the cosmic mind and form the first one sprang the seed of creation. This is pure spiritualistic monism.[14] Darkness and emptiness are also symbols of the first moment. Out of nothing, nothing can come. Nothingnesss is not previous to, but coexistensive with being. The source of being is not another being or anything that can be considered as being an origin out of which things come to be."

The process according to the intuition of the Vedic rishi, is one of concentration, of condensation, of an emergence by the power of love. This love cannot be desire toward. Something, that does not exists, or even a desire comings out of a non-existing being. It is this very concentration that originates the self which is going to be and have that love. Primordial love is neither a transitive nor an intransitive act; it is neither an act directed toward the other no an act directed toward oneself but it is the constitute act by which existence comes into being. Without love there is no being, but loves, does not happen without ardor or 'tapas.' It is fervor, tapas, that makes the being be; they are not separable. The elution between 'Karma' desire and love, of on the one hand, and 'tapas,' ardor and heat, on the other, is one of the universal cosmic laws linking being and the whole realm of beings.

This insight brings us again to that ultimate level where the one is situated. From that depth the sage expresses the most fundamental question about the essential and existential enigma of the universe; what he asks, is the origin of universe, of all this idiom? Who or what, is its purpose, its end, its direction? It cannot be the Gods, for they themselves belong on this side of the curtain. It is beyond the subject and object of knowledge itself. Only he who is beyond and above everything may know-or he may not, for how may there be any assurance concerning it? They hymn concludes with the query. It is openness of this interrogation which allows the universe to emerge and to exist.

Nasadia Sukta RVX, 129

!!129!!

It is self-abnegation of the cosmic spirit. There was no caste system though Purusha Sukta refers to the four classes.

Purusha Sukta

There is a cosmic person (Param Purusha) whose body is the whole universe. He has a thousand heads, a thousand eyes, a thousand feet. He pervades the whole terrestrial space and transcends it. Whatever was or whatever will be-all that is Purusha. He is the lord of immortality. He is untouched by the fruits of actions (Karma). All creation is his grandeur, but he is ever superior to the entire creation. The whole of the universe is only one-fourth of his being, the remaining three-fourths remain in celestial immortality. The inner nature of Param-Purusha is transcendental, though he is immanent in the whole universe. He is both immanent and transcendent. The Purusha Sukta teaches pantheism. These are mono theistic tendencies in the Rigveda.

This is the most important hymn of the Rigveda. It reveals to us the character of the creation, sacrifice. It's all embracing function in which the entire universe is involved. It is neither a merely divine affair, nor a purely human endeavor, nor a kind cosmic process; it is human, divine and cosmic all in one.

Purusha is not only the cosmic man, it is also the personal aspect of the whole of reality. The very concept of person excludes isolation, alienation, and solipsistic solitariness and expresses interconnection and unity.

This hymn of rather late Vedic times, though undoubtedly pre-upnishadic, describes the formation of the world from body of the primordial man. who is so vast that he covers and even overlaps the earth, not only in space but also in time. only one quarter of the cosmic person is visible and emerges into the sphere of the manifold.

From him the shining one was born,
From this shining one man again took birth.
As soon as born, he extended himself.
All over the Earth both behind and before. !!5!!

From this sacrifice, fully accomplished,
Were born the hymn and the melodies,
From this were born the various meters;
From this were born the sacrifical formulas !!9!!

His mouth become the Brahman; his arms
Become the worrier-prince, his legs
The common man who plies his trade.
The lowly serf was born from his feet.

In Vedic age this was one of the respectable belief that there was no child marriage. Women enjoyed a high position in society. They did not observe 'pardah.' Some women were composers of mantras. "One in the many, unity in variety, is the perennial message of the Vedic India. The last Sukta of the Rigveda breathes this out unequivocally thus: Assemble, spoke together, let your minds be of one accord... Let all priest utter the mantras in a common way. Common be their assembly, common be their mind, so be their thoughts united......"

United be the thoughts of all, that all may live happily, that ye may all happily reside. These are the religious belief and ethical values of Rigveda.!!9!!

The soul of any determination resides in faith not in words only but faith in words. The knowledge can be obtained by faith on anything. Various personalities possess knowledge of different fields but true knowledge of any field can be gained by complete faith on it. The knowledge of the absolute, the whole universe can be obtained by perception, comprehension, contemplation and intuition.

At the present age life style is completely changed. There is universalization of education but men is caught in the network of hatred, jealously, evilness and sorrow. There is no peace of mind because peace resides in true knowledge, in righteousness, in nature, in knowledge of absolute. Present education is not talking about life, but it talks about subjects only. To earn money is only goal of life of man. only cognitive aspect is developing, his conative (emotional) level is disappearing and man is becoming unstable and thus losing conscience. He is not able to discriminate between right and wrong. Unknowingly a big imbalance is becoming part of his life. everyone is feeling aloneness. His minds is losing self-control. The senses are becoming boss of man and man is like a slave of his own mind.

Every person wants to live a peaceful and happy life but on the basis of scientific and technological aspects man is putting much burden on his head and losing himself in the teachers worlds. he can't gain happiness. To lead a perfect peaceful and stable life, knowledge of true religion is necessary. He doesn't know the definition of religion. To follow the law of rit is religion. To follow the righteous path is religion. To do his own duty with perfect devotion and dedication is religion.

The foundation of religion is an implicit faith in our own divinity, ceremonies, rules, laws and rituals only heighten our faith in this divinity unity of existent is the law of universe.

Today people are deeply immersed in daily occupations, in high ambitions, in over work, sometimes in the midst of the greatest of the struggles there comes a pause; the mind stops and wants to know something beyond this world. Sometimes it catches glimpses of a realm beyond the senses, and a struggle to get it is the result. Thus it has been throughout the ages in all countries. Man has wanted to look beyond, wanted to expand himself; all all that we call progress, evolutions has always been measured by that one search, the search of human destiny, the search for God. Purusha Sukta relinquishes this search and knowledge of Vedas makes man peaceful, healthy and prosperous.

The Vedas, the Upanishads, the Ramayana, the Mahabharata, the Puranas, The Bible, the Quran and the Gurugranthasaheb are the foundations of universal truth. All these great scriptures teach the one reality, 'Ekam Sat' "Tad Ekam." 'It is an impersonal, universal principle which breathed by itself without breath Bhagvat Gita teaches the dualistic monism, preaches the cult of Vasudeva or Krishna, and enjoins works (Karma Yoga), devotion (Bhakti Yoga) and knowledge (Jyan Yoga) for the attainment of God.

The most fundamental message in the Quran which apply to all mankind are; belief, prayer, and good deeds. As law of Rit of Rigveda, belief and good deeds (righteousness) are absolutely the basic requirement in Islam. Numerous views confirm this. To believe in Allah is the primary requirement, and in this sense we must also believe in Allah's revelation. In Holy Bible it is said that Faith, the belief that God and Jesus exist and are the rewards of those who seek them. Faith gives Christians the assurance that what the Eternal promises. He will do. The person of the Godhead known as the father rules the entire universe. His will is accomplished through his spirit. He is all powerful and possesses all authority. He is the very definition of love and has perfect righteous character. He sent Jesus. His son, in the form of a human to reveal his love, grace and plan for man.

The Bhagwat Gita teaches theism, and regends God as the supreme and perfect person (Purushottam). He is Para Brahman, the holy, eternal, divine person. He is the foundation of the infinite and eternal Brahman, the eternal moral order, and supreme supersensus bliss.

The Gurugranth Saheb promotes the message of equality of all beings and at the same state that Sikh believers obtain the supreme status Sri Guru Granth Sahib promotes the concept of equality by highlighting the fact that we are made of the same flesh, blood and bone and we have same light to God with us-soul.

The Rigveda is the most ancient religious text of the world. UNESCO also proved this fact and regard Rigveda as most ancient text of the world. Rigveda is generally believed to have been compiled into its present form not later than 1300 BC. This is the book of Indo-Aryans, who came to India in ancient times. They shared a common origin with Iranian, Aryans, worshipping the same Gods. There is a striking similarity between the languages of the Rigveda and Zoroastrian holy Bible, the Zend Avesta.

Bibliography

S.No.	Name of the Book	Author	Publisher	Year
1.	A Critical Study of Rigveda (I.137.163) Particularly From the Point of View Paninian Grammar	Dr. Deo Prakash Patenjal Shastri	Pantanal Publication Urmilad Devi Pantanjal	1963
2.	Aurobindo The Revolutionary Philosopher Who Defiles Description	Sri Aurobindo	Vijay Goel Delhi	2010
3.	Beyond the Secret	Brenda Barnaby	Pentagon Press	2009
4.	Comparative Essays	A.A. Macdonell	NAG Publisher	1977
5.	Divine Hymns and Ancient Thought, VI&II	DA Sadashiv A. Dange	Navrang Delhi	1992
6.	Divine Message of Vdea	H. Shriram Sharma Acharya	Yug Nirman Yojna Vistar Trust Mathura	2010
7.	Early Indian Religious Thoughts	P.D. Mehta	The New Order Book Co. Book Sellers and Publishers, Ahmedahad-6	1956

8.	Gita For Every One	Jogindernath Mukherji B.A.	Gopsons Paper Ltd. Noida	First Pub. In 1900–2000
9.	God Loves Fun	Sri Sri Rai Shankar	Sri Sri Publication Trust India	2008
10.	Health and Healing Mantra	R.L. Kashyap	Sri Aurobindo Kapali Swisty Institute Vedic Culture Bangalore	2013
11.	Hinduism	Roshan Dalal	Penguin Books India Pvt. Ltd.	2010
12.	Hymns From The Vedas	ABINASH Chandra Bose	ASIA Publishing House, London, New York	
13.	Indian Philosophy Vol. I	Jadunath Sinha	Motilal Banarasidas	1999, 2006
14.	Indian Philosophy Vol. II	Jadunath Sinha	Motilal Banarasidas	1999, 2006
15.	Indian Philosophy Vol. III	Jadunath Sinha	Motilal Banarasidas	1999, 2006
16.	Mind and Super Mind Vol. I	N.C. Panda	D.K. Print World (P) Ltd.	1994
17.	Mind and Super Mind Vol. II	N.C. Panda	D.K. Print World (P) Ltd.	1994
18.	Philosophical and Sociological Foundation of Education	H.R. Swaroop Saxena	R. Lal Book Depot	2008
19.	Personal Excellence Through the Bhagwad Gita	Swami Sukhbodha Nanda	Jain Book Agency, Jaico Publishing House	2010
20.	Rigveda The Oldest Divine Book	RTH Griffith	Clarendon Press, Oxford UK in the 1880s	

21.	Satyaloka in Rigveda S.40	Dev Datta Shastri VVRI Press Hoshiarpur India		
22.	Shabda Vedah	Karpurchand Kalishah	Patrika Prakashan Unit of Rajasthan Patrika 409 Lakshami Complex MI Road, Jaipur 302001	First Edi.2000 II Edi.2010
23.	Sri Sri Ravi Shankar Celebrating Silence	Sri Sri Ravishankar	Jaico Publishing House	2008
24.	Swami Vivkananda The Living Vedanta	Chaturvedi Badrinath	Penguin Group India Pvt. Ltd.	2006
25.	Tagore Vis-à-vis Kabir	Sanjeev Chaterji	Vijay Goel Delhi	2009
26.	The Complete Work of Swami Vivekanand	Swami Bodhasurananand Advait Ashram Kolkata	Advaita Ashram Kolkata	1951 1959
27.	The Complete Works of Swami Vivekananda Vol. I to X	Swanu Bodhasarananda	Advaita Ashram	1989
28.	The Essence of Hinduism	M.K. Gandhi	Parasight Publishing & Distribution	2009
29.	The Orion'or Researches Into The Antiquity of the Vedas	Bal Gangadhar Tilak	Painting Sleve Page Bar Code-781231' 107195	2011
30.	The Religion and Philosophy of Veda and Upanishad Part I and II	Arthur Berric Dale Keith	Motial Banarasidas Publishers Pvt. Ltd., Delhi	1970, 1976, 1998, 2007

31.	The Religions of India	Edwardwash Burn Hopkin	Munisharam Manharlal New Delhi	1970
32.	Thoughts on Synthesis of Science and Religion	I.D. Singh and Samaresh Bandhopadhay	The Baletivedonta Institute Culcutta	2001
33.	The Sketch of the Religious Sects of Hindus	H.N. Wilson MA	Cosmo Publication New Delhi India	1977
34.	The Vedic Experience for Modern Man and Contemporary Celebration	Raimundo Pannikar	Motilal Banarasidas	
35.	Vedas A Divine Light Part I	Swami Ram Swaroopji	Ved Mandir Prakashan	2010
36.	Vedas A Divine Light Part II	Swami Ram Swaroopji	Ved Mandir Prakashan	2010
37.	Vedas A Divine Light Part III	Swami Ram Swaroopji	Ved Mandir Prakashan	2010
38.	Vedas A Divine Light Part IV	Swami Ram Swaroopji	Ved Mandir Prakashan	2010
39.	Vedas A Divine Light Part II	Swami Ramswaroopji	Ved Mandir Prakashan H.P. India	2008
40.	Veda A Way of Life	Ramanuj Prasad	Pustak Mahal	2009
41.	Vivekananda World Teacher	Swami Adishwara Nanda		2007
42.	ऋग्वेद भाष्यम् प्रथमः भागः मण्डल 1 से 6 तक	Shripad Damodar Satvalekar	Manavutthan Sankalp Samsthan, 119 Gautam Vihar, New Delhi 110010	2010
43.	ऋग्वेद भाष्यम् द्वितीय भागः मण्डल 7 से 10	श्रीपद दामोदर सातवलकर	मानव उत्थान संकल्प संस्थान	2010

44.	वेद–विज्ञान–माला देवी–सूक्त तन्त्रोक्त–सूक्त	प. देवीदत्त चतुर्वेदी	प. मधुसुदन ओझा वैदिक अध्ययन एवं शोध पीठ संस्थान, जयपुन– भारत	फरवरी, 2015
45.	वेद–विज्ञान–माला देवी–सूक्त ऋग्वेद 10.90 कर्पूर–भाष्य	गुलाब कोठारी	आईबिड	अप्रैल 2015
46.	सूर्य सूक्त ऋग्वेद 9.995 कर्पूर भाष्य	गुलाब कोठारी	आईबिड	अप्रैल 2015
47.	अग्निसूक्त ऋग्वेद 1.1 कर्पूर भाष्य	गुलाब कोठारी	प. मधुसुदन ओझा अध्ययन एवं शोधपीठ संस्थान, जयपुर, भारत	अप्रैल 2015
48.	ऋग्वेद संहिता भाग 1 से 10	वेदमूर्ति तपोनिष्ठ श्रीराम शर्मा आचार्य	युग निर्माण योजना विस्तार ट्रस्ट, गायत्री तपोभूमि मथुरा	1974
49.	धर्म प्रबोधिनी एवं भगवत तत्व निरूपक Applied Religion	S.G. Rathi Shikshak Nagar, Indore	S.G. Rathi Shikshak Nagar, Indore 414448	2001
50.	वैदिक कोषः	हंसराज एवं भगवद्दत्त	विश्वभारती अनुसंधान परिषद ज्ञानपुर (वाराणसी) भारत	
51.	ऋग्वेद	राजबहादुर पाण्डे	डायमण्ड पाकेट बुक्स, नई दिल्ली	2015
52.	संस्कृत–हिन्दी– अंग्रेजी शब्दकोष	डॉ. उमा प्रसाद पाण्डे	कमल प्रकाषन	
53.	भारतीय दर्शन	प्रो. हरेन्द्र प्रसाद सिन्हा	मेतीलाल बनारसी दास, वाराणसी, पुणे	प्रथम संस्करण 1063, ग्यारहवाः 2002
54.	आचार्य शंकर ब्रह्मवाद	डॉ. रामस्वरूप सिंह, नवलखा, कानपुर	किताबघर आचार्य नगर	
55.	वेदान्त	चक्रवर्ती राजगोपालाचार्य	सस्ता साहित्य मण्डल प्रकाषन	2005